The Covering

EMBRACING THE MOUNTAIN PEAK
EVEN
WHEN STRUGGLING IN THE VALLEY DEEP

Life is not a bed of roses for anyone. There are no exceptions. But life becomes much harder when we fall down into the victim-valley state of mind instead of rising up into the power of perseverance.

Rosie M. Hill

ISBN: 0615948588
ISBN 13: 9780615948584
Library of Congress Control Number: 2014900216
Rosie M. Hill, Lee's Summit, MO

All scripture quotations are taken from the
Holy Bible, King James Version.

It is with great love that I dedicate this book to David R. Hill, the man God created to "complete me." You have helped make all my temporal dreams come true, walking with me through this ever-changing and sometimes-difficult journey for the last twenty-seven years. Your abiding love provides security in both our marriage and our calling. About twelve years ago, you were receptive to my need to write this story. You understood the most important reason: it could make a difference in so many lives. Through this entire process, I could count on your consistent, unwavering, and faithful support.

To my brother, Cornell (Junnie) Vance, who not only witnessed the things that happened to me along my journey, but who is deeply passionate about this story's reaching the world. After reading *Forgiving Them*, you said to me, "I was there; nobody knows it the way you and I do. I was there, and I know it's the truth—all of it. You are going to help so many people. But there is one more thing I want to say—I don't know why you call it a story; it's the truth." I remember the times we talked about when we were children. I love you and am grateful to have you as my big brother; you are the best.

To my children, Markela Thatcher, Frank Reynolds, and Brian Johnson. You are God's awesome gifts to me; I love you with all my heart. To Kenny Morgan, my son in the Lord. You have been a blessing in ways I will always cherish.

Thanks to my brother in Christ, David M. Hansen, PhD, for his constructive critiques. Thanks to A. Denise Davis, one of my best friends, for her support and insight. And thanks to my friend Tonya Britton for all of her heartfelt suggestions.

Thanks to Michelle Steven, a dear friend, who assisted me in the beginning editing process of this book. She worked with me on my first two books and provided her editing expertise once again. I knew I could count on her as I started with a novel idea, a new story, for a bigger reason. That is exactly what she did at a time when a constructive critique was so important. While I had many ideas to write about, she offered thought-provoking suggestions that were very helpful. Her recommendations were exactly what I needed. I was receptive to her input in the beginning of what was an overwhelming project.

Thanks to Krista Connell, who is one of my best friends. In addition to being my friend, she is an educator, so I was delighted when she said to me, "Let me know if you need some help." Of course, I said yes to her offer. And after reading the manuscript, she suggested particular events that she thought would be great for me to include. Oh, was she right. Some of her ideas hadn't occurred to me, and I took her advice. Yet, many times the process was excruciating, and I would have to set it aside. When I procrastinated, she would gently encourage me year after year by asking me the same question again and again: "How's the book coming along?"

Thanks to Lisa Wilson, who is another one of my best friends. We realized that our friendship was meant for a bigger mission than either of us had envisioned. Lisa's creative credentials were exactly what I needed, and she was delighted to assist me as I completed the manuscript. The interesting thing about Lisa and me is that while I was focusing on deadlines, she would slow me down by consistently asking about more specific details. She positioned herself as the reader. Lisa's help was invaluable.

Contents

Foreword

*M*y aunt has, for as long as I can remember, been one of my favorite people in this world. She is the third oldest of my mother's eight siblings. When I was a little girl, I called her Aunt Nosey." I believe the real reason was that "Nosey" was easier to pronounce for a thumb-sucking four-year-old than "Rosie," but one day I decided to ask her why she thought I called her this.

"Do you know why I call you Aunt Nosey?" I asked in my best smarty-pants tone.

"No, honey. Why?" she replied sweetly.

"'Cause you nosey!" I declared with a big smile.

Instead of getting my mouth washed out with soap and a smack on my behind, this reply drew a chuckle from the adults, including Aunt Rosie. That was the start of a very special bond between the two of us that exists to this day. Even beyond this special relationship, I always looked up to Aunt Rosie because she consistently emulated what a godly woman should be, even when no other adults in our family followed Christian tenets. She was not only special to me; she was unique in her actions toward and treatment of others in her life, including her family.

Family, from the Latin word familia, *is a group of people affiliated by consanguinity (sharing common ancestry), affinity (kinship or relationship by marriage), or coresidence (the same household). At times, those we consider to be our family aren't related to us in the typical sense. For example, in the 1950s and 1960s, it was common that your mother's boyfriend was referred to as "Uncle," making him accepted as a member of the family while covering up the true relationship. And really, who wouldn't like having another uncle around to call on when the ice cream man drives down your block? Or when you need help with your homework? Or just another trusted adult to help protect and guide you in the difficult process of growing up? We all would, of course. Yes, we all would—that is, until the uncle becomes someone to be feared instead of trusted.*

This book is about my aunt's triumph over abuse and neglect at the hands of those in her life who, because of ancestry, kinship, or coresidence, were her family—how, despite her cruel childhood, this little girl managed to become a successful and productive member of society.

We often wonder why God allows bad things to happen. We will question God and ask him why these things have to happen and why they have to hurt us so very much. And while we're welcome to ask, we may never get the answer that would allow us to fully understand. While nothing excuses the abuse of anyone, particularly such a wonderful person as my Aunt Rosie, I'm starting to understand how her enduring this abuse may have served a purpose. In sharing her story, she may give someone the strength to hope for change in their seemingly hopeless situation. She may give someone the ability to break free from unforgiveness or the cycle of abuse, either as the abuser or the abused. She may cause someone to persevere in the face of insurmountable odds simply because that is exactly what she did. I came to realize that Aunt Rosie essentially "took one for the team."

You may be in a situation right now in which you are questioning God and asking, "Why?" Know that if God brings you to a situation, he will bring you through it. You may not understand why it is happening to you or why God allowed it. Remember Romans 8:28: "And we know that all things work together for good to them that love God, to them who are the called according to his purpose." Aunt Rosie was and still is "the called" for God's purpose. God had a purpose for her life, just as surely as he has for yours even if you can't see it or if it doesn't make sense right now. Yes, God has a plan!

Loretha Hayden

The Condition

My skin is dark. That was not my choice—just born that way.
I am called Colored Girl and Negro by polite people.
Prejudiced people call me nigger.
I remember how they shouted out at me just for being me.
They break my heart with those harsh words
I guess I should expect that…Still, it hurts.
Those people are different from me—but in only one way.
So many of those people have hurt me.
Yes, the ones who like me and the ones who don't like me.
The ones who don't look like me and
the ones who look just like me.
They have hurt me to my core.
But what could I do to stop them from
hurting me…stop the pain?
What could I do to change my position
in their eyes? Not a thing.
That is what I believed most of the time.
I was powerless to change my situation. So I thought.
People said they really cared about me…people like me.
Yet without batting an eye, they took away my innocence.
The touch and lack of touch, the words,
the beatings that scarred my back.
And afterward broke my heart. And then crushed my soul.
I could not escape the pain…could not do it.
It was within…and it was without…everywhere I turned.
And so the rare moments of happiness
were erased with fear and anxiety.

Hours of crying and asking, "Why?" flooded my mind.
But *they* are like me. I don't understand; I screamed within.
The other people with ivory covering reject
me. They don't even know me.
But they reject me anyway…just because I am different.
No, really, I don't understand…
Different…yes, I am. But so are they. Why can't they see this?
Their eyes are opened, but their hearts are not.
Who will protect all of us from ignorance?
I know the answer to that question. Yes, I do.
But exactly *how*…that, I do not know.
Like them, I am also ignorant.
It is like a sickness…I know I need help.
So many people are narrow-minded.
How can they see the real problems through blinded eyes?
They can't. But I can.
I see it. I see it clearly!

The Beginning

"Children are apt to live up to what you believe of them."
—*Lady Bird Johnson*

Doctor's Orders

I had heard Dr. Powell prescribe treatments for hundreds of patients in the years we worked together. Suddenly, her prescription was directed at me. But I wasn't her patient. I wasn't even sick. As she passed me at the end of a long day, she turned around, stared at me, and spoke as if my life depended on hearing what she had to say: "It's time to write your story." Later she said, "So many people don't make it through these things as you did…You are wired differently."

Dr. Powell was right. After all was said, done, and written down, the writing healed my insides. *That's what counts, right? What's on the inside?* Mine is more than a story of innocence lost and wisdom found. It's more than finding things aren't always what they seem. It's living alongside what a child is told in spite of what she knows. In this case, it's what's on the outside that counts most of all.

The Foundation

The birth of my journey was January 2, 1949. Sometimes I try to imagine what it was like in the delivery room on my birthday. I see a bouncing little baby girl entering the world, crying up a storm, traveling from my mother's womb where we had been so closely connected to a big world full of disconnections. It must've been a frightening journey. I like to think that as Mama held me for the very first time, I looked into her big brown eyes, wet with tears but lit with a big smile. Feeling the comfort of her arms and learning the security of her touch was all I would've needed to be OK.

However, the birthing process wasn't all that new to her. I was her third child, so I assume she was relieved to be done with the whole ordeal. She was probably looking forward to the recovery—to the end of her pain and getting her body back. I stayed in the neonatal ward of the hospital for about one week before my mother and I went home.

My mother was twenty-two when I was born. Although her age disqualified her from the classification of "teen mom," she was surely not mature enough to raise three children. She was a tall, big-boned, assertive woman with a jovial personality—or at least that's the way she was around her friends, who all lived to have a good time. It was as if life's goal was to work all week in order to party every weekend. Each of them had jobs and worked to be independent people. But on the weekends, they let it all hang out. When the responsibility of parenting competed with the apparent thrill of getting sloppy drunk, the latter triumphed, week after week, month after month, year after year.

When I was born, my mama was married—but not to my father. It was a marriage in name only since she'd had both me and my older brother with another man. I don't remember certain things about our real father—such as his profession or how he and our mother met. I do believe they enjoyed the occasional fling. If we couldn't be conceived in matrimonial love, at least we know there was passion.

Although I don't remember what kind of work my biological father did, I remember he did have a job. I recall how he never lived with us. I also know my father and mother were two of a kind in a way. And I am certain that many of my later decisions were based on the fact that I came from nothing more than the occasional intimate encounter.

There was a flip side to my mom's joviality. She could also be very no-nonsense and a tough woman who took nothin' off nobody. She would cuss a man out if he tried to cross her. She was fearless and demanded to be respected on *her* terms. I remember times when her boyfriend would come to the house and they would have a big argument that turned into a fight. But she was the only one hitting. He would run from her like a child inside the house, and then out the door.

I called her Mama Doe. We kids were never allowed to call her "Mother" because it reminded her of another phrase. "If you call me Mother, you're probably cussing me on the sly." "Mom" was off-limits, too, because that "sounded white," and "we don't talk like that." I never understood why it was such a big deal, but what did I know? I was just a kid.

Oh, how I wanted to gaze into her eyes, to touch her, to hug her, to kiss her and say, "I love you, Mama." How much I wanted her to smile back at me and say, "I love you, honey." My little heart ached to hear something along those lines, but I never did. I'm not sure how a little girl comes to know that a mother is supposed to love her child, but nobody had to tell me how it was supposed to be. I tried everything I could think of to get her to love me. *She's my mother. I came out of her belly. I love her so much because she's my mother.* I would think this over and over again and again.

Picture This

We called my maternal grandma Mama Nan. In many ways, she was more like a mother to me. She usually dressed me, combed my hair, and readied me for the day.

This day was no different. My hair was combed in its usual style with bangs and two long, braided ponytails. The sun's rays had invited me outside to play. At four years old, I was happy playing without toys, friends, or even family.

That day, I wore a light-brown shirt, a darker-brown pair of shorts, white socks, and brown leather-type shoes. Between the sound of the wind and singing birds, it would never have occurred to me that I was alone.

My joy must have been truly apparent because, unbeknown to me, someone noticed. A strange man suddenly appeared and walked toward me. The alley was like a dirt road without grass. On that day, my older sister and brother were not there with me when I met the strange man. I was OK with that.

In those days, I wasn't scared of strangers. I was at ease talking to him. He was a tall white man and was wearing a suit. *He looks different dressed like that. Who is he?* I thought. He was definitely not one of us, first because he was white and second because Negroes in my neighborhood didn't dress like him. He looked like an important man, but why he was here and what he wanted with me was not clear. I just thought he seemed nice.

He asked where he could find my parents. I pointed to the apartment on the second floor. "Right up there."

The front door was open. I noticed that Mama Nan had been standing there. He made his way up and walked inside behind her.

I continued to play in the alley but was extremely curious about what was going on up there. *Maybe he's another salesman. Maybe he's selling something. I don't know.* All I remember is that he was inside the apartment for a short time. When he walked out the door with Mama Nan, they stood there talking for a few moments. Then he walked down the stairs toward me where I was still playing and asked if he could take my picture. Of course I agreed, smiled, and posed against the fence.

My mother had come to the door and watched us from the porch. I didn't know what was going on, but he was nice to me and to my family, and they were nice to him, too. It wasn't the first time I'd seen a man in a business suit. Occasionally a sharply dressed man would stop by to take care of this or that. But this was the first one who showed particular interest in *me*. He took several pictures of me with a Polaroid camera and then gave one picture to Mama Doe for us to keep.

He told my mother to call him if she changed her mind, whatever that meant. I was fascinated by the thought that there was something about me that made him want to take my picture. *What does he want her to call him about?* Whatever was going on was connected to me, and oh, how special that made me feel. Other than that time, I don't remember my picture ever being taken. To this day, I haven't seen a picture of myself alone before the age of four.

After the man left, my mother filled me in. "He wanted you to be on television and in movies, and he was willing to pay for the entire family to go along with you. But I told him, 'I can't do that. All my kids would have to leave town. The answer is no. I know we could probably be rich, but no.'"

I had no idea how to respond. I just understood that what Mama said was final and that I was just a little girl who was supposed to keep my opinion to myself.

Rather than being disappointed, Mama seemed pleased with the conversation. "That was nice of him, but I can't do that," she insisted. She was not willing to uproot me and my sister and brother. She apparently thought the offer was legitimate and appeared to be fascinated by the very idea of her daughter being on television. I don't remember her mentioning any specifics about a role, a specific amount of money, or anything like that, most likely because they hadn't discussed it. Her answer to him was a clear and final no.

I often wondered what that man saw that day as he watched me playing all by myself. *What exactly was I doing that made him notice me? What kind of show or movie did he want me to be in?* I thought maybe he wanted me to be on a program like *The Little Rascals,* but I would never know, and it was quite all right. My picture was tangible evidence of that encounter, and that was enough for me.

I cherished that picture and shared it with many people for years as I told them the story of that bright, sunny day. I often wondered how actors were chosen, especially little, poor Negro children like me. How did they select them? Where did they find them? Who knows? Maybe I had just experienced the typical process. Perhaps he recognized a natural talent in me.

When I was in elementary school, I realized I had a gift to express myself in front of an audience. I was never afraid of performing in school. I was totally confident in my natural abilities but didn't flaunt them. I just wanted to have fun. In fact, the more people in the audience, the more excited I was. Getting into the characters and personifying them was total bliss for me. Then again, I didn't require an audience. I remember reading short books, memorizing them, and then teaching myself to act out all the characters.

One of my favorites was *Marco Comes Late,* a story about a little boy who was late for school and made up a preposterous story to tell his teacher after she scolded him for being tardy:

Little Marco boasted to his teacher about how he planned to be the first
pupil in his seat,
and then bang, something happened on Mulberry Street:
A bird landed an egg on his arithmetic book.
He said he couldn't dare move, and he couldn't dare talk
because if he did, he would have knocked the egg off.
So he stood there stock still and it worried him pink.
Then his feet got quite tired and he sat down to think.
While he was thinking down there on the ground,
he saw something move and he heard a loud sound.

It was a worm that was having a fight with his wife,
*   the most terrible fight he had seen in his life.*
So he didn't know what he must do
*   but he really didn't mean to be late for school.*
The teacher listened and said, "I don't know if I can believe all of this.
Is this really true?
Did all of these things really happen to you?"
*   Marco said, "Not everything. But I did see a worm."*

Another favorite was *A Sad Fat Beaver*, which is about a beaver whose life is difficult because he is so very lonely. He goes on and on, talking about how sad he is when suddenly a small mouse appears at his door. After they meet each other, their lives change, and they live happily ever after.

To this day, I have shared these stories with lots of people, especially my children and grandchildren. The words are indelibly etched in my brain.

People would make comments about how I was "different." "Girl, you'll stand up in front of anybody and perform; I don't know how you do that," they would say to me. Even people outside my family would echo this sentiment: "You're different; where did you come from?" Most of the time, it felt like a compliment, but sometimes I was singled out as an "Oreo," people saying that I was "trying to be white." They said I was dark on the outside, white on the inside. My mother said to me so many times, "You are my white child." She usually stated it as a fact, though, rather than a hostile judgment. All I knew for sure was that I enjoyed learning and doing things different from the status quo in my environment. I didn't mind being different. I was just happy being me all by myself. That's what must've caught that picture-taking man's attention—my exuberant performance without an audience.

These short, seemingly insignificant events created bright spots amid otherwise dark memories. I came to know that being unique was a good thing, a very good thing.

❖ ❖ ❖

Elementary School

In kindergarten, I learned my ABCs, colors, and how to read adventure books. I fondly remember books such as *Dick and Jane, The Three Little Pigs, Goldilocks and the Three Bears,* and other childhood stories. I remember playtime and taking naps every day. I absolutely reveled in being in school with the other children. My desire to learn was insatiable. It was so much fun. Going to school really made my day.

"Boys and girls, go sit down and open your books. We're going to start our assignments for today," my teacher said each morning.

Yes, ma'am, I said to myself with respect and excitement.

My eyes scanned the room, looking at the other children in class. Everyone was laughing, learning, and simply having a good time. My face lit up with joy when I thought about the stark contrast between this atmosphere and the one at home. *Oh my, this is so nice. Look at the teacher. She is so smart,* I would say to myself. No wonder I liked going to school so much. Although I was aware of the contrast, I didn't fully understand how much it affected me then—or how it would shape my future.

When school wasn't in session during the summer, I had some of my best times at the swimming pool and the playground behind the school. I remember what seemed like hundreds of kids splashing in the water, yelling at each other and having a blast. There were monkey bars close to the pool and a steel merry-go-round there, too. I had so much fun hanging from the bars, swinging forward and back, and spinning on that merry-go-round.

I never thought of the games as boring. On the contrary, I was captivated by spending time with my friends, who loved having a good time just like me. *I wish I could stay here forever* I thought when it was time to leave.

Despite my home life, there were times when I felt pleasant and secure. My sister and brother, the other neighborhood children, and I walked to school without fear. When we went trick-or-treating on Halloween, we never gave a second thought about what neighborhood we were in or about being hurt or abducted. Oh, how much fun it was to dress up in our home-made costumes, do scary things, and get lots of candy!

We clearly understood that we were to respect any adult as our authority. We were the children, and they were the adults—plain and simple. Whenever we stepped out of line, we were reminded to "stay in our place" by beatings with cords, belts, tree branches, a hand, or whatever was there at the time. Mama's beatings gave us a clear understanding of rules and policies.

However, it didn't take me long to learn that there was a different standard for adults compared to children. This really confused me. I told her that time and time again, only to be silenced by a slap on my face or beatings, both accompanied by words that pierced my heart. *Why is it OK for adults to do bad things, but I get beaten for doing bad things?* I'd wonder. *What's so wrong about giving my opinion about what I believe? That is just wrong, but I can't tell Mama that. She will beat the living daylights out of me if I talk back to her.* That was called being sassy, rude, and disrespectful.

After kindergarten, we moved again to another apartment. I attended another elementary school. This was quite a change for us. But just as in kindergarten, I absolutely loved going to school. I was so eager to get there each morning, intent on making new discoveries. During class, I was in awe of the adults who were so smart and so kind, and who were there to take care of my education. I was a very good student, receptive to the rules that were there for me to follow. During class time, my attitude was, *the teacher is talking, and I must pay attention so I can learn.*

I saw my teachers as role models and held them in high regard. I understood at a very young age that they helped us and our community in profound ways. I wanted to understand why they were different from most of the other adults in my life. I tried to model this same mind-set at home. I was in awe of their intellect, stature, neatness, sobriety, and professional demeanor.

I hung onto each and every word they said. They took charge of each student using words of wisdom rather than inflicting pain, exercising discipline that kept order while maintaining good relationships. *Something is different about the teachers compared to the grown-ups who are not teachers. What is it? Why is it that way?*

In general, my family didn't have the same opinion of teachers as I did. Teachers were viewed as enemies who didn't really care, who tried to hurt the little Negro children. I was told so many times, "They don't care about you!" To be honest, to a certain extent, I must have believed it—in a way. After all, it was only logical to think that my mother cared about me but strangers (especially strangers who were white) didn't. I tried to convince myself of this since it was what I was told. I was confused and conflicted because, deep down, I didn't believe it at all.

This inner conflict made it hard to respect many of the adults in my environment. I truly respected the teachers and held them in high esteem. But at home, I was told that my teachers didn't really care about me, that they were just there to do their job. *This stuff is just wrong; why are they saying that?* I was confused when what I heard contradicted what I saw. Teachers seemed to show much more care and concern than those people in my life who *should* have cared for me even more. This ongoing state of confusion might explain why I can't remember most of my teachers' names or visualize their faces.

What a shame for a child to be put in this situation when his or her future is based on the need for community, which includes family, friends, teachers, and other people in so many places. How can we learn without teachers, both the good and the bad? As an adult, I would learn invaluable lessons from people of all walks of life—good and bad.

I do remember one teacher's name, however. Ms. Kelly taught fourth grade. Her face is vivid in my mind. I thought she was the best teacher ever. She was such a nice lady, tall and poised with a dark complexion and short black hair with a page-boy hairstyle. She was the only Negro teacher I can remember having, so it makes sense that I both remembered her and held her in such high regard. Since we wore the same color skin, it was also possible (according to what I'd been told) that she might genuinely care about me. I wasn't conflicted in any way about my feelings about this teacher. Ms. Kelly was so nice. In fact, she invited me over to her house, so she must have favored me as much as I did her. Why? Did she see me as a child who desperately needed the love of her mother? I'm certain she must have looked into my young eyes, sensing the workings of my little heart and mind, perceiving that I particularly needed a connection with her to foster my enthusiasm for school and learning.

Other than the recollection of Ms. Kelly, my memory of all my other elementary and junior high school teachers is foggy. I attribute this loss of memory to living in an environment that didn't value my education as I did and to struggling to reconcile that disparity. Going to school was a very low priority for my parents (which I'm certain was a reflection of their parents' priorities), but I must have seen it as a necessary relief in my otherwise largely barren childhood and a hopeful segue to a better life.

What was this all about? What was the big picture for me to see, to understand, and to use as a tool of empowerment and tenacity for this journey of *my* life?

Conversations with Mama

Mama was the parent, and I was the child. I had to remind myself of this every time my young heart and mind got rocked by something she said or did. *Where is the love and affection? What kind of person cusses and fusses and beats her child?* Those kinds of questions haunted me day after day. I couldn't wrap my head around why I was living in such a bad environment.

Whenever I was looking for comfort, trying to understand a situation, or questioning what she made me do, I only made matters worse for myself. Her responding words never failed to pierce my heart. I believed I was justified in asking why I couldn't go to school when she made me stay home to take care of the kids or why we didn't have vegetables to eat or why we had meat only on Sundays.

A typical meal might be spaghetti with butter, salt, and pepper on it or potatoes with butter, salt, and pepper. The day after, we would have "vegetables" because we topped it with tomato paste instead of just butter, salt, and pepper. No fruit, no vegetables, no nutrients, in my mind. Once I said, "Mama, we *need* more food like fruit, vegetables, and meat every day."

"Shut up—your belly is full, so you're getting what you need."

"We need more!" I cried. And I got beat for talking back to her.

Again and again I would ask Mama questions about food, school, and family stuff. What started as my curiosity must've sounded drastically different in her ears. She would yell back at me at the top of her voice, "I'm the captain of this ship! You're just a member of the crew, and don't you forget that!" Oh, how it crushed my heart and soul when she spoke to me like that. Just in case her words weren't enough, the heat from her hand across my face silenced me every time.

I was so afraid of the price I had to pay for expressing my concerns and displeasure. The unfortunate combination of curiosity and innocence overpowered my ability to learn my lesson. So the beatings and fear would silence me again and again. *I'm just a little girl, and I don't know what to do. Why can't I tell her what worries me? Mama is a tough woman, and I must learn how to keep my mouth shut!*

My mother believed that my life was doomed solely because of the skin I was born in. Furthermore, she insisted people would never accept me as equal because of it.

"Remember who you are, girl! You are *not* white—you just wanna be white!" she'd say.

"No, I don't!" I'd cry out. *I just want you to love me. I need you to talk to me, Mama.* I had said that before out loud and was beaten for suggesting that she didn't love me. She would just remind me that I was a child and didn't know what I was talking about.

"You just wanna be rich like those white people. Get away from me, gal," she would say to shut me up.

I obeyed her, but my heart so badly wanted to connect with her no matter what she said to me. *I know who I am, but why does she continue to pound this junk into my head day after day?* I thought. *What is going on with her? Why is she so angry with me for being who I am? What does she mean, I wanna be white? I don't understand what my needs have to do with that at all!*

Clearly, Mama had issues. As time went on, I felt myself detaching from her perceptions about race. Navigating the hostile world she spoke of was an overwhelming problem in itself. I started to understand that somehow she felt threatened by my thoughts and behavior. She took my inquiries personally. The way she often talked about me and described me as her "white child" was something I didn't understand. It didn't make sense to me, but the reality of my skin shade stared me in my face daily. I kept thinking to myself, *Why is that?* It was very confusing to me as a child, but I would learn to live with it. I had no other choice.

I didn't understand at the time that my mother just plain did not like me. *What did I do wrong?* I pondered day after day, trying to figure out the problem. *What can I do to make her love me?* I wanted her love and acceptance so desperately. *She's my mother, and I just want her to love me. Isn't that what mothers do? They love their children! After all, I used to be inside her belly,* which was an absolutely amazing thought to me as a child. I thought about it all the time—our connection was nothing less than a miracle. *Why can't she see that?*

When I offered up my love to her, she would push me away or slap me. Just in case I didn't get the hint, she'd follow it up with a surly, "Get away from me, gal!" I was a pest to her, and she wanted no part of me. How could this happen between a mother and her child? I knew for sure that she didn't like me. I just didn't know why. I longed to figure it out and to change our relationship.

Will she ever understand how to love me? Will she ever change? What is her problem? How will I survive living like this?

❖ ❖ ❖

A Conversation with My Father

When I was seven years old, something incredible oc-curred to me. I didn't think of it as incredible at the time; but as I look back, it truly was. I needed to understand my life. I was keenly aware that the hostile environment in which I was living wasn't what a child should have to experience. I was very distraught that I had not been loved or treated as a child should be, and I needed to know WHY. I don't remember why the magnitude of my sorrow weighed upon me so heavily this par-ticular day, nor do I really know how I had the clarity of mind to take my case to the highest level possible. I just remember think-ing, *I need to talk to God, and I need to talk to him NOW.*

I don't remember exactly how I learned about God as my Father, alive and approachable, and someone I could talk to. No one in my family said his name except before the "d" word, which I heard all the time. Perhaps it was from saying the Lord's Prayer in school every morning; I don't know. Even though he wasn't a tangible presence in my life or in the lives of those around me, I knew beyond a shadow of a doubt that God did exist. I knew he created the world as I looked at the wide, blue sky, listened to the wind blowing, and thought about the changing seasons. I won-dered about the signs of life all around me—countless people, ever-changing trees, vibrant flowers, and the simplicity of green grass. I knew I needed to confront him about what he allowed to happen in *my* life. I needed him to answer one very important question: Why did you let this happen?

I walked into a tiny room that we used as a closet in the apart-ment. I sat on a big pile of clothes, looked out the window up to the sky, and had a sincere out-loud conversation with the Creator of the universe:

> *I know you are God, and I know you made all things. So since you are God, I know you could have kept me from being born if you wanted. So why did you do it? Why would you allow me to be born into a family that doesn't*

want me and doesn't love me? Why? My mother doesn't want me. My father is nowhere to be found. Why? You could have stopped all this!

I was clearly disturbed. I held nothing back and wanted answers. I wasn't asking family or friends—I wanted to hear from God. He alone had the single answer I so desperately needed to hear to the question, *Why?*

After I spoke, I waited for a response. I don't fully know how I could have so urgently posed such a question to a God I didn't even know. What I know for sure is that God revealed himself to me that day. Even if I'd never heard a response from him, how refreshing it was to not be berated or beaten for asking a simple, honest question. But he *did* respond. He spoke to my heart, and I heard the message as if it had truly been audible. It was not something I fabricated like the stories I learned in school or like a pretend playmate. This was a direct connection between God and me. I knew it without a doubt!

After a few seconds, when I stopped talking and complaining, he responded:

"I love you and have a reason for your being born and for your life."

"I want you to go to church and learn about me."

Although I had heard it clearly within my heart, I was not completely satisfied. "I'm just a little girl. How can I go to church? Who will comb my hair? Who will iron my clothes?" I responded.

I may have lacked understanding about these minor details relating to God, but he certainly had my attention. As I look back, it's obvious that Satan, the deceiver, was trying to keep me from having a personal relationship with God. Even though we recited the Lord's Prayer in school, my relationship with God was growing far past a recitation. This must've scared Satan to death.

My grandmother, Mama Nan, had always been there to comb my hair and iron my clothes. She took excellent care of me. But when it came to her opinion about church, she agreed with my mother. All of the adults seemed to be anti-God and antichurch. Friday and Saturday nights were times to party, and Sunday morning, we slept late. So, on a Sunday morning, I knew in my heart Mama Nan would not get me ready for church; neither would she have an outfit ready for me to wear. I was literally on my own if I chose to listen and follow the instructions of my Heavenly Father. After I thought about the situation and spoke out loud to him, the final response I heard in my heart was very clearly, "GO AS YOU ARE." And that is exactly what I did. I didn't have any more questions. I knew that God loved me.

My home life interactions had not changed one iota. I knew without a doubt that since God loved me, he had plans for my life that only he would reveal to me at the right time, with clarity and for the right reasons.

The following Sunday, I woke up with excitement and determination. I washed my face, brushed my teeth, put on my clothes, and left the apartment all alone.

Wearing a wrinkled dress with uncombed hair, a big smile on my face, and overwhelming happiness in my heart, I believed in God, and I was doing exactly what he had told me to do. Even though I had never gone to church, somehow I understood who he was and what he had done for the world because he loved us. As I pause now and look back, it must have been a combination of praying the Lord's Prayer in school, evidence of his creation, and an innate desire to connect with God.

There it was. I could see the church as I walked out the door of the apartment building, just up the street two blocks away. It was a two-story, red-brick building on the corner with a large parking lot and a playground in the back.

Inside, I saw the beautiful sanctuary and instantly felt an awesome sense of peace, unlike ever before. The people were very kind, and the music was breathtaking. The preacher looked like royalty in his floor-length robe. His sermon was interesting. My eyes were fixed on him, and I held on to every word and understood what he was saying—that is to say, the part I was sent to hear.

I must've looked quite messy wearing a dress full of wrinkles with uncombed hair, looking as if I had just rolled out of bed. My thoughts, however, were quite focused. I was about to make a very mature decision that I would remember for the rest of my life. I didn't care about my clothes—I remembered that I had been instructed to "go as you are."

I listened to the message as the preacher spoke. He started talking about baptism. I was so excited. When he invited those interested to come forward, nothing could have kept me in my seat. I believed in Jesus Christ—his death, burial, and resurrection—and I wanted to get baptized to prove it. It was as if I knew exactly what would take place *and* what I was supposed to do at this invitation.

"I believe in Jesus." That's what I told the preacher. "I want to be baptized." As I spoke, a lady also approached the altar. She took me to the back of the church and, with a kind and sincere voice, told me I didn't understand what I was talking about. How could I know about the Bible since I was, after all, just a little girl? I looked at her in disbelief. *What does she mean? I don't understand,* I said to myself. *I know exactly what I am doing, why I am here, and why I should be baptized. In fact, I understand it as much as these grown-ups.* After listening to her and looking at her for a few moments, I realized that she was not going to believe me, and I left it at that. I didn't know what I could say to convince her that I was sure about what I wanted to do. I knew exactly why I wanted to be baptized.

What I did know for sure was that things were different since that conversation in the closet. Now I had a relationship with God and knew what that meant in my life. I had his power to guide me even in the midst of my pain and suffering because he cared about me and had a purpose for my life. From that point forward, I never wavered from his clear directives to go and learn about him.

Shortly after that, I read the entire twenty-fourth Psalm, and my eyes were opened to some powerful truths about life. Soon I learned it all by heart and without instruction to do so. I believed it was an important chapter for me because it was a summary of how God had chosen to reveal himself: "The earth is the Lord's and the fullness thereof, the world and *they* that dwell therein…" The Creator was real to me, and I knew it! There was something about the "they" part that stirred my soul. But my home life would continue to spiral downward. That part of my life—outside my church family—was miserable most of the time. Still, what he uncovered for me was nothing less than miraculous!

The Encounter

Being a child, I suppose I was not as privy to Satan's existence as I was to God's. What my Heavenly Father had set in motion for my life, Satan was already out to destroy. I later learned that what God creates in perfection, Satan tries to destroy in deception.

My sister, brother, and I would occasionally spend the night at my great uncle and his boyfriend's apartment. Yes, I said that right. My grandmother's younger brother, Junior, had a lover named Bill. We were instructed to address both as Uncle even though one never deserved said title.

My sister, Loretta, was the oldest child and four years older than me. As firstborn, she fit the role perfectly in terms of her take-charge attitude. The idea of her being my big sister was a really big deal to both of us. She wasn't just older; she was bigger. I looked up to her as a mentor. She was a very pretty girl, medium height—about five feet five inches tall, polished in her appearance, and very confident in her actions. She was much like our mother, in a way. She had a no-nonsense attitude when it came to dealing with difficult people. She was assertive in conversation and aggressive when it came to defending our brother, Junnie, and me or any cause she felt would benefit both of us.

I don't recall Mama's way of raising us bothering Loretta like it did me. If anything, she seemed to understand Mama better. They got along really well, and I was glad for my sister. But Mama and I didn't seem to connect in that same way. I often appeased myself about the difference with this assumption: *I'm just a little girl, and I don't understand.*

My uncles lived in the neighborhood, not too far from our house. The apartment was on a street that was close to some taverns, an Italian restaurant, and grocery stores. It was a very busy street with downtown buildings in sight and sidewalks where we played games such as double Dutch with jump ropes, hopscotch games with the numbers written on the sidewalk, Hula-Hoop, and jacks. There were no playgrounds or yards around the building, yet we still found a way to have fun with each other and the other kids in the neighborhood.

Behind the room where we slept on the rollaway bed was a door to another room. It was the bedroom where my uncle and his boyfriend slept together. I was confused, but it was none of my business. I just thought to myself, *That's what adults do; I don't understand it because they are both men.* I didn't judge them; I was just confused and dismissed it as another thing I should accept about how things were different in the adult world.

During one of these sleepovers, when I was about eight years old, my sister, brother, and I were all sound asleep in the same bed. (While that sounds fairly odd by today's standards, it was very common at that time to sleep with a few people in one bed. Most of the time when we were young, I slept in the same bed with my sister and brother.) In fact, it was very rare to have a bed all to myself.

One night, Uncle Bill entered the room very quietly, and I awoke to his hand touching my legs. At first I was still groggy from being asleep, but then I was paralyzed with shock as his fingers moved inside my panties and then his fingers further to my vagina. Being eight years old, a swirl of confusing, disturbing emotions arose inside me. But I knew that if I told him to stop or resisted, I would wake my sister and brother and they would find out what was happening. I had no idea what to do. Thankfully, after a few moments of this, he left the room. Despite my horror and fear that he would return, I eventually fell back asleep.

When I awoke the next morning, I remembered what had happened but decided that I wouldn't say a word about it. I knew what he did was wrong, but I was afraid that he would do it again if I didn't tell somebody. Yet, I was equally afraid of what would happen if I *did* tell. *Who should I tell?* I wondered. *Would they believe me, or will they think I'm lying? I have to remember that I'm a little girl and he is a grown man. If they do believe me, will they even do anything about it, or will I just get in trouble?* I decided the safest option would be to just keep my distance from him as best I could.

So the next night, I positioned myself at the opposite end of the bed, where he wouldn't be able to get to me without waking my sister and brother. I fell asleep confident that I'd be safe that night and that it wouldn't happen again. But it did.

Uncle Bill somehow managed to get to me without waking my sister and brother. The same confused, queasy swirl of emotions arose again then and throughout the following day, especially when he would flash that creepy grin at me. That made me nauseous, but I still didn't feel I could tell anyone what he had done.

I was afraid and confused—afraid because I knew what he had done was wrong, and I didn't want him near me again; confused because he had awakened a feeling in my body I hadn't known. After that incident, I privately longed to be touched like that again, but I also knew it was wrong and stayed away from Uncle Bill as best I could. I wasn't even close to being mature enough to deal with this bewildering tangle of emotions. *What is happening to my body? Do other little girls do this? It's a bad thing to do, so I will never tell anybody!*

I remember making up excuses to keep me from spending the night at Uncle Bill's place the next time we were to have a sleepover, or ever again. I'm not sure what I said, but I knew, despite my conflicted emotions, I would never be in that position again—no, never again!

This horrible experience shouldn't have happened to me, but it did. I shouldn't have been distracted from being a child by that man, but I was. That I felt unloved and unprotected by my mother and father was bad enough, but what this man did shaped my understanding of intimacy far too early. I would never forget that time. Never.

Touch of Fear

We lived in a climate with very distinct seasons. There were unbearably hot, dripping, humid summers with occasional violent thunderstorms. There were also frigid, windy, snowy, and icy winters. When these conditions were extreme and dangerous, the six-block walk to school felt more like six miles. Once I arrived, I loved everything about my school. I was genuinely excited about all I was learning, not to mention my fondness for my teachers and classmates.

As one morning progressed, however, I discovered something that brought my otherwise carefree thoughts to a screeching halt. As I sat in class on a beautiful morning, I could tell that something was definitely wrong with me. This was a feeling I had never had before, and I was scared. The strangeness was happening down below, and I soon realized my underwear felt moist. *What in the world is that? I didn't pee on myself, so why is it so wet down there? What in the world is in my panties?*

I didn't hear a word the teacher was saying because I was distracted by what was happening in my body. My first chance to investigate without drawing attention would be at the lunch bell. After it finally rang, I hurried to the bathroom without saying a word to my friends. I was desperate to find out what was happening to me. I ran into the stall, slammed the door, locked it, and pulled my panties down real fast. What I saw was devastating: blood! I was bleeding down there. Blood was in my panties! *What in the* world *is that coming out of me? How did that happen? Why am I bleeding?* I hadn't fallen. I hadn't scratched myself, and yet I was bleeding. I sat there on the toilet, not wanting to leave. I had no clue what to do. I had never heard of such a strange thing in my life! I was so very confused and so afraid of what was going on in my body.

I sat immobilized in that stall until the lunch bell rang. I had to get up and go back to class or I would be in trouble. *People are going to be asking me questions, and what will I tell them? I don't know what to tell them because this is* so *weird.*

I played it cool and pretended that I just had to use the restroom, and that was all there was to it.

I suppose I could've told my teacher, a classmate, or a friend. But no, I didn't say a word to anyone that day because I didn't know *what* to say! I had no idea what was happening to me. I decided the best course of action was to keep my distance from everybody and keep my mouth shut until I got home with my family. That is exactly what I did.

When Mama gets home, she will know what to do. I've gotta hurry. I can't stop and walk with my friends today. I don't even want to talk to them right now.

The moment we were dismissed, I sprinted out of that classroom immediately, running those six blocks in record time. I couldn't wait to tell Mama what had happened so she could help me. This was a serious problem. I was really afraid to tell her because I was scared to death about what was happening to me. *Am I really sick? Will I have to go to the hospital so they can stop the bleeding?* I wondered as I ran home.

Finally I arrived at our apartment to find that my mother wasn't home from work. I paced by the front door nervously in those minutes, which actually seemed like hours, until she arrived. It felt like it took forever until I heard her footsteps on the front porch and saw the doorknob turn. With my eyes open wide and a smile of relief on my face, I was elated by the fact that things would be all right. *Yay, she's here! Mama's home! She will help me 'cause I'm sick.*

I leaped toward her as she opened the door, unable to contain myself. Instead of telling her what had happened (since I really didn't know why it had happened), I thought showing her would be better. I had already taken off the soiled panties and put on a clean pair. I said, "Mama, look," as I held them in front of me. Her eyes grew wide as she looked at my undies, looked at me, and then quickly looked back at my undies again.

She didn't say a word—not one word. I was uncomfortable waiting for her to tell me what was happening to me and what to do about it. But instead of helping me, she remained silent, a long silence that made me even more uncomfortable. She appeared as shocked about the situation as I was! She looked away as she was apparently trying to decide what to say and how to say it.

After what seemed like an eternity, she turned to face me, looked into my eyes as if she had serious concerns. She went into the bathroom and brought out something I had never seen before to place in my panties. She explained how I would need to change it, dispose of it, and expect the issue to return every month. When she assured me that this was a normal part of growing up, I felt a sense of internal calm.

"Something has happened that happens to all girls, but generally they are older than you." She paused as if she was searching for the right words to say. "You are a young lady now, and you could get pregnant and have a baby if you let a boy touch you. So, don't let boys touch you, do you hear me?"

Huh? What? Don't let boys touch me? I thought to myself as I tried to make sure I had heard her correctly.

"Yes, ma'am. I'm not supposed to let boys touch me," I echoed for complete understanding.

"No, don't let them touch you, or you will have a baby," she repeated with a very serious look on her face and a matter-of-fact tone in her voice to make sure I understood.

Yes, I *heard* her but was still confused by what I heard because I didn't understand her. No, I did not understand at all. *What does she mean that I'm a young lady now because I'm bleeding down there? So don't let a boy touch me or I will have a baby?* Imagine hearing that at nine years old! My head was so filled by her fearful words and their ramifications that I couldn't muster any questions. There was nothing left to say and only one thing to do—stay away from boys for fear of them touching me. *I can't be a nine-year-old mother. No way.*

As she looked down at me and imparted those words of caution, instead of feeling comfortable, I stood there feeling worse than before. *What in the world? She is crazy if she thinks I can keep boys from touching me.*

In all fairness to my mother and through the eyes of an adult, I want to pause parenthetically for a moment. I'm sure she was caught off guard simply because I was so very young. The shock must have kept her from thinking through how her declaration would sound to me. Even though I'm fairly certain my sister had already started her period, she was a few years older than I when it happened. My mother said and my mother did what she thought was best, not imagining how literally these words would resonate in my naïve, nine-year-old ears and in my immature mind. Once again, I was just a child facing another adult situation. What little guidance I did get just made bad matters worse for me—so much worse.

I can't let a boy touch me, I kept thinking all that evening and well into the night. *How can I keep a boy from touching me?* I trembled inside, imagining how impossible that would be. *What if a boy touches me accidentally while we're playing outside? What if he touches me before I can stop him? What will I do?* I didn't know how I could possibly keep that from happening, but I was committed to trying my very best. One thing I knew for sure was that I couldn't have a baby at my age. That part was crystal clear.

The big challenge was before me, and I was sweating it like crazy. I had to go to school and keep this secret to myself. *Oh my gosh! What will the kids think of me if they find out what happened? They won't want to play with me. I have to make sure they don't find out. I just have to be very careful.*

The desks in our classroom were connected two-by-two alongside one another. As bad luck would have it, a boy had been assigned to sit right beside me. *What if he touches me? I should tell him not to touch me. No, I'll just scoot over. How in the world can I keep him from touching me accidentally?* I anxiously wondered as I arrived in the classroom the next morning. I moved over to the outer edge of the chair to put as much distance between me and this potentially dangerous boy as I possibly could. And my mind wasn't on what the teacher was saying *at all.* It was up to me to obey my mother and do as she said. "If you let a boy touch you, you will get pregnant and have a baby," I remembered her saying clearly. I had to protect myself at all costs, even if it meant letting my studies fall by the wayside. *This is more important than listening to the teacher,* I thought.

I continued to safeguard myself everywhere else, too—on the playground, on the way to and from school, at home, and even at church. I was constantly on guard, aware of all the boys in my vicinity and maintaining a safe perimeter of space around me. I was still very nervous about the consequences of my dangerous situation, but I felt a bit safer since I'd been able to follow my mother's instructions thus far.

But that changed. One day the inevitable happened. Yes, it did! Despite my thorough safeguards, my classmate's shoulder came in contact with mine as he leaned over to turn the page of the book that was between us. I was devastated. Then I was mad!

Oh my gosh, he touched me! I screamed within. *He really touched me!* I was furious. I got out of my chair on the left side of the desk and circled around to the right side to get a clear shot of him. Then I started hitting him, beating him on his shoulder with my fist. I didn't say a word—I just kept hitting him. He seemed frozen with fear, wide-eyed with shock. He looked at me as if I were crazy, as if he had no idea why I was so upset. The look on his face seemed to say, *What in the world is wrong with you?*

He was totally unaware that I believed he had just gotten me pregnant. What I knew for sure was what he did, and what Mama said rang in my memory loud and clear: "If you let a boy touch you, you will get pregnant." *But I couldn't stop him! I think it was an accident. Why did he do it? Did he know what would happen to me?* I was so mad at him for what he did. *He touched me, and now I'm pregnant!*

I had always been a well-behaved model student. Most likely, the teacher was especially surprised to witness this scene. She yelled from her desk, "What in the world are you doing, Rosie?"

I responded as I pointed to him, "He touched me!" My face was flooded with tears. Not understanding why that would warrant such a harsh response, she asked what was wrong and why I was hitting him. I kept crying and repeating myself—"He touched me!" *What's wrong with her? Surely she understands,* I thought.

The teacher got up from her desk, gently separated me from the boy, and then immediately ordered me to go to the principal's office. I knew I was in trouble for hitting him, but what in the world was I supposed to do? *My whole life is gonna change 'cause of him—what he did!* I thought as I walked to the office. I was devastated.

The principal told me to sit down. He asked me what my problem was and why I had started hitting my classmate. I explained everything to him as best I could—what this boy had done and what was going to happen to me as a result. The principal listened and then stepped outside. When he returned, he didn't say anything to me about being in trouble. He told me to wait outside his office.

My mother was then called to the school, and she spoke with the principal as I waited outside the office. I wondered if they were talking about my being pregnant now and what would happen because of it. My mind whirled with all of the consequences, but my mother soon emerged from his office, and I was told that I could come back to school the next day. That was a bit of a relief, but I still was overcome with what had happened and what would happen to me as a nine-year-old mother.

The journey home was quiet, making it seem almost endless. Thoughts and questions raced through my mind, but I knew it was best to wait for my mother to speak. When we got home, Mama finally broke the silence.

"You won't get pregnant if a boy just *touches* you—only if he gets real close, like to hug you or something like that."

"So, I'm OK?"

"Yes, you are OK. You're not gonna have a baby."

"OK," I cried. *Thank God!*

I was so relieved and grateful and felt myself smiling once again. Yes, I was so relieved to know that, first of all, I wasn't pregnant, and second, I didn't have to worry about a boy just touching me on the shoulder or bumping against me on the playground or in the cafeteria. Even so, I was still very concerned. We didn't hug much in our family, but I knew that other people hugged all the time. This happened a lot less often than just a mere touch, but boys would probably try to hug me. I was also confused by the "or something like that" part of what my mother had said. Still, I knew for sure I didn't want to get pregnant, so I was committed to doing the best I could to obey her.

Too bad I had never told her about "Uncle" Bill's nightly calls. Too bad there was such a gap in my mind between the touching I misunderstood and the touching I knew far too much about. Too bad she and I never found a bridge to walk across where she could learn that "something like that" had long since happened to me. Understanding where exactly the touch was forbidden could have saved me from the paranoia distracting me and my classmates from learning that day. Maybe it's best after all. It might have been too much growing-up news for one week. It might have broken her heart. Then she might have set out to break Uncle Bill! Too bad I still didn't fully understand the new rules about what was possible and not possible now that my body had changed.

Once my mother left to return to work the next day, I went out on the back porch to enjoy a breath of fresh air. Sitting out there, I thought about what my mother had said and the new task that was before me with this change in my body. Then my brother came out to join me a few minutes later. I was so glad to see him. I wanted to tell him about what had happened at school and what I had just learned from Mama. Before I could prepare myself, he put his arms around me and gave me a big hug. *What has he done to me?* This time it was not just another boy; it was my brother. It was not just a shoulder-to-shoulder touch; it was a real close touch, a hug touch. *What in the world? Oh no!* I was ten times more distraught by what I believed my brother had done than by the incident with my classmate.

I sprang from the porch and ran inside to the bathroom, my thoughts reeling once again. I looked into the mirror, imagining my breasts growing large and my belly beginning to protrude. I wept at what I thought I was seeing and cried out to God with tears streaming down my cheeks like buckets of water. I seriously wondered if the blood vessels in my head would explode, my head was pounding with such excruciating pain.

Between sobs, I prayed and prayed, almost nonstop. *Oh God, how am I gonna tell my mother I'm gonna have a baby by my brother?* I was hysterical. This was such a terrifyingly real possibility simply because it was what my mother told me. I was so afraid, and once again it seemed as if it took forever for my mother to return home. *What will I tell her, and how will I tell her? Oh, I have to tell her the truth,* I said to myself. *She warned me, but I didn't know he was going to do that! What will she do to me? Whatever she does to me won't be worse than my having to live with the fact that I'm going to have my brother's baby!* The thoughts just wouldn't stop, raging through my mind like an angry river.

Despite my concerns, I didn't hesitate for a split second. I greeted her crying and said, "Mama, Mama, I'm gonna have a baby." Incredulous, but also seeing that I was very distraught, she patiently asked who did it, when, and where it happened.

I told her it was Junnie. "It happened. He did it out on the porch," I said. Mama looked puzzled and didn't respond at first as she tried to take it all in and determine how to respond.

I continued, "I was just standing out there, and he opened the door, came over to me, and before I could stop him, he hugged me! It was a big, tight kinda hug."

I tried to make it very clear that I tried to stop him but couldn't. Mama was surprisingly calm considering the severity of the situation, or at least what I thought was the severity of the situation. She assured me that I was OK and wasn't pregnant. I was very confused because my brother, a boy, had definitely hugged me, but I was so relieved that I didn't bother to question her about how or why I wasn't really pregnant. I just said, "OK."

After two false alarms, now Mama apparently understood that these vague explanations were only going to lead to more confusion and distress. She seemed to realize she needed to be much more specific. This time, she said that if I let a boy touch me "down there," as she pointed between my legs, I would get pregnant. Because I was so relieved that I wasn't pregnant, I didn't think to ask her why she had told me those other confusing things. I was just very happy to have that weight lifted from me and to know a simple touch or hug from a boy wouldn't cause pregnancy.

A bit later, I learned from my friends that I couldn't get pregnant just by being *touched* that way. They gave me a much clearer picture of how I could and would get pregnant. Knowing the full truth, though, prompted other concerns and thoughts as I began to understand what my mother had been doing with her husband and my father. This may have been part of the reason she was hesitant to tell me the full truth.

Even though I was just nine, I still needed to know the truth because not knowing the truth led me to believe the lies. The lies, no matter what the motives, caused me more pain. Mother Nature's visit was a surprise. Now I knew why she had come, how her presence in my body would change me from a little girl to a young lady.

Time and experience would soon bridge the gap, helping me understand what Uncle Bill had both stolen and awakened. Sadder than his perverted violations was the lost opportunity by my not telling Mama. Could that have brought us closer in the ways I'd longed for—as close as she was to my sister? Would it have made it easier for her to guide me on the day I became a woman, far before either one of us was ready? Who knows? Then again, would she have believed my innocence, even at eight? Even if she had, would knowing the truth have made a difference?

❖ ❖ ❖

A Cut Away

My grandmother, Mama Nan, was tall with light skin and pretty brown eyes. She was born in 1910 but looked much younger than she actually was. My friends would often say, "That can't be your grandmother—she looks so young!" She flaunted it with pride, eating those compliments right up. Her favorite beverage was gin, and she drank it straight from the bottle. She put on makeup every day and wore a nice starched dress and an apron over the top. She penciled in her eyebrows because they were thin, and she wore a wig because her hair was thin, too. She was vain, seemed very happy and confident in her skin, and wore a big smile—especially toward me. I'm so glad she lived with us.

I was secure knowing how much she loved me. In fact, I was her favorite of the grandchildren. She made it clear to me that I was special to her by the way she interacted with me and the things she did for me. She made sure I had my clothes perfectly ironed for school. Even though they were purchased from the thrift store, she took pride in washing, starching, and ironing them, folding them immaculately so they looked like new clothing in the stores, and placing them in the drawer ready for me to wear. My clothes looked brand new every time I opened my drawers.

She also made sure my hair was combed for school. Most of the time, she fixed it in two ponytails with bangs. She smiled as she ushered me out the door to go to school every day.

She would also take me aside from the other kids almost every day and give me laxatives to "clean me out." She didn't want me to be sick. Back in her time, there were all kinds of home remedies. Some worked, some didn't, and some had bad side effects. She didn't realize that chronic laxative use would cause dependency. She clearly thought she was doing a good thing for me. I would learn that she, like many other adults, was sincere in her motives and actions but sincerely wrong in her understanding.

I felt bad, in a way, because she didn't treat my sister and brother as well as she treated me. I knew that preferential treatment was wrong. My older sister and brother were special to my mother, yet hers was the relationship I so desperately wanted. I used this disparity to justify my grandmother's overt favor toward me. It wasn't the same as getting love from my mother, but it was enough to appease me. I needed that to make things OK.

Since I was her favorite, I could count on Mama Nan to protect me. If I got into arguments with my mother, she would always come to my defense. On one of those occasions, something she said stuck with me. Mama Nan said to my mother, "You are hurting her just to get back at me." I had never been able to figure out why my mother treated me so badly. Nothing else really made sense. Maybe this could've been why. After all, it is simply natural for a mother to love her child.

I could always count on my grandmother—until that morning when everything changed.

I was getting ready for school, and Mama Nan instructed me to do something that was beyond my normal routine. I disobeyed her. I honestly don't remember *exactly what* I did or did not do that morning to deserve what happened.

I was only ten years old and wanted desperately to please her. But whatever I did caused her to slap my face ruthlessly. I was frozen with fear. I didn't know it was coming, and the surprise itself made me feel as if I might pass out. *Oh my God, what is going on? Why did she hit me in the face like that? It hurts so bad. God, why did she have to slap me?* It caught me off guard, and I didn't know what to do. I think it hurt my feelings almost more than my face. She had never ever hit me. Now, not only had she hit me, but I felt blood running from under my eye.

After a moment, once I realized what had happened and saw the blood, I started crying even more hysterically. She yelled, "Stop that crying, straighten your face up, get out of here, and go to school!" I desperately tried to stop crying for fear of getting slapped again, and I simply said something like, "Yes, ma'am," and walked to school. Survival was the name of the game.

Surviving was certainly a task I had been used to mastering, but for Mama Nan to slap me like that broke my little heart. I had no choice but to take the abuse. After all, I was a child. She was the adult. She was the one who was right. That was the bottom line, or so I had been told over and over, again and again. I never understood it. There was something illogical about a person being right or wrong simply based on his or her age. Convinced I knew my common sense was correct, I was still unable to change my situation.

When I was beaten in the past, I survived it. So, I decided to brush it off. After all, getting slapped by my mother was a common occurrence, so I knew I would be OK. Getting slapped by my Mama Nan wasn't. That truly hurt! But once again, I had to carry on. It took every ounce of energy I had to be OK with this terrible situation. Perhaps my grandmother treated me the way she treated my mother, which was most likely a reflection of the way her mother (whom I never knew) had treated her.

When I got to school, my teacher asked me what had happened. Not only was my cheek swollen where Mama Nan had hit me, but there was also a long cut under my eye from her ring. I hesitated to answer her because I was afraid. But she was the teacher, apparently concerned, so I had to answer her. She motioned for me to come to her desk away from the other children in class, and we talked about it.

"Oh, Rosie, what happened to you?" she said as she held my face in her hand.

"My grandmother slapped me this morning just when I was leaving for school," I responded with tears in my eyes.

"She slapped you? Is that how you got that scratch under your eye?"

"Yes, fro-om he-e-er we-e-edding r-r-r-ring," I stammered between sobs.

"Oh, honey, I need you to tell me everything that happened. Everything."

My teacher seemed to be very concerned about me, so I told her the whole story. It never would have occurred to me to lie to her. I simply told her the truth.

She sent me to the office and instructed me to tell the principal what had happened. I repeated the whole incident to him honestly and vividly. It didn't occur to me to lie to him either. Little did I know what trouble the truth would bring. I went back to class, soon distracted by the normal routine of a day in my classroom. It was just like any other school day, or so I thought. I had no idea what was happening behind the scenes, no idea at all.

Once classes had ended for the day, I became increasingly anxious about going home and facing my grandmother for the first time since she'd slapped me. *I bet things will be different 'cause Mama Nan has never hurt me like that. That makes me so sad. Will she still be mad? What do I say? I really messed up. Why did I talk back and get myself in trouble?* I questioned myself and practiced my answers all the way home.

Oh, how hard it was to walk in that door. And just as I had feared, things were not the same as they had been before the incident that morning. *Oh, she's mad at me. Why did I disobey her? I'm so sorry, Mama Nan.* She was not happy to see me. She didn't even acknowledge that I had come in the house! This all made me so very sad—and so afraid.

The rest of the day, I was consumed with how I could change the situation. *I should have kept my mouth shut. I was a bad girl, and that is why she slapped me. Things will get better. I know they will because Mama Nan loves me.* Despite my usual optimism, however, I had the sinking feeling that irreparable damage had been done, and the relationship between my grandmother and me was going downhill.

That evening and the next day, I had to fend for myself. *She's looking at me like she hates me. I already got my punishment, so why is she still mad at me?* I was so confused and it was so hard, but I managed to piece things together to get ready for school. It was clear that life had changed in a big way, but I went to school and tried to act as if nothing had happened. The puffy, swollen patch beneath my eye had bloomed with color overnight, a very visible reminder of what had happened just the day before. I felt a resolve in my attitude to push on through and make the very best of this sad situation. I had no other choice.

The school day proceeded as usual, and again I returned home to a very chilly reception. It was obvious to me that my grandmother had not warmed up to me at all. Shortly after I got home, a sophisticated-looking man dressed in a suit knocked on the front door. I let him in. He said he was there to see my mother. I was not allowed to stay in the living room to hear what they talked about, but I assumed it concerned what my grandmother had done.

After he left, my mother told me that I needed to go back to the person I talked to at school the next day and tell him that I had made it up. "Tell him that you lied about your grandmother hitting you. Tell him that you really just ran into the screen door," my mother said. Even without my mother saying it, I was getting the sickening feeling that I'd gotten my grandmother in trouble. I didn't want that. I still saw her as my security—the only adult I could count on to take care of me. Time would prove that I was right. *I didn't mean to get Mama Nan in trouble, but that is exactly what I did.* So, I decided to make things right for us, to fix the problem that I had determined was my fault. Therefore, I was focused on obeying my mother and doing exactly what she had instructed me to do. I went to school the next day and told my teacher I lied and that I really had run into the screen door.

I will never forget the hateful words Mama Nan yelled at me when I "told on her":

"You little wench! You are on your own from now on!"

I didn't say a word back to her. I didn't know what to say. I just looked at the hatred in her eyes and cried like a baby as I thought, *Oh why did I do it? Why did I tell on my grandmother? It's my fault.*

Mama Nan never again treated me the same as she had before the incident. My little world was irreparably damaged. As far as the parent–child relationship, my fears turned out to be a reality. I had nobody in my corner.

Mama Nan had decided to end the loving bond between us. I had no choice but to accept what I could not change and learn how to fend for myself. I don't remember exactly how I made it without her, but I did.

I had to grow up quickly. I taught myself how to wash and iron my own clothes, take care of my hair, and absolutely everything that Mama Nan had done for me. She was bound and determined to make me pay for "telling on her," and there was no mercy for me when I needed it the most. The security of my grandmother's love was gone. Without Mama Nan, I was all alone.

As an adult, although our relationship was better and remained amicable for the rest of our lives together, it was never the same. She became ill, had a stroke, and was bedridden for several years. As I looked upon her frail body and into her sinking eyes, I remembered the good days when she was the only one I could really count on to take care of me. When I spoke to her, she was unable to speak back clearly. But she was able to smile, and that spoke volumes to me. Forgiving her became my goal, and it felt great! I wanted nothing more than to shower her with mercy and grace. Visiting her was a pleasure because I desperately wanted her to know how much I loved her and would not let one mistake sever what was deep within my soul. I would greet her with a kiss on the cheek and say to her, "I love you, Mama Nan."

She would respond in almost incomprehensible words, but I did understand when she said, "I love you." Soon our earthly relationship was severed forever, but our soul connection was restored by the words from our hearts and the outward reflection of our smiles.

Gifts of Mind

One day when I was about ten years old, I had a bright idea. I had acknowledged my mother's rejection and now my grandmother's. I decided to fill the void with another person, a woman who would come to nurture me as I had always hoped my mother would. I had thought of her and dreamed of her, and finally I found her. Her name was Ms. Brown.

Ms. Brown was the epitome of what I thought a good mother should be. She was plump with short gray hair and always had a hug and a big smile for me whenever I visited. I loved the way she dressed with her neat apron. That was exactly what my grandmother always wore. Like Mama Nan, Ms. Brown captured the essence of a mother ready to care for her family. Therefore, she was a suitable replacement—indeed, the best I had found.

In addition to bringing contentment to my broken heart, she brought joy. She gave me the most wonderful little gifts. Every single day, I could count on her to give me something, something tangible that I could show off. Those gifts of love made me feel so special. I loved to talk about my mother-type friend. "She gives me nail polish, candy, cookies, and toys—all of that stuff because she loves me. She gives that stuff to me because I am special to her—very special!" I would proudly tell my friends and my family.

Ms. Brown was in my life at the right time for the right reason, and I was so glad she was there. I understood how much I needed her and was resting satisfied in her presence, in her gifts, and in the fact that I could show my little world that life was good. I was able to show them that I was OK and that I was happy. More importantly, I was able to pull myself up and stand content in what she would do for me. She accepted me and made me happy. How timely! Happiness was just what I needed.

There was only one little problem with Ms. Brown. Actually, it was one big problem. She didn't exist. No, she was not a real person at all. All make-believe. Despite this one problem, she and I had a great relationship. I would daydream about her, and my dreams were wonderful. She was always excited to see me when I went to her apartment nearby to visit, which was very often. That's what I told people, and they all believed me. They seemed genuinely happy for me.

I loved, loved, loved knowing Ms. Brown. What a gift it was to have her in my life, even though she really only existed in my mind. I figured out a way to make the relationship more believable. I acquired the "gifts" she had given me and then showed them off with great confidence. The mission was accomplished; I had it all figured out.

My plan worked just fine. I got the gifts from a grocery store that was less than two blocks away. There was just one more little problem. I didn't have any money to buy the stuff. Since these "gifts" were necessary for Ms. Brown's existence, I realized I had to steal. Yes, I convinced myself to lie and to steal. It was the only way to prove how much Ms. Brown really cared.

Although lying was wrong, the end sometimes justified the means, right? Generating the perfect maternal substitute was serious business, and I had achieved great success. *I know it's not the truth, but I'm not hurting anybody; I just need someone like her to love me,* I would whisper to myself. Obviously it was my little secret, and I was totally content with all my thoughts and with all my actions. After all, I practiced this fairy-tale dream of a mother day after day, and everyone around me could see how happy I was. But that store-stolen happiness soon came to an end.

On one hot summer day, I decided Ms. Brown was going to "give" me something she had not given me before—ice cream. Of course, I was going to steal it and then show everyone what I had gotten from Ms. Brown again. Only this time, I was after a bigger gift—several of them.

I always knew who was working at the store, what they were doing, and where they were doing it. I walked up and down the aisles just looking around, thinking about my next move. Being an inconspicuous little girl, I had gotten away with this pattern for a long time. There were no surveillance cameras, undercover security officers, police officers, or any high-tech security systems that we have today. None of that existed. Since there were usually only one or two people working in that small inner-city store, they were frequently multitasking. It was fairly easy to pocket quite a few things while they weren't looking. I had the procedure down pat. Nobody knew what I was up to, and that exhilarated me.

Per my usual routine, I walked in the door, greeted the owner, and then started looking around the aisles for something to buy—something to steal. Most of the time, I did both. I could buy candy for a penny a piece, but after spending a dime or so, I would come out with so much more. I loved it when I had a quarter, and if I had a dollar, well, I was rich.

That day, I was thinking big but wearing little. I was dressed in just a halter top and shorts. When nobody was looking, I quickly grabbed two small containers of ice cream and put them in my halter top. I figured that if anyone noticed I looked "big" in that area, he or she would simply think I was big-busted like my sister. Like all the other times before, I had a plan and was certain things would work out just fine. That illogical thinking seemed logical in my undeveloped mind. After all, I was still getting away with it.

The containers were cold and uncomfortable in the halter top against my skin, but they wouldn't be there for long. I would take them out just as soon as I walked out the door, crossed the street, and got to the alley. I looked around quickly to see if any-one had noticed, then made my way out the door. I had stolen yet again. Mission accomplished. I held my head high and strut-ted my petite body out the door, just like all the times before, with more boldness that comes only with repeated success.

I walked out the door to find the owner ready and waiting for me. He grabbed me by the arm and said, "Hey, little girl, give me that ice cream and come with me." There it was. Finally, my shame had caught up with me. I bowed my head and wanted to cry, but I held back the tears. *Oh no, oh my God, I got caught!* I was busted. I didn't try to resist in any way. I obeyed him, gave him the ice cream, and followed him.

The owner took me past the cash register on the right and down a long hall behind the dairy section to a small room in the back of the store. I was headed to a place where customers didn't usually go. That room was totally different from the rest of the store. It was dimly lit, cold and barren, and furnished with just a dirty-looking desk, one table, and a few chairs. I shivered as I looked around at the darkness of the room and realized I was in big trouble. *What am I going to do?*

He told me to sit down because he was going to call the police. He said they would come get me, take me to jail, lock me up behind tall steel bars, and I might never see my family again. I cried. Of course, I believed him—every single word he said! *Oh my God, I'm going to jail!*

I was there alone while he was in another room talking on the phone. I heard him saying something like, "I have a little girl here, and she stole some ice cream. Yes, uh-huh. Yes, she's right here, Officer. Yes, OK. I'll tell her you're on the way." He talked loud and clear, as if he wanted me to hear every word. And I did hear every word. My mind raced with fear as I pictured what would unfold.

After hanging up the phone, he returned to the room with an angry look on his face. I knew I was going to jail. As far as I was concerned, his mean look confirmed to me that I'd be locked up. They'd toss away the key, and my life as I knew it would be over. I started crying hysterically as my thoughts ran wild. *I don't want to go to jail!* I screamed inside. Then I seriously prayed that God would help me escape punishment. *Please, God, I'm so sorry. I won't ever do it again. Please help me.* But instead of confessing and telling the truth out loud, I lied to the man. "These big girls told me to steal some ice cream for them or they would beat me up," I stuttered between the tears and sobs.

Probably realizing that he had put the fear of God in me with the police bit, the store owner said, "Where is your mother?"

"I dunno where she is."

I thought she was at work, but I was not about to help him find her. Calling her would be almost worse than calling the police! It was becoming clear that he wouldn't let me go home until he talked to someone in my family face to face. It's really too bad my Ms. Brown was not real and thus not available.

"By the way, what is your name?"

"Rosie."

"Where do you live?"

"Right up that alley and around the corner." As I pointed in the direction of the apartment, I was hoping he would decide to let me go since I lived close by. I quickly realized that was only wishful thinking.

"I'm not gonna let you leave here without talking to your mother, and that's final."

Talk to my mother! Oh no! If my mother finds out, she will kill me!

"What about my big sister since she takes care of me when Mama's gone?"

"OK, go ahead and call her and get her up here."

"Yes, sir."

I dialed the phone and Loretta answered. He stood right next to me as I explained to her that I had stolen some ice cream, how I was in serious trouble, and I needed her to come to the store immediately. There was no doubt my sister would agree that what I'd done was wrong. But I hoped she could at least protect me from going to jail.

Loretta was there in minutes. When she walked into the store and back to the room where I was imprisoned, she looked at me with a mixture of anger and pity. But thankfully she came through for me. She went along with the lie that we had no idea where to find Mama.

"Why did you do something stupid like that, girl?" Even with that greeting, I was so glad to see her.

"There was some big girls who told me to do it or they were gonna beat me up," I responded with a grimace on my face as if I was going to cry.

She had come to my rescue. I was so thankful. Because I was afraid of jail, I had also lied to her about the big girls making me steal the ice cream. I could literally see myself living behind the bars of a prison cell, which was a terribly frightening thought. Come to find out, Loretta never believed a word I said. She'd had no trouble seeing straight through my lies.

She and the store owner went back to the same room where he had called the police, only this time, I didn't hear much from either of them behind the closed door. The next thing I heard was when she opened the door and said to him, "I'll see to it that she never does it again."

I held my head down in shame as my sister and I walked out of the store. Once we had crossed the street, my sister said she wouldn't tell on me. I was so relieved. Even so, what I had done was wrong, and I deserved to be punished—not only for stealing and lying but also for the reasons behind it. Big lesson learned!

I may have been just a little girl, but I understood the real problem, or at least in part. I was determined to deal with it. I was keenly aware that I had a price to pay for lying to make myself happy, by looking for love in things and in people, especially pretend people. I vowed to never take anything from anybody ever again. This also meant that my lying had to stop. Easier said than done, I'm afraid. Lying is a hard habit to break. I still lacked the emotional strength to tell the whole truth. Instead, I did the best I could and told another lie to end a lie. I told my friends and sister and brother that Ms. Brown had moved away. No, it still wasn't the truth. It merely eliminated the need to steal gifts for the fictitious Ms. Brown to lavish upon me.

That day had started with my concocting a mischievous plan to further a lie, but it ended with an invaluable lesson on the consequences of living a lie. This important (and rare) bit of morality guided me through decisions I'd later face. It stuck with me through the rest of my life. I was thankful to have learned such an important lesson so early on despite the lack of more affectionate and truthful role models.

Once imprisoned by the need to have Ms. Brown give me gifts, I later discovered the underlying need to be loved and accepted. Understanding the extent to which I had gone, creating a fictitious character who would love me, I realized I already had my Heavenly Father who was real to me, who was the only constant truth in my life. Never again did I feel the need to create someone to love me.

❖ ❖ ❖

Two Girlfriends

It wasn't so hard to give up lying and stealing. I felt better about myself when I was telling the truth because it pleased my Heavenly Father. From then on, if I lied, it was to obey my mother. I didn't like it, but I didn't have a choice. It wasn't long before another issue emerged, demanding my full attention and leaving me even more troubled and disenchanted with certain grown-ups I knew.

Paula Smith was my next-door neighbor and my very best friend. She was much taller than I was. Her hair was beautiful—long, thick, and jet black. Her mother, Mrs. Smith, combed it into two ponytails and bangs just like mine. Paula was always dressed in the perfect clothes for any occasion, making it obvious to me that she was dearly loved by her family. I wasn't jealous of her—I was in awe of her. I felt the happiest when I was with her, her brothers, and her parents. They seemed like the perfect family.

Paula and I had a lot of fun hanging out with each other day after day. If we weren't going to the store, we were playing together at the park, at the school's playground, or in the backyard. Paula and I also had fun with the rest of the kids in the neighborhood. We played games such as hide-and-seek, kickball, and baseball. We played with the other kids until it started to get dark. Mama had always told us to come home when the streetlights came on.

Having a good friend like Paula gave me much joy. She was a well-behaved girl who never gave her parents any trouble and always respected my family as well. I don't recall a time when either of us was told to leave and go home because we had been disobedient to the adults in the other person's home. For the most part, we were just good kids.

Paula's two older brothers had already moved out, so their apartment wasn't as crowded as ours. Usually it was just Paula, her loving parents (who were significantly older than my parents), and their big, friendly dog. Sometimes I was invited to come in and eat dinner with them, which I thoroughly enjoyed. Their food was different from what we had to eat. I assume it was because they could afford to purchase more and better food from the grocery store. The meat we ate mostly was the garbage that was thrown away at the packinghouse where my grandfather worked.

Even though our apartment was identical to the Smiths', theirs felt like a model home to me. I was welcomed there with open arms and treated just as if I were a member of the Smith family. What a comfort that was to my young, love-starved heart. Their family life seemed always peaceful, loving, and calm—just the opposite of mine.

Paula and I had another friend, Mary. The three of us often played in the park several blocks away from the apartments. Mary and her family lived in a red ranch-style house that could be seen from our backyard and was less than a block away. Paula and I would have loved to have the same relationship with Mary that we had with each other. But for some reason, we were never allowed to go into Mary's house. Her parents wouldn't allow it, and I had no idea why. Paula and I were well-behaved children who simply wanted to play with Mary because she was our friend. However, her parents were adamant that we couldn't come inside the house, yet they allowed us to play together outside.

What was it that kept me from being welcomed into their home? What was so wrong with me—with us? I was even more mortified when Mary came to my apartment for a visit. The same thing happened! She wasn't allowed to come inside our apartment either. *Why can't she come inside to play with me? Why can't I go inside her house? Paula can come inside to play with me, and I am more than welcome to go inside her house to play with her. What is the problem?* I hadn't been a bad girl around Mary's parents. In fact, I always made sure to be on my best behavior because I loved being Mary's friend. As perplexing as this was, Mary and I respected each other's family. We knew neither of us had any contagious diseases that would affect the other. What could possibly be the issue?

I remember a certain day when I went for a visit. I just wanted to play with my good friend Mary. I walked up and excitedly knocked on the door. Her mother called out to answer, opened the door, and had a mean look on her face when she saw it was me.

"Can I come in to see Mary?"

"Mary is busy right now and can't come outside to play."

"Can I come in and wait for her, then?"

"No, you can't."

"Well, can she come inside my house when she gets done?"

"No, she can't."

I sensed something was very wrong but was unable to express what I perceived as prejudice. So, I went home to investigate my thoughts and had the same conversation with my mother and grandmother.

"Mama, can Mary come inside our house and play with me sometimes?"

"No! No, she can't."

"Why not, Mama? You let Paula come over all the time. Why can't Mary come over, too?"

"Because I said so, and that's final!" I didn't respond, but I was thinking hard. "Do you understand?"

"Yes, ma'am."

The truth was I didn't understand why adults treated kids as if they had some kind of disease. There's no way skin color was some form of sickness. Eventually, I realized the real problem. Our parents were racist! I abhorred the very idea. It was absolutely ridiculous—it made no sense to me at all! We had done nothing wrong, so why were we being judged as if we had? We were simply two good girls wanting to play together with a third. Both Mary and I had good manners and didn't cause anybody any trouble. Both of us showed respect to the other's family. Neither of us had a disease that was going to affect the other. *Stupid grown-ups…What's wrong with them?* I didn't dare let those words come out of my mouth, but I sure wanted to.

I couldn't let this issue go. Eventually I got my answer.

"Because white people just don't like colored people," she blurted out to me. "You need to understand that, girl," she added, as if I were clueless.

Yeah, that's right—all white people don't like all colored people, I thought sarcastically. *I'm sorry. I don't believe that's true.*

"OK," I responded.

But it really was not OK with me. In that moment, I understood I was too young to change the situation, so I held my head down and walked away.

This was the beginning of really hearing the same message echoed from all corners of my life.

"Why do you like white people?" colored people would sometimes say to me.

"Don't you know they are just using you? They don't care about you," my mother would say.

I don't know which tone of Mama's was more troubling to me. Sometimes she would use that bitter, angry tone. But more disturbing was her gentle, matter-of-fact version. How sad that she couldn't see past her own experience to help me make sense of mine. It took me a long time to understand, although I strived to gently prove to her and other people that they were wrong about the races. All of "them" don't dislike all of "us" any more than all of us dislike them. I know that because I'm one of "them" AND one of "us."

My friend Mary was like my other friends, and she absolutely *did* like me and *did* care about me. I could understand that what my family said may be true about *some* white people, but it certainly wasn't true about Mary! I could understand that what Mary's mother said about some colored people was true, but it certainly wasn't true about all colored people. It definitely wasn't true about Paula or me.

Nor did I understand some of the other things I was told repeatedly as I got older: "You talk proper—you act like you wanna be white," people would say. "I'll bet that when you grow up, you're gonna wanna be like those white people who have maids and stuff. Yeah, you wanna be white. Anybody can see that."

Their words would echo in my head. *What does that mean, "I wanna be white"? Nah, I don't want to be white,* I'd think to myself. I just want to be me—who I am.

I didn't fully understand until later what they meant by this, or the underlying reason they said it. Even so, something deep down in my young heart and soul cried out to fight against this idea that some people are inferior while others are superior. I could see the stereotypes of the haves and the have-nots, the educated and the uneducated, the suburbs and the ghetto. As sure as I knew my own name, I knew that our inner beings were identical in the eyes of our Creator.

Truly, I didn't want to be a white person. I just wanted to be a *better* person—the best person I could be, as God had created me. I wouldn't accept my family's ridicule no matter how often I was labeled "different" or the "white child." I didn't understand how wanting to be a bright, intelligent girl meant I was trying to be white. I just didn't get that logic and wouldn't accept it.

I did aspire to be different, not simply for the sake of being different but rather to take a stand against the lie of racism that was becoming very evident even at my young age. Those repeated accusations hurt at times, but I held on to my convictions. I simply refused to adopt the same destructive perspectives of those around me.

Paula and Mary were both my good friends, and I will never forget what I learned from the time I spent with both of them.

Mama, Please Help Me

Mama was bold and tough. She was afraid of no one. She would cuss anyone who crossed her—man or woman—anyone who gave her a hard time. And, most of the time when she had an argument with one of her boyfriends, he would back down. "Cussing like a sailor" was minor compared to my mother's X-rated, vivid vocabulary. Her vulgarity was so piercing to my young heart and ears that I could hardly stand it.

We are kids and should not have to hear this nasty language all the time. Why does she have to talk like that? We were exposed to that kind of environment, and we lived in it night and day. Even though we kids heard that language all the time, we were told, "Don't do as I do; do as I say." Yes, we were told that, and we were beaten if we cursed. I also wondered why my mother got involved with men she didn't like. I just couldn't understand why she'd put up with them being mean to her. It didn't make sense to me. Something was wrong with the way she was thinking. Of course, that explicit language tempted a vivid curiosity about what exactly she was doing with these men. I couldn't erase the thoughts from my young mind.

Occasionally, I had to get up with the babies at night, feed them, and change their diapers. As I recall, these were the times she was going out partying or needed to sleep since she had to go to work the next day. I literally remember nights when my mother was in the room with her baby in her bed downstairs, and she would yell out to me, "Rosie! Come and get this baby." In other words, *You come and do my job while I sleep. After all, I need my sleep.* What a life for a kid. Of course, I couldn't complain because I would pay for it.

Some of my responsibilities were just unfair. One was to keep my mother's uniforms cleaned. And since she had only two complete sets, I had to wash them daily. Five days a week, she would come home and take off her uniform, slip, girdle, panties, and stockings, and it was my job to make sure she had a clean outfit for the next day. I would wash them in the bathtub on the scrub board, rinse them thoroughly, wring each piece out, and hang them outside on the clothesline or sometimes in the kitchen over the door to dry. *I have to keep my clothes clean; why do I have to keep hers clean, too? She's an adult; why can't she do that herself? That's just wrong.*

My mother worked at a hospital where she prepared food for the patients and employees. She was very proud of her job. Her attire was immaculate every day. She wore a white uniform dress, white shoes, and white stockings. It was obvious that she really enjoyed working there. I went to work with her several times and always found her smiling, laughing, and having happy-go-lucky relationships with her coworkers. She loved her job so much that she said, "Whenever they close down this hospital, I'm done working." *Really? She's gonna quit working? What's gonna happen to us?*

For now, though, my mother was working, and I was glad about that. During the workweek, she stayed sober. But on the weekend, things were completely different. She would come home from the nightclubs in a drunken stupor, often with a man in tow. I was instructed to not tell anybody they were there spending the night in my mother's bedroom. Even at this very young age, I knew what was happening, and I knew it wasn't right. More importantly, I knew I shouldn't have been told to lie about it— about anything. Caught between my conscience and my mother, I obeyed the latter and joined in the covering.

I remember feeling a certain awkwardness meeting one of these "uncles" while visiting my mother at work. I thought I recognized that bald-headed, short, stocky, dark-skinned man from somewhere, but I was told to keep that to myself and act as if I had never seen him. Not only was he her coworker, but he was also married. Whenever I saw him at the hospital, I pretended as if I didn't know him, just as I was told. Keeping that secret was hard on me—not just because it wasn't right, but also because I believe the secret-keeping helped me lie to myself about how much it affected me. *There he is. I wish he would not come to our house. What's going on is wrong. But I can't say anything.*

In our home, he acknowledged me. At the hospital, we pretended to be strangers. He knew just how to give me the eye, so to speak. No, I wasn't going to tell a soul.

Mama had been married and never divorced, even though she didn't live with her husband Craig. I remember that they seemed to be like friends going their separate ways with other people in their lives.

Her husband was nice to her and all of us kids. I was comfortable around him. I even remember spending the night at his house with him and his girlfriend. He once showed me a picture of him and another man in a boxing ring, both wearing boxing gloves. Somebody had told me he was a real prizefighter. How I loved bragging that I personally knew a real prizefighter!

The last I remember of Craig was that he died of a heart attack. Not long after that, Mama started to receive his social security checks. It's a good thing because money issues would soon get worse. In 1965, after ten years of employment, the hospital doors were closed for business. This was not easy to watch. I knew how much Mama enjoyed working there. She'd also said she didn't know what she would do about money without a job.

What she did, or didn't do, about the lack of income was disappointing. She wasn't much older than forty, if that, and still quite capable of holding a job. True to her earlier declaration, however, she did stop working. *We are already poor. Why would she just quit working? So what if that hospital has closed? Can't she go find a job at another hospital?*

Again, she was the adult and I was the child. I gave her the benefit of the doubt, assuming there may have been something I didn't know. Still, it appeared that she was simply tired of working and didn't consider how we children would be affected by her decision. The message to me was that when you don't want to work, you settle for less, even if your family suffers as a result of it. That is exactly what happened. From that point on, Mama raised us three kids only on the social security checks after her husband died. We were dirt poor.

Expectation, Disappointment, and Betrayal

I was twelve years old, but my life behind closed doors did not reflect my age. I was living in a horrific environment, it seemed, every day of my life. But this day was going to be different, unlike any I had experienced at home before. That is what I was promised. That is what I believed would happen.

It was a wonderful Saturday morning in 1961. I awoke excited about what was going to happen that delightful spring day. It was the perfect day outside—the sun was shining so brightly. It was also the perfect day within; my heart was racing, irresistibly over-powered with anticipation. *What a great day it's going to be!*

That day, all was well with me because I had plans, really great plans, unlike any I'd had before. In fact, I was so happy that I jumped out of bed, not giving a second thought to going back to sleep as most kids my age would do on a Saturday. Usually, my older sister, older brother, and I were awakened at the crack of dawn to do our chores, which was depressing. I felt like one of the servants called on for duty instead of a child enjoying the nurturing that children need. This day was different. Getting the work done was not the most important thing on my mind; having fun with my friends was.

I quickly left my tiny room and hurried to the bathroom. When I looked in the mirror, I could see the excitement lighting up my face. I had exciting, happy, and childlike plans for that day.

It was time for the annual carnival, a two-day event to be held Friday and Saturday from 6:00 p.m. until 10:00 p.m. at the elementary school two blocks away. I had never been allowed to go to the carnival before. But this day was different. Mama had said yes this time, and I was overjoyed! Truthfully, I wanted to go both nights, but Mama had said that because she was going out, I had to stay home Friday night to take care of my baby sister and brother, which was not unusual. Oh, how I wanted to go both nights, but to my great relief and joy, she assured me that I could go Saturday, and I was pleased with that.

Saturday evening came, and I had done my chores—the house was immaculate; the diapers and other clothes had been washed by hand on a scrub board and hung out to dry; the bottles were ready for the baby; and everything else I was expected to do was done. I had taken care of anything that might prevent my evening of fun with my friends.

Time seemed to be standing still as I sat watching the hands of the clock. Finally, it was 5:45! My girlfriend would arrive at any moment now, and we would be off to have lots and lots of fun. A few minutes later, there was a knock at the door, and I ran to answer it. There she was, ready to go to the carnival. Yes, the time had come!

"Hello! Are you ready to go?" she asked.

"Wait a minute. I gotta get some money," I replied. I left her standing in the doorway and walked quickly into the kitchen where Mama and her boyfriend, Sam, were talking. "Mama, I'm ready to go!"

"Go where?"

What does she mean, "Go where"? I thought.

"To the carnival, remember? You said I could go."

"Well, uh…uh, you have to take care of these kids," she replied. "I'm going out."

"You said I couldn't go last night, but you promised me I could go today!" I shouted in protest. *I never get to do anything fun like other kids. All I do is work, work, work, work like a slave! I'm not a slave, Mama. I'm a child—a child, Mama—your child!* I didn't dare say that aloud. *What is going on here? I don't believe what she said. Oh no, this can't be happening. This is wrong—this is terribly wrong!*

I stood there for a few moments in turmoil. I felt hollow on the inside—as if my life as a little girl had been taken away—as if I had no hope to ever be like other kids, free to enjoy laughing, playing, and just having fun. I craved that so much—just having fun—if only for one evening. Now *that* had been taken away. Yes, taken away from me. And I was powerless to change my situation—powerless to give myself what I needed so desperately. I needed to feel like Mama's precious little girl. But I felt like Mama's servant. That's what I was really feeling inside my heart and my soul, but I kept it inside to avoid punishment. *Oh my!* I thought. My heart was so heavy. Tears streamed from my eyes like rivers of running water. Pain was rocking inside my head, and anger engulfed my mind. I could not believe what I was hearing. I was furious that my plans had been changed again.

"You promised me! You said I could go to the carnival!" I shouted back at her again.

"Shut up! Shut up!" Sam yelled at me.

I heard the door slam. My friend had gone. *I should have known this was too good to be true. She's gone. This ain't right,* I thought as I stared at my mama motionless, frozen in fear for a few seconds. But I was screaming on the inside and unable to keep it all in any longer.

"You said I could go!" I repeated to Mama, ignoring her boyfriend. "That's not right!" I shouted at Mama.

Suddenly, I felt the heat of a hand upon my face and pain in my body as I hit the floor. The blow came not from my mama but from her boyfriend, who had decided he had heard enough. I stood up, dizzy, and my vision was blurred from the blow to my head. Yet, I continued questioning Mama—rather, yelling at her. "Why, Mama? Why did you let him hurt me like that?" I just wanted to go have fun with my friends—that's all. I didn't do anything wrong. "Why, Mama?" I cried.

I'm just a kid, just a kid. Why does this always happen to me? Why? I repeated inside my hurting head. *I should have known it was too good to be true, that it wasn't gonna happen.*

"He has a right to hit you. He has done more for you than your daddy ever did!" Mama's words hit me that day, words that would leave deeper scars than any physical wound.

What? He has a right to hit me? What does that have to do with anything? This is not about him. This is about me—your daughter, Mama! I thought as I tried to figure out why I was being hurt so badly. I was hurt physically, but the emotional pain was devastating. Blood was running down my little face. Although I could hardly see and stood swaying, struggling to keep my balance, I continued to yell, "Mama, Mama, Mama, you said I could go!"

She stood there with a blank look on her face, just stood there and said and did nothing. Oh, but not him—he was determined to shut me up.

"Shut up! Shut up!" Sam yelled again, running toward me with blatant hatred in his eyes.

I stood there and thought again, *Why can't I be like other kids? I haven't asked for much. I just want to be a child and have fun sometimes. I don't understand.*

I continued crying out, "Mama promised I could go!" I was defiant even though I knew more pain was probably coming.

Then that hateful man grabbed me and punched me in the face, fist flying as if he were beating a man, not spanking a child. He knocked me to the floor. When I stood up, he hurled me across the kitchen into the wall as if he wanted to destroy me.

There was nothing I could do or say to stop what was happening. Battered, feeling betrayed and abandoned, I changed in that moment. I had to distance my mind (and body) from the ones who were supposed to protect and love me. I vowed never to speak to them again.

I managed to struggle my way to the bathroom. I looked in the mirror, and my face looked awful! *My body hurts all over,* I thought as I walked out of the bathroom. I stumbled as I went up the steep wooden stairway, holding my forehead in my hands. I was in such pain. Finally, I reached my tiny bedroom and fell on the bed. "Oh my God, my God," I kept repeating. "Please help me!"

My heart was broken into tiny pieces. My head and body felt as hollow as a dark, empty tunnel. *Why?* I continued to ask myself with accelerating intensity. The anger was boiling up in me like a volcano about to explode. Vengeance shadowed my sadness and self-pity. *I will get him. Yes, someday I will make him pay,* I thought as I sat up on my bed. *I'm gonna call the police right now.*

I stumbled across the hall to Mama's room to use the telephone. I called the police and shook with fear as the phone began to ring. I thought of hanging up, but I felt anger shouting in my ears, sending chills down my spine and saying, *Do it! Do it!*

I thought the police would never answer. "Answer the phone! Answer the phone!" I repeated anxiously out loud.

Finally, I heard a woman say, "Police Department."

I hesitated for a few seconds. *What do I say? How do I say it?* I wondered.

"Police Department," she repeated.

The words began to tumble out of my mouth. "H-h-h-he, m-m-m-my mother's boyfriend beat me up," I stuttered between sobs. "He hurt me so bad. Please come get him! Take him to jail!" I cried.

"Wait a minute, honey. Calm down. Where are you?"

"I'm at home, upstairs. He beat me up, and I'm just a little girl. He's a grown man!" I cried in an angry voice.

"Where is your mother?"

"She's downstairs with him!"

"Put her on the phone. We'll have to get her consent to pick him up."

"No! She's on his side!" I stammered.

"I'm sorry, honey. There is nothing we can do without your mother's consent."

What? There's nothing they can do? The police can't help me!

I didn't know what to say. Stunned, I couldn't believe what was happening. I stood there for a few seconds in disbelief and then hung up the phone. I felt trapped, as if I were sinking in quicksand. "My God, my God, why are you letting this happen to me?" I cried.

I returned to my room and curled up on the bed in a fetal position facing the window. I stared out the window and kept talking to myself and praying to God. "Oh, God, why, why did he beat me? Is he drunk? Why, oh why?" I cried. The tears kept falling for hours. My pillow was sopping wet when I finally drifted off to sleep.

The next morning, I woke up thinking for a few seconds that I'd had a bad dream. As I moved to get out of bed, I knew it hadn't been a dream. *Oh, it hurts so bad!* The pain stretched from my head to my feet. Finally, I managed to sit up. "Oh, oh!" I groaned in agony as my feet touched the floor.

I stood up slowly, grimacing from the pain that shot through my body with each movement. I walked down the stairs to the bathroom, where I stood in front of the mirror and stared at my broken and bruised face. My eyes were swollen. My face looked lopsided, and my lips had doubled in size. I was devastated as I saw what had happened to me.

Tears ran down my face as I reflected on the beating that had disfigured my face. The tears began to flow even faster as I thought of the reason it had happened. *I don't know why I have to be beaten when I speak up. I just don't understand. And by him. Usually Mama would slap me around. But him?—and with his fist! Why did he have to beat me like that? If I had deserved it, then maybe.* I struggled to make sense of it. *No! Nobody deserves that,* I corrected myself. I continued this dialogue with myself as I slumped over the basin. I was still in such pain.

The silence was eerie as I walked into the kitchen. Everyone was gone except my baby brother, who was sound asleep. I looked at the wall and then quickly back to the spot on the floor where I'd lain in pain. I screamed inside as I thought of all the details of the previous night. I was the only one hurting this morning and wondered why.

Where are they now? How do they feel this morning? I thought, hoping their guilt would find its mark and bring remorse and a reason. *I'm glad they're not here. I don't ever want to see them again,* I reminded myself.

As the days passed, I tried to hide the signs of abuse from others. I winced a little less each day as I combed my hair. My eyes were swollen, and I often wore sunglasses to cover the obvious. The severity of the beating became more real as some people did not even recognize me.

While I was in physical pain for a long time, it slowly faded. But the emotional pain lasted for years, leaving an indelible imprint on my mind. I wrestled to emotionally understand why my mama had allowed this to happen to me. Still, I loved her. She was my mama; that bond could not be broken. Sam, however, I hated with a passion that touched every fiber of my being.

Over the next few months, thoughts of that day lingered in my mind. I tried to erase it. I tried to understand it. I tried to forget it. But I was fighting a losing battle. I wanted to wipe him off the face of the earth so that he would never hurt me again.

❖ ❖ ❖

Trapped for a Reason

"Life is like photography. You need the negatives to develop."
—*Unknown*

The Cost of Gifts

When I was thirteen, we lived in a house that didn't feel like a home. Yet, it was bigger than the apartments we lived in when I was just a little girl. The chaos had moved right along with us, just to a bigger area.

I had an Aunt Beth, my mother's younger sister. She looked like my grandmother, Mama Nan. She was tall, thin, light skinned, and had a vibrant, bubbly personality. She loved to party and cussed like a sailor, but she was always nice to me.

Her boyfriend, Jim, was really nice to me, too. He was nice to all of us. By nice I mean that he would always bring us candy and stuff, which made us very happy. We called him Uncle Jim even though he wasn't married to my aunt. My sisters, brothers, and I loved to see him coming to bring us treats. We really, really loved that!

But one day, while the two of us were alone in the house, things changed. He had smiled at me and began to look me up and down. There was something terribly wrong with the way he was looking at me. The look on his face was devilish, and his approach was making me very uncomfortable. What he said to me was even worse. "You sure are growing up to be a nice-looking young lady, all developed and everything. You know, I've been giving you a lot down through the years; it's time for you to give me something." *Oh my God, what is he about to do to me? He's a grown man, and I'm just a girl. What in the world is wrong with him?* His eyes were undressing me. My heart was beating so fast I could hear it and feel it pounding in my chest. After standing there for only a few seconds and sensing him moving toward me, I ran upstairs and locked the bedroom door so he couldn't get to me.

He came after me, knocked on the door, and tried talking differently. "Oh, I was just playing with you, girl. You can come on out."

I was a kid but not a fool and said no. Finally, he went away. I heard him walking downstairs. Even when I heard him close the front door, I was still afraid to come out. I believed he was setting me up to think he had left and was sure he would attack me when I walked downstairs. I stayed locked in the room for what seemed like hours until my mother came home.

After that day, whenever we made eye contact, Jim had a little smirk on his face and appeared to still want me to "give him something." There was no mistake about it.

Yes, I understood his intentions. And to make sure he wouldn't hurt me when I was by myself and unable to get away from him, I decided to tell Mama. *I will tell her everything he said to me, how he was acting, everything. I remember what happened to me before when I didn't know what to do. I was scared back then. Not this time. I will tell her what he did, and she will give him a piece of her mind. She ain't gonna let him get away with that.*

Within a few hours, Mama was home. As soon as she opened the door, I told her. "Mama, Uncle Jim came in the house and was looking at me funny. He was eyeing me all up and down, smiling and stuff. Then he said, 'You're all grown up now. I've been giving you things all the time. It's time for you to give me something.' I was so-o-o-o-o scared!" I stuttered.

Mama frowned and, with hate in her eyes, said, "What? Shut up, girl. You're just so fast, prancing around in front of men like you do. He wasn't gonna do nothin' to you. Just shut up and go away with yo' fast self."

She totally dismissed everything I said, totally turned me off. She didn't believe me, her own daughter. That was crazy to me. *Oh no! Really? You don't believe me? You're my mother. You think I would make up something like that?* I thought to myself. But in the end, I obeyed her. I did exactly what I was told to do—I shut up and went away.

By the way, "fast" was a term used for "bad girls" who set out to entice the boys. Mama acted as if I were lying to her, as if it were my fault. Nothing could have been further from the truth. But she didn't believe me, and it hurt me to my core.

The next time Jim came to the house, I trembled inside with fear, thinking about what could have happened to me. He always acted nonchalant as if nothing had happened. But we both knew what had really happened. And since Mama didn't believe me, I took matters into my own hands and kept my distance from that dirty old man. It was so hard to understand that Mama believed him and not me, her daughter. *I'm her little girl, and she believes him. I don't understand that.* It was hard living with her decision.

Oh, Daddy, No, Daddy

My father, whom I always called Daddy, was a jovial, short man with a medium-brown complexion and medium body frame. I resembled my father. One thing nice I inherited from him was his smile. He smiled all the time, and when he took me around his friends, they would comment about how I had to be his daughter because I looked just like him. I was also proud of him because he was one of only about three people in our family who had his own car, which meant he had a job to pay for it.

Daddy didn't live with us and, therefore, I expected to see him only occasionally. There was no consistency, nor was there a nurturing relationship. I had no issues with that, no sleepless nights wondering why. I simply accepted it as a fact that was common among a lot of people. Unlike the disconnection from my mother, which left me deeply troubled, I just thought it was OK for my father to be different. He never disciplined me in any way, never beat me, yelled at me, or cussed me out as my mother did. In my childish mind, this made him a nice father, the better parent. Because he was kind to me, I made excuses for him, ignoring his behavior. I didn't have a clue where he lived most of the time. I really didn't understand the role he played (or was supposed to play) in being my father. He just was. He was nice to me. I was OK with that.

I also liked Daddy a lot because he brought me candy when he came to visit. Sometimes he even took me out to buy me clothes, brand-new clothes, which Mama couldn't afford. I was thrilled about that because those gifts made me feel as if he really did care about me even though he wasn't around all that often.

Whenever he did visit, I could see the delight in his eyes as they connected with mine. This was something I never felt with my mother. He was a nice guy in my book simply because he was nice to me. That was the way I saw it. The expectations I had for my relationship with him were fairly low, almost as if he were Santa Claus. I knew he'd come around only on rare occasions to bring me these tokens of love. No strings attached to his gifts—I felt safe with him. He was my daddy, and that made me happy.

One thing about him was different—and it was interesting compared to all the other adults in my life. It was his position on eating out. He never went to restaurants and would frown and say, "That kinda food ain't good for you. You don't know what's in it, who cooked it, so I ain't eatin' nobody's food 'less I know them real well."

I was surprised to see how he thought eating out was a bad thing for his body, but had no problem getting sloppy drunk. I guess he just wanted to have a good time hanging out with certain people. I told myself, *It's just another thing adults do differently than children.*

Daddy was popular, the life of the party, a real swinger. His friends' faces lit up when he visited them. He smiled from ear to ear right back at them. *He's so nice. They really like each other,* I often thought as I witnessed the interaction. Never did I see him argue with anyone. I never heard him cussing anybody out. To tell the truth, he did cuss a lot around me, but he was always making some kind of joke to make people laugh. I was used to people around me cussing and therefore was not surprised or offended. I guess the difference was that he was not cussing me. He was not angry with me and, in my mind, he was just an adult, and all of them talked like that.

However, his moral behavior fell short of what I expected of a parent. Though my expectations of his fatherly role were low, I knew that some of his choices were very wrong. I remember a time when he bragged about having a girlfriend my age. It was as if it was funny to him, and he was very proud. He loved young ladies. In fact, he married a fifteen-year-old because he got her pregnant. I remember how he laughed that she was "jailbait," how he "robbed the cradle" and had to marry her. He said, "If I didn't marry her, my butt was going to jail." There was no question he had violated her and then married her to avoid punishment. That was a double whammy, two wrongs that didn't end up making things right. Oh, how my heart broke for my little sister born of this marriage, and for our daddy, too. I often think of the poor decisions we sometimes make, gut-wrenching and irrational.

In my adolescent years, it was great to escape my sad life at home to visit my father. He lived in a house with another family who were his friends. Even though he didn't own the home, it was his house to me nonetheless. The laughter and fun there was a stark contrast to the void of love where I lived. When I would ask my mother for permission to go to Daddy's house, the answer was usually yes. It was a big, two-story house in the inner city with one bedroom, a large living room, a dining room, and a kitchen. The only bathroom in the house was on the first floor. The kitchen was very small compared to the huge living and dining rooms. On the second floor, there were three bedrooms. The anticipation of visiting him always made my day.

Whenever I spent the night, all of the girls in the house played together. We had a great time, and at night, we all slept in the same bed upstairs.

One night, the adults had been drinking a lot and partying, while we kids just played and had fun. On this particular night, my father decided he wanted me to sleep with him. I didn't have any reservations about that because he had always been kind and protective toward me. This night was different. The girls were all upstairs piled into one bed, as usual, and Daddy was alone. "Come down here and sleep with me tonight. I'm your father. It's OK for you to sleep with me."

He says it's OK to sleep with him? What does he mean? He's a grown man, and I am a teenager. I don't think that's right. Oh, but he's my daddy, and he won't do anything bad to me. He's not like that nasty man who touched me down there, I thought. Still, I felt uncomfortable, even though he had said, "It's OK." Although I told myself to trust him, deep inside, I was really afraid.

I lay there with my eyes wide open, unable to sleep. I must have sensed something wrong. He moved closer to me and was cuddled behind me, wearing only his undershorts. *Why isn't he wearing his pajamas?* I thought. *That ain't right.* I tried to console myself by remembering that he had said, "It's OK." When I realized he was finally asleep, I was so relieved. *Yes, it's OK,* I thought. Eventually, I fell asleep as well.

However, later that night, he moved even closer to me and put his arm around my waist as he cuddled me. Suddenly, I felt our bodies connected in the wrong place, and he began touching me inappropriately. I said to myself, *Maybe he is having a dream, thinking I am his woman and not his daughter.* That appeased me, but I still knew I needed to get out of there. I moved when I heard him snoring and drifting off to sleep again, and I quietly got up out of the bed and went upstairs with the other girls.

The next morning, the look on Daddy's face was strange, but I pretended that I was unaware of what had happened. I just wanted to think that it had been a big mistake. However, he invited me to sleep with him again, but I wouldn't, and he didn't force the issue. *Why does my father want to sleep with me? He's a grown man. He doesn't need to sleep with me. That's not right. When you are an adult male, there is absolutely no reason on God's green earth that you should sleep with a young girl, especially your daughter!*

We never talked about what had happened, and I never told anybody. But I always made other sleeping arrangements when I stayed at his house, like before that incident, or I didn't stay there at all. I could rest only by believing that it had all just been a big mistake.

I wonder if he has done this before to other girls, I thought to myself. *What kind of man is he?* I remembered that was why he had to get married to avoid going to jail—because he couldn't keep his hands off young girls. *I am not just any girl; I am his daughter! What in the world was he thinking? That is the problem. He was not thinking like a father. Surely he was just dreaming—drunk or both.* I elected to suppress the fear and disrespect I started to have for him after that night.

Several years later, Daddy moved out of town. I was glad I didn't have to see him in that house again. He seemed to be happy with his decision to leave and start a new life in Chicago. His new girlfriend had a house, so he moved on to that relationship. He would drive back home every once in a while. And he would always come to visit me.

Even though I felt uncomfortable in our relationship, I went to visit him a few times. In fact, he paid round-trip airfare for me, which was really exciting. I had never been on an airplane before. I loved it! That wouldn't have happened without Daddy. So, I focused on the good and dismissed everything wrong. What he did for me made me feel really special. Indeed, the past was behind us, and we were forging ahead. I just dismissed it all as poor judgment on his part, with no irreparable harm done. Like every other problem I had, I would make the best of my situation.

❖ ❖ ❖

Sounds in the Ghetto

Mama couldn't afford the rent for the house where we lived, so we had to move out and settle for an apartment that really wasn't fit for human habitation. It was on the second floor of a dilapidated building.

The entryway from the stairs opened into the large living room. The porch off to the left had a dangerously short wooden railing, supposedly to prevent falling. Beyond the living room was an open space meant for a dining room, but we used it as a bedroom. To the right were two other bedrooms, with the bathroom in between. The kitchen was behind the dining room that doubled as a bedroom. There was also a back porch that was very small, with narrow, steep wooden spiral stairs leading down to the backyard. The trash was kept on the back porch.

The whole building was infested with rats and roaches, so many that it would make your skin crawl. The bugs decorated the walls of the kitchen, pranced on the tables, and shared our meals night and day. Both the roaches and the rats really came out in massive numbers at night, and when we turned on the lights, they would scurry to the cupboards. Others moseyed around comfortably as if they owned the place. The rats lived among us, too, moving from one room to the other day and night. They weren't quite as bold as the roaches, coming out more at night than in the daytime. I could hear them running to and fro as I lay in bed at night. I absolutely hated to go to the bathroom at night because I could hear and see them running from room to room. Whenever I had to go to the bathroom, I would stomp on the floor to get them out of my way so they wouldn't run over my feet.

One night I was awakened by a bug crawling into my ear. What a horrible, ghastly feeling! Every time it moved, I screamed, "There's a bug in my ear!" I pressed my finger to my ear, trying to suffocate it, and I pleaded with my mother to take me to the emergency room to have it removed. I thought about removing my finger so it could crawl out, but the feeling in my ear each time it moved was absolutely unbearable. So, when it moved even a little, I would push my finger in deeper to stop it.

Mama agreed to take me to the hospital, which wasn't far away. All the way there, I kept my finger tight in my ear because I couldn't stand the movement it made otherwise. When we arrived, we were quickly escorted to a room. The staff could see me holding my finger in my ear with a frown on my face. As I sat on the cart in the emergency room, the physician instructed me to remove my finger. I figured the agony would soon be over. He had a syringe in his hand, like what I had used to clean my baby brother's nose. Within seconds of my removing my finger, he put the syringe in my ear as suction and pulled the roach out. *"Oh yeah, it's out!"* I cried.

I saw it hit the floor alive, and the physician stepped on it before it could get away. I was so relieved. It was out and it was dead. I shivered at the thought of what had happened and immediately made a plan of action to make sure it never happened again.

Every time I went to sleep, night or day, I put pieces of toilet paper in my ears. When cotton was available, I used that instead. Since I knew the bugs would continue to crawl in the bed, I had to protect my ears just in case one landed in my ear again.

To this very day, I sleep with earplugs. Although I have convinced myself that I can relax better when noise is muffled, I'm no doubt protected. On the slim chance that one single bug might make its way into my home and onto the bed, find my face, crawl in my ear, and wiggle itself inside, I remain safe. No matter where I am, I sleep with earplugs.

I had to go back to live with that kind of infestation until I was old enough to live on my own as an adult. I had no other choice. When I confronted my mother about having to live in that environment, she said sarcastically, "Sorry, Rosie, we can't live like the white folks. We are poor colored people."

We lived in that horrible place simply because it was the only kind of apartment Mama could afford after she quit working. Yet, she played that race card over the matter. I resigned myself to the fact that I had no choice but to accept my situation, but I vowed that when I grew up, I would never live with roaches or rats ever again.

Saving on the water bill was another issue. We were allowed to take a bath only once a week on Saturdays to save water and therefore save money. No matter how dirty we were, we couldn't take a bath until the appointed time. We were told to just wash the main stinky body parts. We cherished our Saturday baths, and I realized that that was the way it was going to be until I was an adult.

Once, when our water was cut off, I thought it was due to a money issue. But when I talked to my brother Junnie, he said the problem was with the pipes. The basement had flooded, and we had to move. For sure, we didn't have water in the house at all. The three of us kids took gallon containers and went to the service station at night to steal water. We made several trips to get enough to get by. It really felt strange stealing water, but we had no choice. I'm glad we didn't have to do that for very long.

Our nutrition remained sadly lacking in the downsized apartment. We almost never had fruit. Breakfast was usually sugar and butter sandwiches. Even though my grandfather brought home the throwaway meat from work every day, there usually wasn't enough for the children. The adults had choices of pig ears, pig feet, chicken feet, skins, chitterlings, and hog maws nearly every day.

All of us kids had special treats on Sundays and special occasions, but these were definitely exceptions, not the rule. Generally, we had mustard greens seasoned with lots of bacon grease. We had fried corn cakes, which were corn bread-batter fried with lard, making thick pancakes. On these occasions we had a real full meal with meat, such as chicken or chitterlings. And we always had greens and macaroni and cheese or fried potatoes on Sundays.

For dessert, we ate delicious cakes. Mama Nan would always bake her cakes from scratch. She never measured anything, but you couldn't tell it by the taste. Sometimes the cake was so light we couldn't cut it, so we just ate it out of the pan with our fingers. She was OK with that. We really loved Mama Nan's Sunday desserts.

There was also a local takeout restaurant. They had delicious pig ear sandwiches served on a bun with horseradish and a slice of onion. Yummy-yummy! We loved those sandwiches and were delighted when someone would give us a quarter to buy one.

Sometimes we would walk a few blocks up the street and around the corner where we knew a man was selling food outside his apartment. It was worth the walk to buy whole white potatoes. Oh boy, those potatoes were smoking hot with so much red pepper we could barely eat them, but we loved those hot potatoes.

Truthfully, I enjoyed the potatoes; yet, somehow I knew there was something wrong with eating just starchy foods for breakfast, lunch, and dinner six days a week. I hesitated mentioning this to my mother because of her reaction to my telling her things like that. In times like these, I was certain the parent and child roles had been reversed.

My mother would say, "The reason ya s'posed to eat is to get full, so shut up." So, in order to get full, our dinner meals consisted mostly of potatoes or spaghetti with butter, salt, and pepper one day and with tomato sauce the next day.

One day, I got up the courage because I thought she might not understand that we truly needed a better diet. I wanted to make sure she understood what I understood.

I said, "Mama we *need* to eat more fruits and vegetables."

"Shut up. You don't know what you're talking about!" Then she slapped me across my face and said, "I want you kids to get what you need, and that is a full stomach."

Even though I knew I would suffer the consequences of "talking back" again, I cried out, "We *need* fruits and vegetables." She cursed at me and slapped me again, so I realized it was best to keep quiet. *I have to keep my thoughts to myself.* I walked away and cried.

I stopped talking about my concerns, but my thoughts were racing like a mighty wind. *I will be different when I grow up. Yes, I will. My kids will have good food, and I will listen to their opinions.*

They don't have to always agree with me just 'cause I'm the mother. Kids understand things that sometimes adults don't understand. I know this is true.

It seemed that the adults in my life played down the importance of everything I deemed most important: God—the Creator of the universe and all therein; nurturing—the love of a mother for her child; and education—the vehicle that removes bondage and opens a world of knowledge essential to a productive life. For some reason, they just didn't get it.

Terrible Teens

I continued on a downward spiral. I made more mistakes and suffered as a result of it. I struggled each day wanting to be a little girl but being forced to play the role of mother. I wanted desperately to go to school but many times got a beating simply for asking and insisting that I *needed* to go to school. The beatings continued. Tree branches, belts, and hand slaps came when I complained about not being able to go to school or out to play, not having the right food to eat, or having to take care of my sisters and brother.

Each Saturday, we were awakened early in the morning to clean the house. My mother would yell at the top of her voice, waking us out of a deep sleep, "Loretta, Rosie, Junior! Get up and get this house clean!" Immediately, we got up or quickly suffered the consequences. The usual routine included mopping the floors and cleaning the baseboards by hand. Mama wanted us to get the house spick-and-span—spotless.

In addition to what my older sister, brother, and I did together, I had other chores that were my responsibility alone. I had to wash my own clothes by hand on a scrub board, which I didn't really mind. All kids had responsibilities, and there weren't any automatic washing machines when I was a little girl. I was totally OK with that; it made sense to me.

Before long, I wasn't the youngest. In the years to come, there were six more to follow. The task of making sure my little brother had clean diapers was my job, too. Every day, the dirty diapers were taken off the baby and placed in a tall tin can. After flushing the feces, I took the diapers, placed them in clear water in the can, rinsed them again, and washed them in the bathtub until they were thoroughly cleaned. My job was to be certain to "get all the soap out, rinse the diapers over and over, again and again until the water was clear." That's what Mama said to do, that is how she said to do it, and that is exactly what I did.

My sister and I took turns in the kitchen, doing the dishes and other stuff. We were told that was "the girls' job, and boys should not have to wash dishes, cook food, and things like that in the kitchen."

It was also my job to sterilize the baby's bottles every day, make the formula, and fill the bottles every night before going to bed. OK, fixing baby bottles was not the job for the sister but rather for the mother, so why didn't the logic of ruling who should do what apply in this situation? *Why do I have to do all this work? I'm not nobody's mama. This is just wrong*, I would think almost every time I had to do it.

It seemed as if the only thing I was meant to do was take care of my baby brother and my baby sister. I felt like a stepchild and Mama was my stepmother. Only that wasn't true. Sometimes I wasn't even allowed to go to school if she needed me to babysit. That made no sense to me at all.

I constantly thought about what I was not allowed to say out loud. So, I talked to myself all the time. *She doesn't understand what I need. She's my mother, and she doesn't understand her own child. I need to go to school just like other kids. How can I learn how to take care of myself when I'm a grown-up like her? How will I ever learn about how to work—to get a job? I mean, I need to know how to read, how to do math, and all the other stuff they teach in school. Yes, I want to go to school, but why doesn't she understand that I need to go to school? Why am I in this situation—a little girl who is forced to do what most little girls don't have to do? I mean, the kids at church don't have to do what I have to do. The kids at school seem to walk around happy-go-lucky all the time. Why is my life so different? This is so hard for me to understand. I know it is wrong. I don't care if she keeps beating me for talking back when she tells me to shut up because this is just wrong.*

I was bombarded with messages that bewildered me every day. I couldn't escape my emotional prison.

School Daze

It was the first day of junior high school. Like previous first days of school, the students briefly shared some personal information. As I sat in my seat looking around the classroom, I saw lots of new faces, and I wanted to get to know everybody. At the very top of my agenda was to get them to know *me* by sharing my story. I couldn't wait until everyone was told to stand up and say something about themselves. In addition to that statement, most of the time there was a question I was eager to hear: "Does anybody have anything to share with the class?" Usually as soon as the teacher mentioned it, I would shout, *I do! I do!* on the inside. If the question wasn't asked, I was very disappointed. At any rate, I had to wait for the question so I wouldn't seem like I was a big show-off. The truth is, that is exactly what I wanted to do—show off my prize possession: the picture that was taken of me when I was four years old. I had tangible proof of a very special time in my life, and I couldn't wait to show my new friends and tell them the story behind it.

My opportunity came on that very first day of seventh grade. I was thrilled to show off my picture and tell everyone my story. I passed it to the next student behind me, who then passed it to others while I was speaking. Yes, I was very proud of that picture. Not only did it have a special story behind it, but it also was the only picture I had of myself. I didn't know what I looked like as a baby or a toddler, so that picture was my pride and joy. So, with a smile on my face and warmth in my heart, I shared this happy occasion with my new classmates.

I was not at all prepared for what happened next. Shortly after I sat down, it became apparent that someone didn't share my enthusiasm and decided to let me know it. The student behind me handed me my picture. It had been destroyed—torn into tiny little pieces. I looked at it and was so hurt. *Oh no, why? Why would anybody do that to me? That's awful. I would never do that to anyone and hurt them that way!* I fought hard to hold back the tears because my heart was broken. It wasn't just a picture they destroyed but a tangible reminder of one of the few really special memories in my life.

At home, I was accused of acting "white," thinking "white," and wanting to be "white." Yet, there I was sitting in a room full of children my own race, humiliated and betrayed, obviously by "one of my own." How ironic that Mama questioned my loyalty, as if good and evil aligned themselves with black and white. That day, I saw the enemy in no race but the human race.

I felt as if a little piece of me had been destroyed as I looked around, knowing someone in my class was pleased by hurting me. After all, I knew what it felt like to have my little heart broken into pieces, to feel abandoned. And now it was happening again. There was yet another void in my life. I felt empty on the inside like I had felt all too many times before. I stared at the pieces and tried to make sense of what had just happened, and I wished I could have turned back the clock and not have shared it. *Someone must have been jealous,* I thought to myself. *But why would they do that?* I held my head down on my desk, and again I fought back the tears. *If only I would have known, if only I would have known, if only I would have known,* I kept repeating, *I would not have brought it to school.*

Of course, nobody knew who did it. And knowing wouldn't have brought my picture back. I had absolutely no baby or toddler pictures, or anything of the sort to be able to connect myself visually with my childhood memories. Now, the only picture of me alone as a child had been destroyed. I realized that I could not undo it, and crying would not bring my picture back. I also tried to forget about what I could not change. I had to focus on learning from this situation the same way I learned from my situation at home.

When I went home, I found something else to hold onto. There was one picture of me with my older brother and sister. I remember instantly thinking I didn't look like a happy child in that photo, but at least I had that substitute picture and the memory that could not be destroyed. So, time after time, I look at the picture with my mind's eye and smile about the memories.

I saw, for the first time, that not only do people harbor prejudice against those of other races, but they also resent members of their own race. I realized, too, that hurt people *hurt* people.

So many people miss this connection and assume a victim mentality. They come to believe that the other person, the other group, or the other race is the problem. In my case, it was a member of the human race who had felt satisfaction in destroying something that would hurt a member of his or her own race. Clearly, *he or she* had issues, and eventually I understood that point. I rested knowing that God knew who did it and why. It was just a thing, a tangible item that was gone. The memories would last forever. That picture could not be taken from me. I can still "see" it clearly, and it is beautiful.

First "Love"

I was fourteen when I met Laurence, a boy four years my senior. I was starving for love and affection. He saw how vulnerable I was and set out to seduce me. He had an agenda to prove to his homeboys that he could score at will. I was so naïve at the time.

On the days I *was* allowed to go to school, a group of us would get together after the last class to talk and hang out. We would gossip about other girls who were bad because they weren't virgins. We would bully other girls and pick fights with them. We were excited when someone was having a fight and would laugh about it. Our favorite after-school topic was boys. We spent a lot of time giggling about who was cute and who was not. There were about six of us who clearly wanted attention as we flirted with trouble, grinning at the boys who had the reputations of being tough. Gang boys who were much older were there to check out the girls and to make trouble.

We understood their reputations but still enjoyed the attention we got. It made us feel good when they said things like "You sure are cute." We just giggled. We did not view their comments as simply a game to manipulate us. However, one particular day, the conversation turned disgusting and vulgar. One boy who had been eyeballing me singled me out with a question: "Are you doing the sex thang?" he asked in a vulgar way.

"No! I'm not, and I'm not gonna!" I said adamantly.

"Oh yes you will," he responded with a slick grin on his face and a confident tone.

"Oh no I won't," I repeated confidently and walked away, disgusted.

As we continued to walk home, I said to my friends, "Yuck. He must be crazy if he thinks I'm gonna do that with him." We scoffed at the game he was playing.

"Yeah, he's pretty slick"; "a real ladies' man"; "we know what he's all about"; "he really acts like he can get you," my girlfriends said.

"Yeah, I know, but that ain't gonna happen." Then we dismissed the conversation abruptly since we were done talking about that garbage—that nasty stuff.

I was both shocked and disgusted by what the boy had said. I wasn't giving in to that. *No way! After all, I could get pregnant.* I was *very* clear on that point now, and I was determined not to let him use me like that. I was also clueless about the strategy in his deception, absolutely clueless. Clearly, he had done his homework and thought I was the perfect target—vulnerable, with low self-esteem, and obviously adoring the attention. He was undoubtedly confident that he could and would abuse me. I imagine he even bragged to his friends about what he was going to do to me and how he planned to go about it. Still, I was determined it wasn't gonna happen to me. I was absolutely sure of that.

One day, he was all by himself and followed me home from school. When he showed up at my door, I wasn't afraid that he would attack me. After all, my older sister and brother were there. Since I already understood what he was up to, I was ready to tell him off and send him on his way to find some other stupid girl to go along with his sex games. Not me.

When I opened the door, I was surprised at first and said to myself, *Why is he here? I made it clear to him that my body is off limits. What is this all about?* But what he had to say caught me totally off guard. He gently cupped my face in his hands, looked me straight in my eyes, and with the most sincere look on his face said, "I love you. I want to marry you someday."

I kept on staring into his eyes, trying to absorb what he had just said. After a moment of silence, all I could think to say was, "You *love* me *and want us to get married* someday?" I continued to stare. *Oh my God!* I couldn't believe what I was hearing. *He loves me!* No other words would come out of my mouth, but my mind had no trouble concocting a sea of thoughts at this new proposition. *Finally, for the very first time in my life, somebody loves me! Somebody wants me!*

These words were like cool raindrops on my desert heart, prompting a flowering of beautiful, idyllic thoughts of what my young heart desired. I instantly delighted at the thought of getting pregnant and having a family with him, of being happy forever. I imagined what it would be like to have my own children. I would raise them very differently from how I had been raised. I would try to be such a good mother. *I could see it now: my husband and I with our child, our own little white house with a picket fence, a dog, and a cat.* I'm sure he was also very happy to see me smile. He was clearly delighted at the thoughts he sensed were going through my head, knowing that his scheme had worked, and had worked well. I'm sure he walked away laughing about how easy it was to get to me and how oblivious I was to his ploy. He had planted the seed in my receptive, naïve mind, and all he needed to do was to wait until the time was right.

Not knowing at all what was behind his words at the time, I was suddenly filled with such happiness. *Finally, someone will turn my life around!* I thought. I was on top of the world imagining how my life would finally change. *I will have my own family to take care of, and we will be very happy. I'll make sure of that. He will be a happy husband, and our kids will be so happy because of our love for each other. We will take good care of them.*

All too soon, though, I learned what was really behind his declaration. He called me and wanted to find some time when we could be alone in a place where nobody could find us. After all, he reminded me, he loved me so much, and he wanted so badly to show me how much. Starving for the "touch of love," I was totally on board with learning and experiencing what true love was all about. *Mama and Daddy never told me they love me. They have never touched me like that, looked at me like that, and made me melt with happiness like he does. This must be all right. I'm a little bit scared. What if he is lying? I don't think he is,* I thought as I remembered not just what he had said when he came to the house but how he had said it, how he had touched me. I had totally blocked out of my memory his very first question for me after school. I had forgotten both his question and my determined response. Totally forgot about it.

Blind to his deception, I gave in to him. There was no one home at his friend's house. In the name of "love," I lost my virginity there in the attic. It was so painful, so cold and dirty. But he assured me it would change as we continued to do it since we "love each other and will get married." The tenderness was something I had been missing. Even though I knew deep down it was wrong to have this kind of a relationship with him, I pushed those thoughts away with the things he had told me.

Eventually I got pregnant and was really happy that the new life I had envisioned was starting to develop. Yet, once I told him

I was pregnant, our relationship changed abruptly. I was starting to see that those beautiful things he said and the other lies he had fed me were all just part of a scheme to get what he wanted. I started to think he didn't really love me. Yes, I could see the handwriting on the wall, but it was too late. And I had made a huge, irreparable mistake.

I didn't see much of him the next few months. Then, one day, he wrote the most loving letter to me, asking me to give him another chance. It would've been clear to anyone else that I'd been had. Still wanting to believe he truly loved me, I was so happy to finally receive a letter from him. He told me he was in jail for six months for traffic tickets. He apologized for what he had done to me, and I gladly accepted his apology. I didn't question him for a second because I was pregnant and in love. I didn't want to be without him or lose hope for our happy family. I believed that this time he was serious about us and our relationship.

Family Dynamics

My grandmother, mother, and sister were all teenage mothers who had dropped out of school to raise their babies. There were many other relatives and friends of my family in the same boat. No one was ashamed because, sadly, it was accepted as the norm. How ironic that my behavior as a teenage parent was not a potential problem.

I had not been afraid to tell Mama I was pregnant because I knew she would be OK with it. I remembered how she had treated my sister and how she had said, "These things just happen. We will take care of the baby." I also knew I could live with her while I was planning to move out someday soon with my new husband and eventually with my first baby. In the meantime, I had to figure it all out. Mama started treating me as if I were an adult—kinda—but in a good way this time. I could talk to her about stuff, and she seemed willing to listen and give me her opinion. I had lots of questions about my new life, especially about getting married.

She'll have to sign for me to get married because I'm too young. Then everything will be different in my life—so much better. I need to talk to her about that right away so I can tell my boyfriend.

"Mama, you know you'll have to sign for Laurence and me to get married, right?"

"Yeah, when yaw get ready, just lemme know. If he wants to stay here until then, that'll be OK. Whatever yaw decide to do, we can all pitch in and help you." She kept talking, assuring me that everything was just fine.

I was so proud to be pregnant, so excited and focused on what I believed that entailed. I was going to be a mother! The very thought of that brought happiness to my soul. The child inside me would be mine forever. My baby would be attached to me, and I would experience the joy of being loved in a very special way. I was clueless about the responsibilities of becoming a mother. Mama didn't beat me anymore because now I was pregnant. She didn't expect me to work as hard for the same reason. I knew for sure I'd be a good mother and therefore concluded that everything would work out great for my new family. After all, I'd be with a man who loved me so much that he planned to marry me. We were going to be a real family, and I was excited about it. Since I had been forced to play the role of an adult with my younger sisters and brothers, I felt prepared to be a mother. That is the reason I liked being pregnant with my own child. Yes, I was proud of the idea of being a mother at the age of fifteen. I was sincere in my thoughts but was sincerely wrong in my reasoning.

Even though I appreciated Mama saying, "We will take care of the baby," I knew it was not a good situation in which to give birth. I decided to seek help from the people at church—my pastor and his secretary. When I spoke with them, they were clearly disappointed in me. At the same time, they were happy to intervene on my behalf. They knew I had made a terrible mistake, but they also knew I wanted and desperately needed to make one of the most important decisions of my life: whether to keep the baby or give it up for adoption. Equally important, they encouraged me to go back to school.

Determined to help me, Ms. Phillips, the church secretary, set up a meeting with my mother at a home for unwed mothers. We couldn't afford to pay for it, so the church graciously offered to help, and my mother agreed to let me stay there. Here, I could learn about my new life as a mother and also attend classes to complete my education.

The home for unwed mothers was an interesting place in the urban community. Lots of girls were there, but most were white, from out of town, and planning to give up their babies for adoption. I found that quite interesting but understood how important it was to their families to keep their pregnancies a secret.

We were assigned chores to do every day such as cleaning, helping in the kitchen, and, of course, doing our own laundry. We kept the home nice and clean, and we had structured class times for school and, for those of us who were keeping our babies, we learned parenting skills. We also took sewing classes and learned how to make clothes for our newborn to wear from day one. In general, we accepted each other as individuals who were trying to make the best of our situations. And so we all got along with each other really well.

We assembled for school in a large classroom Monday through Friday. We had individual desks just as in regular school. Teachers from the public school system were there to teach us, test us, and encourage us to study and focus on the importance of education. That wasn't a problem for me. I definitely understood that. In fact, I was really happy to have the teachers in my life at the time I needed role models so badly. It was a joy to attend class every day, especially given the circumstances. While I was at the home, I'm happy to say I met my goal by completing school that year.

My church family was very helpful during this difficult time. They went to various organizations to see what could be done about my schooling and did not rest until they found the place for me to get help. At that time, pregnant girls weren't allowed in public schools. Although the church staff never judged me harshly, they did counsel me to learn from my mistakes, to hold my head up high, and to not repeat the same mistakes. I so appreciated them and vowed to learn from my mistakes, and I did, for a while.

However, when Laurence got out of jail, their words of wisdom fell on deaf ears. I believed him again. He tricked me again. It was devastating. But I really did learn from it—eventually.

The idea of having my own child was awesome. Indeed, this was going to fill the void in my life. I was ecstatic, but there was so much to learn. How childish to have said to myself back then, with a huge smile on my face, "I think I'm pregnant. Yay!"

The final stage of pregnancy was not fun at all. My water broke, and I was definitely in labor. The labor pains were awful: pain in my lower back that increased in duration and intensity. I had never experienced pain like that before. But, after several hours in the hospital, I was given a shot in my back, which took the pain completely away. In fact, I had no feeling from the waist down. Relieved now and free from pain, I lay there with great expectations about my soon-to-be-new family.

The nurses and doctors were very nice and compassionate toward me, and that made my experience a pleasant one. The idea that I was about to have a baby was absolutely amazing, that a child had been growing inside my body! *I can't wait to see my baby. I already love this child so much. This is my baby.* It was more than I could comprehend. What I knew for sure was that my life would change. My baby would automatically love me because I was the mother, and she was part of me. I would love my baby back no matter what happened in our lives. I was so happy about experiencing that kind of love.

Finally, after nine months of anticipation and the process of labor, my dreams became reality. My little baby was born March 10, 1964—a beautiful little girl with lots of straight hair. She had all her fingers and toes, wiggled a lot, and smiled for me all the time. Right away, the connection was evident as I played with her. I loved taking care of her. I understood how important it was to nurture her, and that is what I did. I would take care of her and protect her with every fiber of my being because she brought unexplainable joy to my life. She was a gift from God to me, and I was grateful to him for her.

Where Is My Baby?

After I'd been duped and dumped by Laurence for the second and last time—with a second pregnancy to boot—I began to look back and remember why and how this second baby was conceived out of deception. Initially, Laurence's release from jail did mark our fresh start, the second chance he so sincerely requested in his letters from jail. He came to me right when he got out of jail, explained how he still wanted to marry me, how his mom would help pay for the wedding and would give us a house. He added, "But we don't want our little girl to be an only child. That would not be good for her." He said, "We need to make another baby so they can grow up together." I bought it all—hook, line, and sinker. His plan to mess with my head and stay in my bed worked.

When I was sure I was pregnant, I told him, anticipating a smile on his face because we were going to be a real family, as he'd said. With a big smile on my face I said, "Guess what? I'm pregnant now!"

"Are you sure?" he asked.

"Oh yes, I am very sure," I said happily.

Then he looked at me with a disgusting frown on his face and said, "Who you been…? I've been in jail. It's not my baby."

I was devastated! "What? What are you talking about? You know this is your baby!" I reminded him of our plan. Then I stopped trying to explain, to remind him, to talk about it at all. And I replaced my words with tears of anguish that flooded my face. He looked at me again, laughed at my tears, and walked out the door. I didn't hear from him for months.

How I wish I'd listened to those kind people at church who would've given anything for me to have made a different choice, I thought after I realized how foolish I had been.

I was not going to be a victim. *Life goes on—I will not ever be used by him again.* He had hurt me to my core. Oh, but for the first time, I had learned my lesson and was over him for sure.

And there was a third time he tested me, not with getting pregnant but with getting married. He even involved his mother who assured me he wanted to marry me. She would help us with the house, my dress, and in any way she could. But I was done.

After Laurence's good riddance, I met Fred, a friend of my older sister, who liked me just as I was. He seemed more captivated than intimidated by my pregnancy. For now, he was a keeper.

Finally, the day came for my second baby to be born. I had packed the receiving blanket, gown, diapers, and everything I needed to bring my baby home from the hospital. After bonding with this child in my belly for nine months, I couldn't wait to see my new baby. *Will it have all its fingers and toes? God, please take care of my baby.*

"Oh, the pain is so bad, but it will all be worth it. I can't wait until this part is over," I said to my new boyfriend, Fred, who was right there by my side.

"Yeah, soon it will be over, and everything will be all right," he responded.

I was at the same hospital for poor people, the one where all the colored people went. From my point of view, the process was like before, but a little different. I noticed that the nurses were checking on me much more frequently than last time. I wondered if my baby was sleeping because it wasn't moving that much, but that was just a passing thought.

Then, it was time to deliver. I was wheeled on the cart to the delivery room. After I was positioned for delivery, they pulled the baby out, just as before. I caught a glimpse of my child out of my peripheral vision, but I didn't hear a cry. Immediately, they took the baby out of the room, cleaned me up, and took me back into the ward where mothers were taken after delivery. I remember the nurse saying, "It's a boy," but I couldn't understand why they didn't let me hold him. *Why did they take him away? They will bring him to me in the room when they clean him up,* I thought. I just assumed they had to get him ready or something, and then they would let me hold him. But that didn't happen.

Finally, the nurse came in, pulled the curtain around me, looked in my eyes, and said, "I'm sorry, honey, but your baby is dead. He died about three hours before he was delivered."

"He-e-e-e's dead? What do you mean he's dead?"

"Yes, honey, he's dead. I'm so sorry. You had a stillborn. But you are young and will be able to have more children later," she said with a very professional attitude.

The nurse turned from me and walked away.

I was absolutely stunned. "My-my baby—my baby is dead!" I cried. *Oh my God, how did this happen? What did I do wrong? My baby boy is dead. What did he look like? Why didn't they let me see him?* My mind was racing all over the place.

I rang the call bell for the nurse because I had questions and could not believe what had happened. She came quickly.

"Yes, honey, what do you need? Are you in pain? Do you need some medicine?"

"I *need* to see my baby," I cried.

"I'm sorry; they have taken him away, and we can't bring him back," she said in a matter-of-fact tone.

I can't see him. I will never see my baby. Oh, God, please help me understand why this happened. Please, God.

I needed more answers, and when the doctor and nurse did their rounds the next day, I was determined to get them.

"Please tell me again exactly what happened to my baby. *How* did he die?"

"The umbilical cord was wrapped around his neck, and that is what killed him. Sorry about that. You had what is called a stillborn baby."

The umbilical cord was wrapped around his neck? How did that happen? Oh, my poor baby.

"How did that happen?"

"We don't know."

They didn't have any sympathy for me at all. At the time, I didn't understand why.

I was in the hospital the typical seven days. Each day, I woke up hoping I had been dreaming, only to remember the truth. Before I left for home, I had been comforted by my Heavenly Father that he alone understood what was best for me, and I needed to focus on the gift he had given me in my daughter. After I "heard" him in my heart, I rested, satisfied that everything would be all right.

Years later, I thought about that day and that entire situation, and while I remembered the pain, I realized that I grew up that day in more ways than one. I became a bit smarter but didn't realize I had so much more to learn. *I will learn from this mistake. There is no point in crying over spilled milk.*

Of course, I continued to make mistakes. But God knew about the deception, about my future, and the fact that I didn't need another baby at the age of sixteen. He made all of that clear to me—about the boy who had robbed me of purity, seduced me to dream of a great family, and accused me of being a tramp. He was dead wrong about me.

Working on the Journey

"Everyone has a story; make your own worth telling."
—*Patrick Ricketts*

Jobs for Security

A single mother at fifteen, I realized I needed money to take care of my daughter. So, one day, I headed out the door to find a job. *I don't know where I'm going. I don't have any experience, and I'm not really old enough to work, but I have to get a job somewhere to take care of my daughter. There is a café up on Twenty-Seventh Street. I'll go up there and check it out.*

The walk was about fifteen minutes or so, and the day was perfect for a good walk. The mission before me made the trip exciting. *This will be great because it's close to home. Oh no, there isn't a* HELP WANTED *sign on the window, but who knows? Maybe they need some help. If they hire me, I won't have a problem getting to work,* I thought as I prepared to introduce myself.

The small storefront restaurant had a bus stop right outside the door. This was the bus I had been taking when I traveled from place to place, but I had never gone inside the café. It took extra money to do that, and I didn't have extra money.

The name of the café was painted on a huge window in bold, colorful letters. Through the big window, I could see the people inside enjoying their meals. There were about a dozen tables. It looked very inviting, and I was excited at the prospect of working there.

Ready for the task ahead, I held my head up high, opened the door, and walked right in. People were eating breakfast at a long counter to the right. Most of them were men. I figured they had breakfast and then most likely got on the bus to go to work or walked home through the neighborhood as I did. They all seemed like family as they laughed and talked with each other. It was interesting to see how they interacted with the owners, as if they knew each other personally. *I bet these people come here all the time. They probably enjoy hanging out with each other, eating a good meal, and having fun. That's great. I really want to work here,* I thought.

Instead of ordering food, I just stood there by the door and waited to get the owner's attention. She was obviously very busy, but I was very patient. Finally she stopped, looked at me, and walked over to where I was standing.

"May I help you?" she asked. It was obvious I wanted to talk to her.

"Yes, my name is Rosie, and I'm looking for a job."

"Do you have any experience?"

"No," I said timidly, scared of being rejected.

"Well, how old are you, honey?"

"I'm seventeen." I had heard you had to be sixteen to get a job. *I hope she believes me. Here I am, so far from the little girl stuffing her halter with stolen ice cream, convinced I would never lie again unless I was told to. Today I am a young mom with a real live person to care for, who loves me no matter what. I will take care of her no matter what it takes, no matter what it costs me. I will return home and cover her little being with hugs and kisses and worry about the lying later.*

"Well, I don't know." She hesitated, looked at me, and appeared to be sizing me up. I just knew she was thinking that something wasn't right, that I had lied about my age—because I did. But to my surprise, she decided to give me a job.

Maybe she feels sorry for me. Who knows?

"Can you start right now?"

"Yes, ma'am, I can." *Wow, I did it!*

"Come over here and sit down. OK, I'm gonna teach you how to be a waitress. First of all, you go to the table and say, 'Hello, what would you like to order?' You take this pad and write down what they want and give it to the cooks."

"OK."

"When the order is ready, the cook will let you know. You go over, pick up the food, and take it to the customer. The main thing is, you need to be really nice to the customers, and you will get big tips. That is where you make most of your money."

"OK, I can do that."

"I'll give you twenty-five dollars a week, which I will pay you in cash every Friday."

"Thank you. Thank you!" I was so excited!

Within a few minutes, my first customers came through the door.

I waited for them to sit down. I let them look at the menu for less than a minute. Then, I went over to the table. I was ready for the task.

"Good morning. What can I get for you?" *Yes, after just a few minutes of training, I'm serving my very first customer, gainfully employed, and so happy about it!*

I took the customers' orders, served them their meals, gave them the ticket, and gave the money and the ticket to the owner, who worked the cash register behind the counter. She gave me the customers' change. Then I gave the change to the customer. I found out that no one was allowed to use the cash register but her.

By midmorning, fewer people were showing up sporadically to sit at the counter and enjoy a cinnamon roll, piece of cake, or pie and coffee.

Finally it was time for lunch, and I was prepared, since I now had worked a few hours. During lunch, there was a different crowd. Most of them sat at the tables instead of the counter. They looked at the menu and ordered things such as homemade chicken and dumplings, fried chicken with mashed potatoes and gravy, mustard greens, and all kinds of desserts. Oh, how the customers loved that finger-lickin'-good soul food!

I continued the same routine from breakfast. It was a piece of cake.

At the end of the first day, I reflected on how great it had worked out. I had served lots of people who were there to enjoy a good homemade breakfast or lunch. Most of the time, they came in as a group. But on occasion, some people, again mostly men, came in alone to read the paper as they enjoyed their meal.

I walked home a happy little girl, feeling like a responsible grown-up. *I did it! This is gonna be great. I made lots of money in tips today, and I'm gonna get twenty-five dollars Friday. Yay! I can't wait!*

The next four days were the same: laughter and great music in the air, just what the customers needed to make them want to come back again and again. Of course, I wore a smile and had a plan to serve and receive money for my services. So, each day my hard work, coupled with my cheerful personality, paid off.

This is a pretty good first job, I thought. I loved feeling that I was being a responsible mother by earning money to provide for myself and all my daughter's needs.

Finally it was Friday, payday. But my attitude about the job changed abruptly. I had a few concerns about some advances toward me. At first, I dismissed them. I decided to be a big girl and just focus on doing my job. But I had to be honest with myself. Some of the male customers started making more aggressive passes at me. Perhaps it was the end-of-the-week crowd, a different group of people. I didn't know for sure, but things were clearly different. Maybe the men had been plotting a seductive move but were waiting until now. One man sitting at a table looked at me, winked, tilted his head up, and mouthed the words, *Come over here.* I ignored him, and then he spoke out loud. "Hey, Little Mama, come over here and sit on Daddy's lap."

"Sorry, I'm working," I said politely. *Oh, how sick is that?*

"Well, can we get together when you get off? I like you."

"No, I have to go home." I walked away, trembling on the inside.

These inappropriate and suggestive remarks made me feel very uncomfortable. I tried to remain kind, and I tried to ignore the comments. Later, a man went beyond flirting and actually patted me on my behind. I struggled with how to handle that because I really needed the money. I tried to rationalize it. *He didn't hurt me; he just touched me and laughed. That's wrong, but surely I'm tough enough to deal with that.*

It didn't stop there, though. Another man started flirting with me and touching me inappropriately. At first I allowed it. I rationalized that I was in a safe place there at the restaurant, that I needed to focus on doing my job and receiving my wages. After all, I had a child who was depending on me to take care of her.

That same day, a female customer approached me and said, "You are a cute little thing. You can quit this job, and I will take care of you if you let me." I was mortified! Her eyes were piercing with lust, and her facial expression was very sensuous. It was obvious that I was in the wrong kind of environment.

Finally, I realized I couldn't—or rather wouldn't—work in a situation that made me so uncomfortable. I finished out the day, got my twenty-five dollars, and never went back.

Even though I didn't always know exactly how to articulate them, I was subconsciously learning how to set boundaries—learning how to focus on not only what was happening in my mind but also what was happening on the outside.

Disconnected Workers

Off I went looking for a new job. I heard I could get hired as a bus girl at an upscale eatery. This job was totally different from my first job. I wasn't going to get tips or get paid in cash. I couldn't walk to work because it was too far away. I would have to take the bus. I was OK with all that. The only drawback was that I would have to lie again about my age because I was too young to work legally. You had to be sixteen. Again, I simply convinced myself it was OK because I really needed a job.

I went to an office to fill out the application. The brief interview went well—short, sweet, and to the point. I was hired immediately. Apparently, there was high employee turnover. No wonder they didn't ask for my birth certificate or anything like that. They were pleasant. I was pleasant. They decided to give me a chance.

Ready for the job, I did everything I was told to do and reported to work early the next day. Being a bus girl wasn't a prestigious job, but it would definitely provide me with money to support myself and my daughter. That was most important in my mind. Of course, I definitely wanted to do a good job and earn my wages.

The building was huge on the outside and spacious and very elegant on the inside. I had never been in a place like that before. I was awestruck! I saw a large room with beautiful tables, fancy chairs, large chandeliers hanging from the ceiling, and breathtaking décor. I heard soothing music, which made me feel light and happy the minute I walked in the door. To my right was a room called the Blue Room. It was for the overflow part of the cafeteria.

Straight ahead and then to the right was where people stood in line and went around the dividing rail to select their food. It was so colorful, so appetizing, and oh, so much food. As customers entered the line, there were trays, eating utensils, napkins, and beverages such as water, tea, and soda. Behind the glass protector was a mouth-watering variety of salads, entrees, and desserts. Everything was lined up perfectly.

Behind the lines were employees dressed in uniforms with hairnets on their heads. They were very kind to each customer and smiled as they gave them their food. There were only ladies, no men. *They all act so happy—like they really love what they do. They seem so organized.* Absolutely everything was spick-and-span, obviously well thought out. Whenever they were low on the hot food, the servers called to the kitchen downstairs and told them what they needed, and within minutes, the food was there. It was kind of like an elevator for food.

At the end of the line stood tray girls, waiting to help each customer with his or her tray. The girls wore pink uniforms that were starched to perfection, and all of them were very pretty. As soon as customers paid the lady at the cash register, the tray girl would take their tray, escort them to their table, and remove the food from the tray. They would then put the tray in a section that was out of sight.

Working there was much better for me than working at the café. I felt safe in this environment, at this location. As with my other job, I found ways to make working fun and challenging. Clearing and cleaning off dirty tables was easy, but it had to get done in a timely manner. I would get the tables cleaned in record time, ready for the next customers. I made sure the tables and chairs were spotless, the salt and pepper shakers placed properly, and any crumbs on the floor cleaned up. I could then walk away feeling good about my job. Being in positive competition with my coworkers, pleasing my boss, and most of all feeling good about my accomplishments were very important to me.

After about a month, however, I began to lose my focus. Something was really bothering me that I had deliberately dismissed. I couldn't ignore it any longer. I had made friends with some of the tray girls, but I couldn't eat lunch with them. They ate lunch in the Blue Room where customers would sit, but I—and other people who looked like me—ate in a shabby-looking little room with a wooden floor on the lower level, out of sight.

The racist practices were unnerving. The people who served the food, carried the trays, and waited on the tables were all white, as were the headwaiter and supervisors. However, the people who cleaned the tables, ran the dishwashers, and emptied the trash were mostly colored people. I found it quite interesting, however, that the people who cooked the food on the lower level, unbeknown to the customers, were more colored than white people. They were out of sight. They were allowed to cook the food but not allowed to serve it.

Nonetheless, none of the colored people were allowed to eat upstairs no matter what their job was. To my surprise, there were a few of them, one a bus girl who had worked there for almost two years and accepted this practice as if it were no big deal. So, no matter what your job was, if you were white, you ate your meals and took your breaks in the Blue Room. If you were a colored person, you ate your meals and took your breaks in the basement. Nobody disobeyed the rules, even though the people I ate lunch with were really disturbed by it.

I was so curious about how the colored people managed to be so happy-go-lucky working in such a situation. I finally got up enough nerve to ask Stephanie, another colored girl, about it.

"How long have you been working here?"

"Almost two years."

"Almost two years? You have got to be kidding!"

"Yeah, but I like my job."

"But how do you deal with the fact that you can clean the tables in the Blue Room, and you can watch other employees eat in the Blue Room, but you're not allowed to eat in there with them?"

"You know that's just the rules. That's how it is."

"And you don't have a problem with that?"

"I mean, I don't like it, but I can't change it. And I need my job."

I didn't have anything else to say. I was shocked. I walked away and thought about the conversation we'd just had. *Maybe she can keep working here, but I can't do it anymore.*

It *was* a big deal to me. While I didn't want to cause problems for anyone, I had to be honest about how disturbing the segregation was to me. I couldn't change the situation, so I had to change my attitude about the situation. And that is what I did. That was my goal. But I wanted to wait until the right time, and I certainly didn't want to cause any trouble.

I stayed there a little longer to give it one more try. I had learned from the other employee who seemed content to accept things as they were—not to rock the boat, so to speak. Then one day, the supervisor yelled at me rudely, accusing me of not cleaning a table fast enough. First of all, it wasn't my table. She had made a mistake. Yet, she didn't care enough to own it—or to apologize when she realized it. It was as if she didn't feel she owed me an explanation or anything like that because of who she was—and who I was. I could see the handwriting on the wall and decided that's it; I am done working here. It was time to leave. It was time to find the right place where I could work and be comfortable in the environment.

Trusting My Heart and a New Heartbeat

Fred, my boyfriend, who was by my side after I was pregnant and rejected, proved he really wanted to marry me and became my husband. He had been married before, and each of us had a child. We were a blended family. He was happy to leave it that way, but I wanted a child with him. This love was for real, and I was certain of it—certain of it because he told me he loved me. In fact, his exact words were "If I could have somebody like you, I wouldn't ever want anyone else in the whole world." With that statement, he had me. That's all it took. This time, it was sincere in my mind just because he said it. Seriously. One thing's for sure: I believed him. I trusted him to love me forever just because of the words that came out of his mouth.

This is hard for me to admit, but I remember saying to him after we were married that I would always be with him, never to divorce him no matter what. I didn't stop there. I said, "Even if you mess around with another woman, I'll understand that you will grow out of doing that one day, and we'll be happy when it's over." You see, that's what I was told: "Every man will do it because he has to get his run out." Literally, that's what I was told—just expect it to happen because all men fool around on their wives.

Since I loved him and wanted to spend the rest of my life with him and our other two children, a baby between the two of us was going to be just perfect—in my mind. My husband did not agree, but I ignored his opinion. And the reason I ignored his opinion was that I wanted to make him happy. I mean, he married me, which meant he was serious about our relationship.

I stopped taking birth control pills because I knew he would come around once he got the news. I figured our bond would be even stronger because I wanted a baby for myself and also as a gift to him. I was certain that my motives were genuine. But while my motives were genuine, my logic was absolutely ridiculous—but not to a seventeen-year-old.

I set my plan in motion. My plan worked. I was happy, but Fred was livid when I told him I was pregnant and even more so when I explained the reason why! Yes, I was totally wrong and thinking like a seventeen-year-old kid. Nevertheless, we were going to have a baby, and I was very excited. *He will be just fine when he sees our baby. I know he will.*

That child-bride/child-mother decision was rooted in what children do. And I was thinking like a child. Without a parent or teacher with whom I totally bonded, I messed up again. Basically, the marriage was over soon after it had started—only I didn't understand why at the time. After all, I was so immature, and a mother of one, preparing again to be a mother of two.

Nine months later, my next child would make a grand entrance into this world. His arrival was one I will never forget. I was about to experience the true meaning of the word *labor* in preparation for another baby. The labor started late at night, and it continued into the next morning, afternoon, and evening—and through the night. It was really tough, and like countless women, I didn't think I could endure the pain. Between the screaming, crying, and begging God to help me, I managed to smile inside at the happiness in having my family complete with my soon-to-be bundle of joy.

Everything was ready for our new baby. I had a going-home outfit, the bed in our apartment, formula, and absolutely everything the baby needed. I just needed to hold on, realizing that he was worth every single pain. But after I had been in labor for almost twenty-four hours, I reached a point of desperation. I thought a full day of labor was absolutely ridiculous, and I felt that they—the doctors and nurses—could surely help make this a little easier. But they refused to. I imagined them saying, "Little girl, if you're grown enough to get pregnant at seventeen, you're grown enough to deal with that decision, so shut up and stop your crying."

No, of course they didn't say that to me, but they did have a nonchalant attitude toward me. I knew that they had my chart and could see that this was my third child. *I think they're trying to prove a point to me because I'm so young. Maybe if they make me suffer, that will make me think twice before I get pregnant again. That's why they're treating me this way,* I thought.

Finally, a nurse came in to check on me. I had been in pain for almost twenty-four hours, but she looked at me and said flippantly, "Oh, honey, it's gonna be a while."

As soon as she walked away, I said to myself, *Oh no it's not!* I began to bear down as hard as I could. *I can't stand this pain another minute!* I started yelling, "Nurse, nurse!"

She ran back into the room, saw me deliberately bearing down, and said, "Stop that! Stop bearing down!" I felt like saying, "To heck with you!" but I held my tongue. At that point, I couldn't stop it. She looked under the sheets and said, "Oh my, it's coming!"

You got that right. There is no way I'm gonna keep going through this much pain—ain't no way! I kept my thoughts to myself. Her actions told me she had absolutely no sympathy for me—none at all.

The baby was coming, and so were several nurses as they moved quickly into the delivery room. The time had come, and I was eager to meet my baby. After all, I had planned to have this child and wanted to spend my life nurturing my child to be a happy baby and a happy child, and to have a life different from the one I had. That was my objective from day one, and I was ready—past ready—to meet my baby. Within minutes of my arrival in the delivery room, my precious son was born.

When he came out, they cut the umbilical cord immediately, took him to the side where I could see him, and hit him on his bottom. He cried. Oh my God, that was music to my ears. They wiped him off, put him on a scale, took some measurements, and told me his height and weight. "He looks great. Congratulations!" the doctor said.

"Thank you," I replied. Then they took him away. I couldn't wait for them to bring him back to me. *What if they don't bring him back? Wait—why am I thinking like that? They will bring him back because he is perfect. Everything is all right this time.*

Shortly after I returned to the ward, they brought my baby to me. My husband and I examined him and saw he was absolutely perfect. He had the right number of fingers and toes. He had wavy hair and was a healthy-looking baby. We had already decided that if it was a boy, his name would be Frank.

As I held him in my arms, my heart was filled with joy. "Honey, Mommy loves you *so* much. I'm *so* happy to see you." Actually, happy does not really describe how grateful I was. He was out, he was with me, he was alive, and he was well. It was truly an answer to prayer. I was captivated by the way he smiled, frowned, and bonded with me as only a child who is loved can do. This was my son, and I would take care of him. I would see to it that he would have a good life. As I looked into his innocent eyes, I spoke words of love to him and promised him a life different from mine.

When Frank was a toddler, he was a typical boy, getting into things all the time. He was as fearless running inside the apartments as he was running outside in a huge backyard. He was happy and energetic. There was no stopping him. While he was a very happy child, he was also very mischievous. He had me wrapped around his finger—and knew it. When I tried to discipline him, he ignored me. It was a problem, but I wasn't about to spank him for any reason. I simply couldn't do it. I didn't see physical discipline as necessary in my immature mind. I saw it as pain, and I could not look him in the eyes and hurt him. This was a big problem because the one thing I did know was that to spare the rod meant to spoil the child. My personal experience clouded my understanding of exactly how to discipline my children.

Once, my son cut a big chunk of hair from his head right in the very front. I scolded him and told him he would get into trouble when his father came home. He decided to fix the problem. He went and got some water and put his hair on his head as if to paste it back on. We just laughed at him as I scolded him very gently. I was glad to see that he was a child who simply had fun, a happy child. I was pleased with that.

Although in elementary school Frank had lots of friends and good grades, when it came to behavior, he had problems. He seemed to have a lot of energy. He would finish his assignment but then disturb other students. The teachers would send us notes or write on his report card, "Frank does well on his assignments, but when he finishes them, he starts interrupting his classmates rather than sitting quietly." *He's a boy, just a happy child. It's no big deal,* I reassured myself. I didn't see his behavior as disobedient because I was in denial.

Things were different when he got older and went to high school. We had moved to another city. When Frank was focused on the task before him, he would let nothing deter him from his goal. I remember vividly how he wanted to be a part of the football team, which had only one other black student. He wanted desperately to be on the team and seemed totally oblivious to the fact that there were no black kids. Apparently, he just saw people. I was so thankful he was mature enough to remain focused. But something happened. Something was said. I wish I could have prevented him from hearing it.

The coach had to decide what was best for the team. Some boys would make the team, and others would not. To my surprise and to my son's credit, Frank's talent plus his positive attitude paid off. He was chosen.

But soon he overheard the wrath of a parent: "You mean you're gonna put that black kid on the team and not my son?" Frank heard it loud and clear. Yet, he was a mature young man who refused to let anyone deter him from achieving his goals. Yes, he had made the team and did an outstanding job in school.

When he became a man, he continued to have that can-do attitude in everything he decided to do.

Mama Got Saved

My mother had been living a happy-go-lucky life. She was content in what she was doing every day and every night—until something happened, bringing her to the place of praying night and day for my brother Junnie .

He was in the army—gone for two years. Mama prayed and asked God to bring him home. She completely changed the way she was living. She joined church, became very involved, stopped drinking, and stopped going to nightclubs. She became a different woman. God answered yes to her prayers and brought my brother home safely.

I remember a time when she became very ill. Sickness consumed her body, and soon she was in the hospital's intensive care unit. The problem: she was almost in a coma from diabetes. Unable to choose what she wanted to eat, who she wanted to associate with, and how she wanted to be in control, she had to rely on strangers God used to take care of her.

She needed healing, mercy, and grace. That is exactly what she got—from the Lord Jesus Christ—when he became Lord of her life. She began every Wednesday with a one-hour Bible study in her home. Everybody in the house would have to be involved. She never turned back; her life was never the same. God had changed her heart.

Vision at the Five-Star Restaurant

I found myself looking for a job at the third eatery, the Buttonwood Restaurant. I wondered whether this would be my "third time's the charm" or "three strikes and you're out" situation. The principles would set the stage for my future working with a purpose that I was "selected" to understand, to accept, and to enjoy.

In many ways, this restaurant was much like the previous one in terms of its appearance and the manner in which it was organized. What I really liked about it was that it was a fresh start, a new opportunity to forge ahead in a place where I could learn, grow, and earn a salary to be self-sufficient. That was the most important reason to work in my mind.

The application and interview process was no different from before. In fact, it was pretty much identical. I filled out the application and had an interview that went well. I told the truth about my age. I was seventeen. After a few days, I received a phone call that I'd gotten the job.

I took the bus to work each day, just as before. When the roads were icy and it was bitter cold, I would sometimes take a cab. But rarely was I absent, or even late for that matter. I understood the importance of being dependable, so I planned ahead.

My most vivid memory is watching my coworker friend Helen make salad dressings. She was a Negro who had salt-and-pepper hair usually in one or two braids. She was a petite lady with a giant, happy-go-lucky personality. Watching her work was a treat. And the fact that she was almost my grandmother's age amazed me. Most likely, I was subconsciously thinking of Mama Nan when I worked with her. She was a great mentor who, through her actions, taught me the principle of working hard to achieve excellence. I loved watching Helen use those gigantic containers to make salad dressing. *What a woman,* I often thought as I witnessed her vibrant personality and tenacity to get each job done with precision.

Making salad dressing was messy, but I was excited to witness the behind-the-scenes process. It was Helen's job, and she was proud of it. Her attitude spoke volumes to me about enjoying the opportunity to choose the type of job you love and loving the job you have chosen. The first time I saw how the green goddess salad dressing was made, I was simply amazed. *Oh, that's how they make it. Wow!*

Green goddess, named for its green tint, is a salad dressing typically containing mayonnaise, sour cream, chervil, chives, anchovy, tarragon, lemon juice, and pepper. Before the popularity of ranch dressing, green goddess was one of the most popular salad dressings on the West Coast.

My job title was salad girl. As the name implies, it was my job to prepare salads for the day. This included making a variety of salad dressings. Making the salads was great fun, and I loved the sense of accomplishment as I gazed at the final product. Sampling the salads was absolutely delightful. After all, I had to do the taste test to be sure everything was great. Of course, that was the objective of the taste test—or the rationale I used at the time. It was a full day's work to prepare a large variety of salads for lunch and dinner and then tidy things up for the next day. A girl could work up an appetite. Unfortunately, my childhood desire for healthier foods was made up for in the ready access to taste testing.

Although Helen never knew it, she impacted my life as I witnessed her work ethic, which included two principles: focus on the task at hand with the end result in mind and embrace the journey as part of the mission. I found myself wanting to do a good job simply because it was the basic requirement for the job. But, to be honest, I also wanted to please Helen. I loved the feeling of making her proud of me. Most important, I was earning the right to get a paycheck and the right to spend it according to *my* needs—and my wants.

I worked in the salad department for about six months, mastered the process—including making the dressings from scratch—and now was ready for a new challenge. The issue was not boredom but rather an opportunity to gain new skills and become a more productive employee. The results would also equip me for a raise, which was always incentive to work hard, learn more, and prepare for the future, no matter what job I had.

I found myself pondering the grill and fry cook position. Promotion was in my mind. A new challenge was right around the corner, and I had decided to go for it with the same can-do attitude. The process was easy. I requested the change, and it was granted. Many years before, I realized the value in this principle. When I needed direction, taking the first step to ask was most important to achieving my goals.

I set goals daily as I prepared breakfast orders for the customers in a very systematic and timely manner. Everything was important, from the beginning of the shift to the final cleanup and preparation for the next day. When the waitresses attached the ticket to the order wheel and told me what they needed, I was excited about filling their order. It was a win-win situation. The waitresses got great tips, and I felt on top of the world because I proved myself to be a hard worker. I had a good job and was proud of being an excellent fry cook.

Billie, one of my favorite waitresses, was a white lady with short hair. She had a husky voice and a bubbly personality. The customers loved her, and I was simply delighted to rub elbows with nice people like her. Billie would turn in an order and say, "Short stack, bacon, and sunny. Make it walk." That meant two pancakes, three strips of bacon, and two eggs cooked on one side only, to go. When I had the food ready, I would yell out, "Short stack, bacon, and two sunny-ups walking." When Billie heard the order, she came quickly, removed the ticket, inspected the food, and smiled. Mission accomplished!

Another expression was "eighty-six," which meant we were out of an item. For example, if we ran out of ingredients to make eggs Benedict, someone would yell out, "Eighty-six on the Benny." I had never heard of eggs Benedict. It consists of half an English muffin topped with Canadian bacon or ham or bacon and poached eggs with hollandaise sauce. So, if we ran out of the muffins or the sauce, we wouldn't have eggs Benedict.

I really enjoyed working as a fry cook. I mastered all the techniques to work on my own very efficiently. I was delighted with my accomplishment. However, once again, I was still not satisfied. I had an insatiable desire to learn new things. There was only one other area where I could and wanted to work. In the back of my mind, I thought, *There is no way I can be a baker. You have to be really smart to do that. I've seen John do it. I know he wouldn't want somebody like me hanging around him.* Of course, I had to find out for sure. It just seemed as if he needed help, and I was the best one for the job.

Now an assistant baker job was on my radar. As before, it took only a request for me to get promoted to that position. I had proven to myself, and apparently to others, that I was a hard worker. I was very dependable and had done an outstanding job. I must add that I could not have learned without good teachers such as Helen and Billie. I was keenly aware of their role in my success.

John was also an outstanding teacher. He was a white man, about my father's age. He stood at least six feet tall with white hair and a potbelly. I thoroughly appreciated learning from him. We made every kind of dessert I had ever eaten or heard of. We made all varieties of pastries, from rolls to cakes to pies. You name it, we made it. To top it off, we made the desserts from scratch! *Wow,* I often thought as I learned the process. My final desserts resembled John's. I was so proud of the new skills I had mastered. I learned how to work solo, and John noticed that I could do the job. I was so pleased with my new skills! I was also content because I worked with all these kind, hardworking people.

I worked in the bakery the longest of the three areas. As far as I was concerned, I was content to work there forever. However, as long as I have memories, I will never forget what happened next. It was life changing.

It was amazing, to say the very least.

While standing in the salad department during the lunch hour, I was struck by a thought that rendered me motionless. For the very first time, I had an abrupt change in my attitude about this job. Two years had gone by, and I felt thoroughly appreciated, but I sensed I was needed elsewhere.

As I looked out at the customers relishing their time together, I had a moment of clarity. *They are here because they want to be here, not because they need to be here. But I'm supposed to do something different. I'm supposed to be a nurse. Patients need nurses who are kind and compassionate. That's who I am. That's what I'm supposed to do.*

In my mind I saw myself lying in mud, as negative thoughts about my life surfaced. *OK. I can do one of two things. I can stay down there and blame somebody for it. I can blame my mother for the way I was raised. I can blame the color of my skin. Or, I can pick myself up, clean myself off, go back to school, get my education, and be somebody. I want to be a nurse. I'm going to school to learn how to be an LPN. That is what I'm gonna do.*

That vision was over as abruptly as it started. I yelled out for all to hear my new revelation, which was as clear to me as the nose on my face. *Wow!* I thought, as I began to absorb the implications of my revelation. It was real, so real that I had to share it.

I walked through each area of the kitchen, telling everybody what I was going to do. "I'm gonna quit this job and go back to school. I'm gonna be a nurse!" I said to everyone who could hear me. I was absolutely ecstatic and sure of a calling to move on and start my career. Without hesitation, I walked away. I went to the personnel department and told them my plan to quit my job. I gave my two weeks' notice right away.

They looked at me as if I had lost my mind. This was totally out of character for me. After all, I was dependable, a hard worker, a person who really loved my job and my coworkers. Yet, I was quitting. It didn't make sense to any of them. In fact, they laughed at me and my "vision." I was unaffected by their remarks. I was changed only by the vision.

John said, "Why would you want to work as a nurse, especially an LPN? You can eventually become a baker and make a lot more money doing this job."

"I know," I responded. "But this is what I'm supposed to do—be a nurse working with sick people. I have to leave."

I absolutely knew it was time for me to go, and I was going to find myself working as a nurse in a hospital helping people. I knew that for sure. Only nobody had told me that. I figured that, as promised, my Father loved me, and this was something he had chosen for me to do. I pondered that in my heart and was certain of my new decision. I had all the proof I needed.

No one took me seriously. Not one person. I had worked with them for two years. Two weeks later, though, as promised, I did not show up for work. However, I did show up early that morning at the training site, ready to start my career.

My first step was the Neighborhood Youth Corps (NYC), established by the Manpower Administration. NYC administered various training programs, including on-the-job training (OJT) through the Concentrated Employment Program (CEP). There was an office in the inner city. I would go there to start my career. That was my goal.

I learned about these government-funded programs that offered alternative education programs for youth. High school dropouts, such as me, who were not allowed to return to traditional schools, were given a second chance. We would have the opportunity for tutoring to obtain our GED, be taught life-changing academic skills and, in general, be coached to become productive citizens. I knew I was on the right track in following my strong intuition.

Each person who qualified could enter the program by self-referral and was placed according to his or her specific needs. To qualify, I had to be a minority between the ages of fifteen and twenty-one, according to the income poverty guidelines. I definitely qualified.

There were opportunities posted to learn skills for many jobs throughout the city. This was an affirmative action program to counter the effects of a history of discrimination. It would increase the representation of women and minorities in areas of employment, education, and business from which they had been excluded. Participants could train to be a cashier, secretary, salesperson, nurse's aide, or LPN. LPN training had my attention, and I was going for it. An opportunity to be in the medical field was a realistic objective for somebody like me.

From day one, I vowed to earn the right to receive the help for which I would be extremely grateful. A handout was not what I wanted but rather an opportunity to learn and give back to our society. This was my plan and my sincere promise to my Father in gratitude for another gift he was about to give me.

Finally, I was there at the Manpower Development Employment Office. The building was in sight, the starting place for my new beginning. *Oh, I can't wait to get started working as a nurse. This is who I am; this is what I was born to do. To say I am happy would be an understatement. I am thrilled beyond belief. Wow! Why me? I don't know. I don't understand, but I thank you, Father, for choosing me.* It was hard to hold back the tears because I was so happy. My heart was overjoyed, and the smile on my face revealed just how happy I really was to have this once-in-a-lifetime golden opportunity.

I had taken the bus to the agency and was right there early and ready to go for it.

I opened the door, walked in, and spoke to the receptionist sitting at the desk.

"May I help you?" the young Negro lady asked in a pleasant tone.

She appeared to be about twenty-five and was dressed neatly. I told her my name and said, "I'm here to sign up for the LPN training program."

"I'm sorry, but we don't offer that training anymore."

"You don't offer it anymore? But I just heard about the training recently and thought for sure I could get it."

I didn't tell her *why* I was so sure about it. I didn't tell her about the vision I had had in the middle of a salad bar. I didn't think she would understand. Nobody else did.

"We do offer a variety of training programs, but we just ran out of funding for the LPN training. Would you like to sign up for anything else?"

I didn't answer yes because I didn't know what to say.

"Will you get more funds and start the LPN training again later?" I asked.

"No, we won't."

I wanted to cry. *I can't believe this. Oh no!*

"But I quit my job because I was sure this was exactly what I was supposed to do," I said, trying to hold back the tears.

The lady must have sensed my sincerity and my desperate need for the job.

"Just have a seat over there, and let me see what I can do."

What can she do if they don't offer the training for LPNs anymore? What in the world am I going to do now? This is horrible!

What had happened in the salad department at work was real. Yes, it was.

The woman went into another room and closed the door. When she emerged, she was with another well-dressed Negro lady who was also very articulate. She looked like a real boss.

She looks really smart, I thought as I sized her up.

"Hello, Rosie. I'm Angela Stevens. So, you quit your job?" she asked.

"Yes, ma'am, I did. I really thought I was going to get into this training program."

"OK, let me tell you what I will do for you. We will hire you here to be a file clerk. There's one catch. You cannot tell anyone you are just a trainee. OK? At least that way, you still have a job. Would you like to do that?"

I don't know what to do, but I know I need a job. "Yes, ma'am, I'll take it. Thank you very much," I said with gratitude.

Ms. Stevens took me back to another room with lots of papers, folders, and index cards on the desk. She taught me how to file information about trainees already in the program and how to work as a receptionist. The pay I would receive for the position was the same I had at the restaurant, which was enough to pacify me. But honestly, I still felt empty inside. I was very depressed that I apparently had gotten it all wrong.

I worked there for more than a month and had come to terms with my situation. Day after day, I thought about a dream that would never become my reality and how disappointing that was. By the same token, I was very grateful to have a job.

Then one day, a lady came into the office to speak to my boss. I was working as the receptionist at the time, and my boss was standing by my desk. She spoke directly to Ms. Stevens. She said something like this:

"Hello, we're looking for five people among the trainees you have who have the potential to learn a new skill that tests the brain. As you know, the hospitals don't have the minimum number of minorities they must have. We'll choose five people and then narrow it down to two. These people need to have the motivation to learn how to be an electroencephalographic— that is, an EEG—technician. I know you have about two hundred fifty people enrolled in this program to choose from. We need five."

Ms. Stevens looked at me, then back at the other lady and said, "We'll look through our files and see what we can do. Surely we can find five people. Thank you. I'll get back to you with the five trainees."

"Thank you," the agent replied and walked out the door.

My mouth dropped open, but I could hardly speak. My heart was running like a freight train. I wanted to jump up and down at the thought of working at a hospital as a technician. *Oh my God! I, the high school dropout, born and raised in poverty, have the opportunity of a lifetime to be an EEG technician working with the brain!* The thought of being equipped to help those who cannot help themselves was absolutely overwhelming.

"Wow, deep in my heart, I believe I'm supposed to work with patients. Becoming a nurse is what I wanted at first. But to learn about the brain and to do the test to help people know how their brain is working is absolutely perfect for me. This is an answer to prayer. This is what the vision was all about."

"I believe you're right," she responded.

Immediately, she examined the other trainees' records. She selected four who appeared to have what it would take to become EEG technicians. None of them were people I had ever met. All of them were apparently qualified by the guidelines and had proven themselves worthy of the opportunity to get the job.

Later, Ms. Stevens contacted them, explained the position, and scheduled the five of us to go through a series of tests: a dexterity test to check our ability to use our hands properly, a basic academic test to determine our level of comprehension, and several interviews to determine our ability to work with patients.

I was ecstatic about the process and did well on all the tests with the exception of the GED pretest. My score revealed my status as a high school dropout. My test score revealed where I was when I attended Central Junior High School. That was the situation, and there was no denying it. The other four trainees were in the same boat. Determined to forge ahead and work hard to pass my high school equivalency exam, I felt I had a good chance of being selected. I realized it would be a tedious process. But he knew I could do it; I was clear about that.

Mission-Mindedness

Being nineteen years old, a mother of two, and in a now-troubled marriage with Fred, I had to trust a power greater than mine to guide me ahead. Clearly, I had lacked the foundation needed to make the best decisions. Yet, something was directing me to pursue a calling greater than I could imagine. And I knew it.

Chosen as one of five competing for an incredible job, I felt my adrenaline flowing in great anticipation. The five would soon become two, and the idea that they might choose me was surreal. Right before my eyes, the selection process was narrowing. My life could possibly change forever. *The personnel department is right there,* I thought as I walked straight ahead. *My application has been filled out, and I am ready for the interview.* I entered the office to fill out the official forms for future employment. There were other people sitting around who were there for the same reason.

When I walked up to the reception desk, the lady looked at me with an inquisitive expression on her face. Here was my cue to identify myself and explain that I had already been preapproved among five people and was here for the interview. With confidence, I told her my name and reason for being there. "I have an appointment to see Mr. Byrd."

"Have a seat. He'll be right with you."

"OK, thank you," I said and sat down with the other applicants.

Mr. Byrd came out, introduced himself, directed me to his office, and said, "Have a seat."

He was a chubby man dressed in a fine suit and tie. His pleasant smile put me at ease. He looked through all the paperwork and asked me important questions such as what I would do for a babysitter and how I planned to handle times when my children were sick. He was trying to determine if there was anything that would keep me from being able to do the job if I was selected. I answered all of his questions with confidence and without hesitation. Judging from his response, I did a good job. He said, "Thank you, and good luck."

I was glad to be done with that interview. *I did great!* I thought as I left Mr. Byrd's office.

The next day, I met the neurologist and the supervisor. I wasn't as comfortable meeting them. In my eyes, they were bigger than life. They were real professional people working in a hospital. *Oh my goodness. OK, I can do this. My interview went well with Mr. Byrd, and it will go well today,* I thought.

Finally, there I was, sitting in the office of Dr. Abernathy, chief of neurology and board-certified neurologist. It was a small room but plush and polished. There was a large, rich-looking mahogany desk covered with important-looking papers and complicated-looking medical books. Dr. Abernathy sat in a big, high-back swivel chair as he talked to me. I could feel his eyes searching and looking through me, sizing me up with every word I said. This interview was very important to me, and I wanted to make a good impression.

After what seemed like a long interview, he ended it with a couple of questions that caught me off guard. "*Why* do you want this job? *What* will this job do for you?"

"I feel that if I get this job, I'll really be somebody," I answered softly, timidly, and unrehearsed. My answer was spontaneous and sincere, which appeared to connect with him. *I really want it bad,* I thought. Dr. Abernathy stood up from his big executive chair, walked around to where I was sitting, reached out his hand to me, and said, "You *are* somebody."

Something just happened, I thought to myself. *I think I'm going to get the job by what he just did, what he said. Oh boy, I got it!* I perceived that he was pleased with the sincerity of my response to his question and that he had chosen me at that very moment to be one of the two trainees.

I tried to read his mind: *She seems to be all right. Her application looks good. Yes, there is some potential in this young lady. I'm going to hire her.* I smiled at the thought. *She wants a chance to get ahead, and I'm going to give it to her.* I smiled again. *Ooo-wee!* I thought, careful not to show my euphoria.

After a brief pause, as if Dr. Abernathy was searching for more to say, there was a knock at the door. *It must be the supervisor,* I thought, and it was.

"Come in," Dr. Abernathy said. A woman walked in. "This is Rosie, one of the applicants. Rosie, meet Rachel. She is the supervisor, and she will take you and the others to the EEG lab. Once you all get to the lab and see the machine, some of you might decide to back out."

Why would anyone back out? This is a once-in-a-lifetime opportunity. You'd have to be stupid to do that. I know I'm not gonna back out.

"It's very nice to meet you," I said, hoping that was the proper thing to say.

Rachel was tall, about five feet nine, and slightly overweight like me. Her casual outfit was not quite what I expected. I thought maybe she'd be wearing a white uniform like most of the other employees. She wore thick glasses that made her eyes look distant and smaller than they actually were. *She must be blind without those glasses,* I thought. Her hair was cut in a short shag style, and she had that take-charge kind of demeanor. Underneath the exterior, I knew she was a very intelligent woman from whom I could learn a lot.

Rachel stayed for a short time, and then she and I joined the other four applicants (one male and three females), and we talked about our chances of being chosen.

But before Rachel and I had left his office, Dr. Abernathy had said, "Good luck. I don't make these decisions alone because I would probably make a mistake."

If you don't make the decision, who will? I thought. My doubt was short-lived because I was certain of getting this position. It had my name written all over it.

The five of us began talking as we followed Rachel. "I'll bet they're gonna choose you, and I don't know who the second person will be," I said to Natalie, another applicant.

She said the same thing to me: "I'll bet they're gonna choose you, and I don't know who the other person will be."

Rachel led us to the next phase of the interview process. We walked down two flights of stairs, through a long, cold hallway, and into her office.

Her office was in the basement, with plain brick walls, a small desk, and no windows—quite different from Dr. Abernathy's. *Oh well, she is not the doctor, so that's the reason her office looks different,* I thought.

"Have a seat," Rachel said with an authoritative voice that made me feel uncomfortable. I felt intimidated by her powerful position as the boss.

She remained standing and began to tell us about the job and the training program.

"The training will be divided into two sessions, clinical application and classroom work. You will each work with the patients directly every morning from eight to noon. After lunch, you will be in class. At the end of each week, you will be tested on what you have learned. You are expected to learn all the material in this book," she said as she picked up the curriculum and showed it to us. "The entire program will take one year, and you will only gain more knowledge with experience. It is important that you understand that. Do you understand?" she asked.

We all nodded and said yes.

I took it all in, mesmerized at how organized and professional Rachel was.

I was hoping and praying, or rather praying and hoping, that I would be one of the two chosen to receive the training. After all, working with sick patients in a hospital setting was my calling in life. Many things had taken place to bring me to this point. They were miraculous, without question. I also felt Natalie would be a strong employee, having observed her to be quite confident in her statements, poised in her posture, and immaculate in her attire. She stood out from the other four, who were nonchalant and, in my opinion, not as prepared for the interview. *Oh yes, she will get the job for sure. I know it,* I thought to myself.

I told my family and friends that I was certain I would get the job, judging from the interview. The opportunity to begin a career as an EEG technician, helping physicians treat patients with problems affecting their brains, was certainly my future.

I never will forget what my friend Brenda from the Buttonwood Restaurant said when I told her I was certain I'd get the job. "If you get that job, you'll really think you're somebody special and forget about all of us little people."

Her words pricked my heart. I responded, "I will never forget from whence I came." My statement silenced her; and she just grinned and walked away. I'm not sure she believed me, but I rested confident in the truth. I had promised my Father to prove my gratitude by being the best I could possibly be and to touch people's lives to bring glory to him. That's exactly what I planned to do.

All my family and friends expected me to get the job because I had told them about the interview. Within my heart, I knew from the time Dr. Abernathy ended the interview with the words, "You *are* somebody," I had it. As I predicted, approximately one month later, both Natalie and I were thrilled to find out we had been chosen. The training would begin in March 1969.

We would be paid two dollars and fifty cents per hour, with one trainee working at one hospital and the other at a second hospital. But that didn't happen. The physician at the second hospital would not accept either one of us. Even though our boss was reluctant to tell us the whole story, we heard it from other people who worked for the physician at the other hospital. The problem for him, according to the secretary, was that "having a Negro working with him would be bad for business."

Dr. Abernathy said he'd take both of us, but the hospital could not pay the original amount promised since the plan was to hire only one trainee. We were offered one dollar and ninety-one cents instead of two fifty per hour to train for this position. It took me only a split second to accept the lower wage. *I'm grateful for whatever they pay us. After all, we're being paid to learn, and that's great!* There was no need to argue about what was promised. There was no need to get angry because one of us was not accepted because of the skin we were born in. It was all going to be just fine. I was absolutely sure of that.

On our first day, Natalie and I reported to Rachel's office to get started with class. She was clearly ready with books containing all the information we needed. I was really impressed. We sat down at the table, and she stood over us showing us pictures, writing on the board, and having us refer to the handouts she had given us.

"These are the basic parts of the brain, their locations and functions..." She named each of them as she pointed. "Now, these patterns you will find on the EEG tracings: alpha, theta, delta, and beta." *Wow!* I thought. She explained every detail and then said, "I want you to know all of these by tomorrow."

Natalie and I looked at each other. My eyes got really wide at the thought of having to learn so much in such a short amount of time. *This must be a joke. How can we possibly learn all of this in one day?* I thought.

But I went away ready to face the task with tenacity. Oh, how happy I was at the thought of learning everything Rachel would prepare for us. After all, this was a huge endeavor. That "I can do it" attitude was what I needed to succeed. I was always mindful of that and refused to let the difficulty of the task hold me back. However, this mountain was steep. I took it one step at a time.

All of Rachel's classes were like that—overwhelming. It was as if her goal was to make us work as hard as we possibly could. That is exactly what she did. Yet, instead of feeling encouraged by her, I felt as if she resented me especially. I was not as assertive as Natalie, who had a no-nonsense kind of attitude. Not me. I just needed to focus on learning. *She must resent us inner-city high school dropouts. Maybe she wants to prove we will fail. That is probably the reason she is so hard on us, especially me because I'm such a pushover.* I quickly realized that thought was there to distract me, so I pushed it out of my mind.

I also recall a time shortly after I was hired when we were alone, and Rachel began talking to me as if she were a mother instructing her child. I was quite disturbed by that conversation. She looked at me as if to say, *I really want you to get this message loud and clear,* when she said, "I want you to understand you will always be at least one year behind me and six months behind Sharon." Sharon was another student who had completed half her training.

I didn't respond. *What does she mean by that?*

"You see, it will always be that way because you started after we did," she added, as if trying to drill it into my head so I would not forget.

"OK," I said because I knew I should respond pleasantly. I wouldn't tell her what I really thought about that logic. It didn't make sense to me.

I get the message, I thought. *She is telling me not to get the big-head attitude.* It was a little strange that she felt compelled to tell me that, but I accepted what she said because she was the supervisor. I was grateful for the once-in-a-lifetime opportunity to learn from her.

Rachel's hard, taskmaster-style training would pay off. That was something I knew for sure. I kept my thoughts to myself. I could only speculate about her attitude, motives, and agenda, but I was certain about mine. Without a doubt, I could achieve any task set before me. If—no, *when*—I happened to encounter difficulties, and if I actually failed one of the tests, I was already prepared and understood that when I tried and gave it my best, it would be good enough. My mottos were "Quitters never win, and winners never quit" and "Nothing beats a fail but a try." I faced each task with confidence that somehow I would get the job done. And I always did.

The coursework was really hard but very rewarding. I was determined to master it. Rachel taught us all the pertinent information: medical terminology, neuroanatomy, neurophysiology, machine instrumentation, and proper technician–patient interactions. As part of our practical training, she showed us how to measure the patient's head. That was the most time-consuming part of the test. Measurements had to be taken with a specific system to ascertain that the electrodes would be on the correct part of the head. It was a five-part system and consisted of mathematical steps for each part.

When each placement had been marked correctly, the area was prepped, and the electrodes were filled with a conductive paste and placed on the correct spot. To hold it in place, a piece of tape or gauze dipped in melted wax was used to seal the electrode securely. Adequate application was checked with a special instrument.

Now that the setup was completed, it was time to check the electrical activity of the brain. Performing the EEG was a complex system to learn. Looking at the sixteen channels of squiggly lines on the paper and learning how to make sense of it was overwhelming at first. Sleep patterns, wake patterns, and normal and abnormal patterns all looked different. This made each test unique in terms of learning how to read and document our opinion for the physicians to critique.

I have to say that Rachel was an excellent teacher who clearly adored her job. She was a perfectionist and expected the same from us. However, at times, it appeared as if we had to work extra hard just to prove ourselves. Sometimes I felt as though she resented the way we got our jobs through Manpower Development's training programs specifically for minorities. I was not looking for a handout—not at all—but rather an opportunity.

Natalie and I understood the importance of doing our jobs according to predetermined guidelines. By that time, I had proven myself and simply wanted to give back to my patients by treating them the way I wanted to be treated if the tables were turned. Lives were at stake. I had not been handpicked but rather heart-and-soul-picked for this position.

Achieving excellence was in the forefront of my mind each day as I stepped foot in the hospital. Dr. Abernathy trained us to that end. Because of him, my career start was incredible. I will never forget what he told me right from the very start of training: "You two are going to be the best technicians in this city. You will go to the neurology conferences each week, and at first you won't understand most of what you hear. One day, that will change, and there will be very little you don't understand."

We were only a few weeks into our training when Rachel came in one morning with a shocking announcement. "You will measure the first patient's head today, Rosie."

"What? But I don't understand how to do it yet. Can I wait a little longer?" I asked.

"No, you will never learn until you start doing it," she replied emphatically.

Why do I have to go first? Why is she making me do it this soon? That's not right. I was so nervous. My mind began racing. *What if I do it wrong? What if I mess up and make the patient's test turn out wrong? What will the patient think? He will know I don't know what I'm doing. How can I possibly fake it? I can't! It will take me forever!* The thoughts were spinning in my head.

"Your patient is on the way," Rachel said.

"OK," I said in a soft, sad tone.

"You have to get started with your first patient sooner or later, young lady. So, get ready."

I was very nervous, but I had to compose myself right away. That is exactly what I did. As I was rehearsing in my mind how I would handle this patient, Rachel looked back at the testing room with a scheming smile on her face.

"Your patient has arrived," she said.

"OK, I'll be right there," I responded.

I took a deep breath and prepared myself for the task. It would be hard since this was my first test. Still, I could and would do anything I was expected to do for my patients. I changed my attitude about the situation. Now equipped with a positive approach, my thoughts were different. *I will just be open and honest with this man,* I thought as the tension began to dissipate. *I will do the best that I can, and my best has got to be good enough.*

Now that the anxiety was gone, I was delighted to begin the practical part of my training. After all, this was an extremely important phase that I could master only through hands-on experience. I had seen Rachel measure and apply electrodes, and it seemed very easy. I realized that one day it would be easy for me, too, when I learned the technique as well as she had learned it. Not only was I ready, but I was excited about the challenge and what would be the memory of my very first patient.

Although this self-talk helped calm my nerves, I was still disturbed as I pondered Rachel's motives. *Why is she making me do this patient now without warning? Oh well, it doesn't matter what she thinks. I just know it will be OK,* I thought. *I am OK now. I am ready for this patient.* Someone not made in flesh and blood was trying to distract me; I understood who and I understood why.

So, I walked out of the lab into the testing room where my first patient was waiting.

"Hello, Mr. Jones," I said with a genuine smile.

"Hello," he responded calmly. But I could tell by the look on his face that he was afraid.

"I'm going to do a test on you today to check your brain activity."

"Does it hurt? Will you have to shave my head?" he asked, still wearing that look of fear.

"No, sir, it doesn't hurt at all, and no, I don't have to shave your head. But I do want to explain something to you." *Yes, this will be easier for him to relax and easier for me to do the test if I just tell him the truth,* I thought.

"Sir, I'm in training. And you are my first patient. To be quite honest, I really don't totally understand what I am doing." I paused to gather my thoughts before going on. *Honesty works.* He looked at me but did not respond. I continued, "My supervisor is in the next room and will check me as I go along to make sure I don't make mistakes that can't be fixed easily. I want you to know I can't do anything that will hurt you. It will just take a while for me to get it done until I get the experience."

I could see the creases of worry on his face gradually melt away. I touched his shoulder and looked into his eyes and calmly said, "Let me assure you it will be just fine. Just think about this: I will always remember that you were my very first patient—such a pleasant man like you. Years down the road, I will look back on this day and remember you as I began my career."

"Yes, and I will be proud to know that I had something to do with your success," he said with a big smile on his face.

Oh, how relieved I was to get this obstacle—this step—behind me.

It was great to see what was happening in that moment. Discrimination and segregation were simply a way of life at that time. This might have been this man's very first interaction with a Negro. I was bound and determined to make it special. This was a time when most of us colored people worked in house-keeping or kitchens. We weren't nurses, technologists, and physicians. Yet, change was in the making, and I was blessed to be in the very midst of it.

I began to measure his head with a red china marker using a metric tape measure. I used my cheat sheet to follow each of the five steps. I kept stopping to erase mistakes with an alcohol wipe until all the measurements were perfect. I was not in a hurry, not even a little bit. By this time, I was focused and excited to complete this awesome new task. The measurements took about an hour, which was actually the time allotted for the entire exam. But it didn't matter to me. I refused to get uptight about it. After all, I had a delightful patient, and I was off to a fantastic start. *Yes, I have to start sometime, and this is the time,* I thought as I looked at the clock and realized how long it was taking.

After completing the head measurements, which is called the 10/20 measurement system, it was time to apply the electrodes. This process also took a long time because perfect application was my goal. Nothing less would be acceptable. Twenty-five areas were prepped for good contact. I filled each electrode with the conductive paste and applied them to his head. Now I was ready to perform the recording portion of the test, which would require about half the time it took me to prepare the patient.

Rachel had been hovering over me and constantly asking me questions while I was working with the patient. I needed the distraction like I needed a hole in my head, but I tried to hide my frustration. She wanted answers explained in detail backward, forward, and in hypothetical situations. This was difficult, to say the very least, but she was the boss, and I had to learn how to multitask, another skill I would need to master for my future.

I remained pleasant, hiding my real feelings throughout the entire test because I thought it best. Truly, I didn't have the guts to tell Rachel how forceful I thought she was being and how her extra pressure was making me, and probably even the patient, very uncomfortable. However, I was already looking forward to having a candid conversation with her about that when the training was over.

After six months, the basic portion of the training was over, and I had learned all the pertinent technical information needed to perform the test, even though I needed much more experience under my belt. The remaining six months would be spent applying what I had learned for all types of patient-testing situations: in the ICU, with psychiatric patients, with children, and with both cooperative and uncooperative patients. I kept reflecting on what Dr. Abernathy had said when he told me that he was going to make us the best technicians in the city. I was beginning to feel totally competent and secure in my knowledge and ability to accomplish even the most complex tasks.

By this time, we were not just doing the tests but were very efficient, adept at interpreting the EEGs accurately as well. Dr. Abernathy instructed us to read the EEGs and put our interpretations of the studies down in writing, even though we were just technicians. This forced us to learn even more than was expected. That was his goal.

One day, Dr. Abernathy said to me, "You know, one of these days, a patient might have an EEG test and we need the results immediately. What happens if I'm not around? Even if you make a mistake, write down your impression of the test. This is the best way to learn."

I understood it was OK to make a mistake because a mistake is never truly a mistake when one is learning. That was called living life tenaciously—positively in my opinion.

Another thing I remember vividly: Dr. Abernathy would correct my grammar every now and then. One day, I was talking to him about a patient situation. I said, "I seen her do it [not sure what *it* was]," and he corrected me right on the spot.

"You don't say, 'I seen'; you say, 'I saw.'"

"OK, thank you," I replied and walked away to study and learn from my mistakes. Clearly, he saw more than the color of my skin and what he had to do for an employee. He cared for me like a father, as if he were divinely instructed to empower me. *Hmm.*

Armed with confidence and the main part of the training behind me, I finally had that conversation with Rachel I promised myself six months before. I told her that I felt she had been really hard on me, that her attitude and actions sometimes made my life as an EEG technician trainee miserable. I was not rude—just assertive. She looked at me and just listened as I was talking, folding her arms and nodding as if to encourage me to keep going. She allowed me to get everything off my chest without interruption. I needed that and appreciated her attitude.

"Well, at least I'm a good technician," I said, shifting gears from anger to confidence. "Rachel, I want to be registered someday," I continued. "But it will be so hard for me to pass since most people don't." *And I'm not smart like you, and I don't think I can do it,* I added in my mind. Rachel was already registered by the American Board of EEG Technologists, one of only a few in the state of Missouri and one of less than one hundred in the entire United States of America. That was totally impressive since the pass rate of the written and four-part oral exams was very low. She was teaching me. *Wow!* "I really don't think I can do it," I confessed.

"Yes, you can do it, Rosie," she replied with a genuine-looking smile on her face.

"But I'm not as smart as you are," I argued.

I will never forget what she said next.

"Listen, and always remember this. If you take a lot of mud and keep throwing it up against a brick wall, most of it will fall, but some of it will stick each time. You can do it. You will have a lot to learn. But as you study, lots of what you are learning will stick."

The analogy was simple; yet, I really heard her and deemed the words to be sincere. *Oh yes, if I keep learning more and more, keep going to neurology conferences and meetings, and just keep learning new information—keep studying like I'm doing now—I can be certified someday. Oh yes, yes I can!* I thought.

"Rosie, I want you to learn—I really do. You have great potential, and I know you're going places. I have always known that about you, and *that* is the reason I was so hard on you. I know what you are made of. Now, *you* have to know that as well."

What I heard surprised me. All this time, I was thinking she had been hard on me because she was making me earn the opportunity I'd been given. If I'm honest, I would say I thought she was prejudiced. But she was just like Dr. Abernathy, wanting me to excel and be the very best technician I could be.

"Thank you! Oh, thank you so much for all you have done for me, Rachel."

"You're welcome. I have enjoyed seeing you learn," she said with a smile.

I thanked her for her coercive training style because she had equipped me with foundational skills that set the stage for a future of tenacity. She had been selected to bring out the best in me. Finally I could see that clearly, without any negative self-talk.

I was internally motivated and seized the opportunity to learn from my past. It was a good thing because years later, after I had learned all I needed to know in the lab, my position would change.

Seven years later, Rachel quit her job to move away and start a family. Therefore, the department was without a supervisor. Her official title was chief technician. Dr. Abernathy wanted me to replace her. Although there was strong opposition by a few people, I had been trained by a board-certified neurologist. With that, coupled with my positive attitude, I accepted the job offer.

I became the supervisor and, as with my training to be a technician, I was focused and tenacious in my efforts to succeed in this new position. Rachel was invaluable to setting the stage for my career. Her no-nonsense attitude *plus* my insatiable desire to learn was the perfect combination for my success. I'm deeply grateful for the role she played in my position—my mission field.

Thinking Out of the Box

Amazing Sister

Early in my career, I had a personal family experience that set the foundation for my understanding of, interactions with, and reactions to patients. As far as timing, I had learned to closely observe what was unfolding right before my eyes. What happened was not just another part of my academic studies. This was not an assignment to investigate and master. This was a rare situation, yet one I observed up close and personally. I will never forget the many messages and life-changing principles within this single event. Yes, as the saying goes, "this hit home," reminding me of the importance of family and the need to interact with others, while I remain mindful that they are also part of someone's family.

Four years my senior, my sister Loretta—I call her Retta—was the oldest of the nine children. My brother is two years older, and I was the youngest of the three. Nine years later, the second set of six came rapidly. Initially, I wanted so badly to be a big sister so I wouldn't be the baby. But after I had so many responsibilities with my siblings, I changed that tune. Such is life. We are never satisfied with things as they are and seek to find something better. After I get this…if only I had that…when I go there…the list goes on and on.

As a child, I always wanted to be like my big sister. Retta got a gold tooth when she was fourteen, which was common in our family. It was a fashion statement. She was allowed to bleach her hair strawberry blond at that same age. She looked beautiful to me, and I couldn't wait to add the golden touch to my smile and the glimmering beauty to my hair. After all, my sister was beautiful, classy, self-confident, and fearless like our mother. Loretta appeared to be on top of the world, and my goal was to be right up there with her.

Retta was highly esteemed by so many people in school, so I felt proud to say she was *my* sister. This was especially true when I needed her to bail me out of trouble, such as that time at the grocery store when I got caught stealing. When I got into a fight as a child (which happened a lot), I knew she had a reputation as a fearless fighter, and people were afraid to mess with her. I could count on her to protect me because she would beat up anyone if I needed her to do so.

I found security in having a sister like Retta. She was my role model in just about every area of my life and my young mind. When she decided it was the right age to start smoking, get married, and have children, I wanted to follow in her footsteps even though she would always say to me, "Act your age, and stop trying to be me." But I rejected anything that I didn't want to hear. The bottom line was that I loved her and wanted to be like her. Right, wrong, or indifferent, that was never the point. The most important thing was about our relationship. I loved my big sis, Retta.

When Loretta was a young, vibrant woman in her twenties, her life changed. Suddenly, she became sick. This acute illness directly affected her husband and three children because she couldn't take care of them. My sister was unable to change the situation. The whole family wanted to help, but that didn't happen. So, all we could do was wonder about what was going on, worry that it might be something serious, and pray that God would take care of it.

Since we all agreed that there were drastic changes in her personality and none of us had the answers, we decided to take her to the hospital to get help. After all, that is where you go when you realize something is wrong with your body and when you determine that it requires emergency medical intervention. There are doctors there, experts who understand the ills of the human body and who can examine you, determine a diagnosis, plan a course of action to treat the illness, and therefore make you well again. So, we took Retta to the emergency room.

While in the waiting room, we talked among ourselves, trying to pinpoint the cause of her problem.

"Maybe she's been taking drugs."

"Oh, but she would *never* take drugs."

"Maybe her husband did something bad to her."

"But she is a fighter and wouldn't allow him to get away with that."

"Maybe something frightened her, and she is in a state of shock."

We all had our opinions, but none of us had the answer. It was an enigma. That something was terribly wrong with Loretta was all we knew. And we were on a mission to find out what it was so she could get back to normal.

The facts: we witnessed an abrupt change in Retta's personality. She started complaining of dizziness and was somewhat nonchalant, yet appeared to be very concerned about what was happening. We heard her concern. Everyone in the family could see that something was wrong with her. Her husband could see there was a problem; her children could see there was a problem and, most important, Mama knew something was terribly wrong. Let me tell you, a mother knows. All the people who loved her and knew her well understood something was wrong—but we didn't know exactly what. We needed the doctors to help us identify the problem so she could receive treatment.

If you didn't know her, your opinion might have been different. Judging by her looks and the way she communicated, there weren't any major issues or obvious signs. You would have to know her demeanor and personality first. We heard her say she was dizzy, and we could see that this disturbed her.

When Retta's name was called, we went into the exam room with her. We were certain they would find the problem, treat her, and everything would be just fine. *The doctors are smart. They will know what is wrong, and they will fix this problem,* I assured myself. I was confident in their expertise and their compassion. After all, people who work with patients are smart, and they really care. That's the reason they do what they do.

The physician who entered the examination room was typical of the professionals with whom I'd been working. He wore a long white lab jacket; spoke in a kind, compassionate, and very professional manner; and got right to asking pertinent questions.

"Hello, Mrs. Carson. My name is Dr. Knight. What brings you here today?"

"I don't know," she said, perplexed.

"What is your date of birth?"

"January nineteen, 1945."

"Can you tell me what today is—the date, month, and year?"

She gave him the correct answers. So far, she was doing fine.

"So now, why are you here today? What can I do for you?" he repeated clearly, to be sure she understood the question.

"I don't know," she said, and shrugged her shoulders.

"Who is she?" the doctor asked her, while pointing at me.

"Rosie," she replied with a big smile, confident with her answer.

"But you don't know why you're here?" He asked again to be sure of her answer.

"Uh, no, uh, I'm not sure." She stumbled on her words.

Dr. Knight continued to ask Loretta pertinent questions to check her neurological status, and she appeared to answer correctly. She was able to identify her entire family and state the date, time, and place appropriately. But she consistently denied being dizzy, and she was clear in the fact that she did not know why she was in the emergency room.

Clearly, the physician had difficulty with what he heard her say, and what we, her family, said she had been complaining about—the reason we brought her to the emergency room. It didn't add up, and none of us understood what the problem was.

After all, she was sure about the other facts in her life. She had demonstrated that the memory area of her brain was intact. The doctor could see that she was not rude, combative, or anything that would indicate blatant mental status change. However, since he did not *know* her, there was no way for him to ascertain that there had been an abrupt change in her personality. He had no evidence to prove that. I understood his dilemma based on the limited neurological information I had learned.

That is the reason I attempted to get him to fully understand the problem in order to make his assessment through the eyes of the family. We needed him to give us the benefit of the doubt— to trust what we were saying. So, when he walked out to gather his thoughts, chart the information, and make his decision, I followed him to talk with him privately. Looking him straight in his eyes, I said matter-of-factly, but not in an argumentative manner, "There is something wrong with my sister. She has been saying, 'I'm dizzy.' Her personality has changed…"

"I have no way of knowing what her personality was like before," he said very calmly, as if trying to avoid a confrontation. "She says nothing is wrong. I have examined her and can't find anything wrong."

"So what are you going to do?" I asked.

"There is nothing I can do, so I'm going to send her home," he responded.

"You're going to send her home? That's it? I know something is wrong—we all know it. We're her family," I said, disappointed.

"I'm sorry. She says she's not dizzy and doesn't understand why she's here. Maybe something is going on with her that she doesn't want anybody to know. I don't know, but there is nothing else I can do," the doctor said. He walked away and didn't look back.

I stood there silently as I watched him walk away—watched him give up on her.

Why won't he take our word for it? Doesn't he understand that we wouldn't bring her here if there wasn't a problem? That's not right, not right.

Arguing would have been futile, so I just vented along with everyone else. I went back inside the room. And after the physician made his final decision, said and did all he would do, we left the hospital and went to our homes.

In my opinion, the problems with that physician that day were many. He didn't trust the family who knew the patient better than he did. He didn't know which test to order to evaluate major brain problems. He refused to second-guess his initial opinion. Perhaps he perceived our hostility and allowed that to blind him to the primary objective of taking care of his patient. *He* had the upper hand. *We* needed his help. But he sent her home anyway without ordering lab work for a blood and urine sample, a CT scan, or an EEG to check her brain functions.

The result: in a very short time, his decision would be proven wrong, and my sister would suffer the consequences of that decision.

Retta became more withdrawn day after day. This very active, extroverted, and energetic young woman became apathetic, complained of dizziness even more, and was clearly ill by anyone's standards. Her speech changed, as did her entire personality.

At this point, hospitalization was no longer an option but a necessity. We, her family, were all in accord.

My niece, Retta's daughter, called me and said, "Mama was walking to the bathroom, and she started peeing on herself, and she had a nonchalant attitude about it."

"She what?" I interrupted. I wanted to hear the whole story, but it really didn't matter. Enough said. At that point, we all realized beyond a shadow of a doubt that we had to get her back to the hospital and insist she be admitted. We were not going to take no for an answer. We decided to take her to another hospital. We couldn't afford to have a repeat of the same logic, or rather lack thereof.

When Retta was in the emergency room this time, things were quite different. I wasn't with her, but my niece told me the whole story. She was examined thoroughly, and the physician listened to the history of what had taken place both at home and at the other hospital. Without hesitation, he admitted her to the hospital. That was what was needed to find the cause of her problem.

However, they quickly determined that Retta's mental status change was due to a psychiatric condition. So, off to the psychiatric ward they took her. We couldn't argue with that because we had no earthly idea what was wrong. By this time, she was visibly ill, even to people who didn't know her.

She continued to decline. Week after week, she got worse. Suddenly she was not speaking at all, not eating anything, and drooling at the mouth. She showed no expression no matter what subject we talked about. Nobody understood what was happening, including the entire medical team. "What is going on with her, and why can't the doctors figure it out?" I would say again and again. *Oh God, please help my sister. No one can help her but you. Please, God,* I prayed. It seemed as if I was losing my sister. Physicians weren't helping her. I tried to remain confident God could and would help her, but my faith wavered.

Finally, a physician had an enlightened moment and decided to order some tests. What a novel idea! (Yes, that was intended sarcasm.) At any rate, they ordered an EEG, which is the test I had recently learned to do. And guess what? Yes, it was abnormal. Who would have thought? (Sarcasm again.) Subsequently, they ordered a CT scan, and lo and behold, that was abnormal, too. Seriously—why hadn't they done that a month ago? Yes, both tests were abnormal and definitive for the cause of her acute personality change. Those tests revealed the reason she had an abrupt change in her behavior. The frontal lobe is considered to be the emotional area—the personality area; therefore, decision making and problem solving are affected when that area is damaged. It was.

Why did it take months for health care professionals to simply check her out to rule out underlying problems? They didn't believe the demanding family members. They didn't give our family the benefit of the doubt, and my sister paid the price. I was livid—*livid!* We elected not to act overtly on the new facts, our feelings, or the impact on my sister. Rather, we chose to find the good in this bad situation.

Personally, I was learning so many principles to live by during my career. I was taking it all in like a sponge. First, I decided that if a person is breathing, he or she was and would be important to me, period—no ifs, ands, or buts about it. Therefore, I would really listen and really hear what patients were saying and what they were not saying. I deemed the family's input as valuable information because, after all, they would know my patients better than I would know them in a short visit. For every patient I would have, somebody cared for that person deeply and wanted the very best for him or her. What happened to my sister became a real mission within my heart and my mind that would be another driving force for me to treat patients as if they were *my* relatives because, in a way, they were and are part of my family—the human race.

Shortly after obtaining that definitive information from the EEG and the CT scan, Retta was scheduled for surgery. She had a craniotomy, which is the surgical removal of part of the bone from the skull to expose the brain. This procedure was done to obtain a biopsy, a medical test involving the removal of cells or tissue for examination to determine the presence or extent of disease. Part of the frontal lobe, as noted by an abnormal section on the CT scan, was removed, and then the bone flap was replaced, sutured, and protected with sterilized dressing. The biopsy was sent to the pathology lab for investigation.

The report was prepared, and we were all ready to finally hear the results. The chief neurologist came into the waiting room where we had gathered and revealed the underlying problem that had caused Retta's abrupt personality change. He said, "From the biopsy report, Loretta has a form of multiple sclerosis. It's an atypical form in the way that it has affected her differently than it affects most people."

Even though we didn't fully understand all the medical jargon, we were content in knowing that something was wrong with the front area of her brain, and that was the reason she behaved as she did. Now we were waiting for her to wake up from surgery so she would be well, and then everything could be back to normal. But that didn't happen.

Following surgery, it is normal for patients to be "out of it" for a while—maybe the rest of the day. But my sister didn't wake up as most patients do after surgery. She was comatose, unresponsive to commands. She stopped moving, and her prognosis was grim according to the experts. This went on for more than a week. Finally, they called the family to come together for a meeting about her condition. *Oh, God, please help my sister,* I prayed, *because we can't help her.* We continued to speculate about her condition, continued to pray, cried, and once again expressed that we were not able to fix her.

The chief neurologist came into the room again to give us an update on Loretta's condition. By this time, she had been in the hospital for several weeks and remained unresponsive. Then one day, we knew the doctor was about to deliver bad news by the serious look on his face.

In a matter-of-fact tone, he said, "We are here to help patients get well. That is what we do. But we are unable to help Mrs. Carson get well. We are sending her to a facility where they can make her comfortable." He said that as if he had rehearsed it before speaking with us and wasn't going to stop until he asserted the bottom line.

I paused for a few seconds, gathered my thoughts, and said in a nonthreatening, pleasant but assertive tone, "I understand that the hospital is for patients, but *you* don't understand, sir. She is not *just a patient* to me; she is my sister. She is not *just a patient* to my mother; she is her daughter. No, sir, she is not *just another patient* to my nieces and nephews; she is their mother. She is not *just a patient* to the people who know her and love her. But she is simply another patient to *you*—not to *us*. She is special to each of us." These words were unrehearsed and came directly from my heart.

The doctor was taken aback. Since I had said all I needed to say, I stopped talking and waited to be certain he had understood *our* position based on *his* decision. I was determined because I knew, just as I had known before, that something was terribly wrong. I understood the doctor's point of view based on his opinion, the rules of the hospital, and the tunnel vision that was apparent. He had a plausible point, but we saw things differently from our point of view. Our focus was broader, and our hearts focused on our love for one who was unable to defend herself. We had no earthly idea about all the facts behind the decision to remove her from the hospital. We knew only that they had given up on helping her and wanted to send her to a nursing home. We just said no.

The doctor hesitated for a moment, as I believe he was surprised that we were taking a stand against his advice, his mandate. Then he repeated what he had said before. "Like I said, we have done all we can do, and we are going to send her to a facility. In fact, we are sending her out on Friday as planned."

We just looked at each other in disbelief.

We didn't know what more to say, so we didn't say anything else to him. Then he said, "Sorry," and walked away. We didn't know what we were going to do, but we were adamant that Retta wasn't going to a nursing home. I winced at the thought of what might happen.

I was done talking, but my mother spoke up. "You know, I was talking to this lady, and she said she wanted to come and pray for Loretta. But here's the thing. She has a request. She said, 'I don't want anybody in the room—just Loretta, me, and God.'"

We all agreed and prayed together right there in the waiting room. We trusted God would somehow answer our prayers through this lady.

I never saw the lady, but I heard what she said, and like the rest of the family, I stood in agreement. So that evening, while no one was in the room with my sister, she did what she said she was going to do. When she came out, she gave my mother an awesome report.

This is what she said: "Just as Loretta walked into this hospital, she *will* walk out."

We all joined together praising God for what we believed he was going to do without a single shred of evidence. This lady, a stranger to me, was sent to pray for my sister. She did so much more. She told us what God had placed in her heart. She was not a medical doctor, and she didn't claim to have any gifts of healing. She was simply a servant and a messenger. With our faith in God, we believed her and waited to see what would happen. The lady was unwavering about what she wanted to do for my sister and was certain about what God had revealed to her.

That Thursday, the day before the hospital staff planned to force Retta out, I walked into her room as I had on numerous occasions and saw her lying there, not moving and not talking. Only this day was different. I walked over to the bed and once again called my sister's name. This time she responded. She began to moan and move! My mouth fell wide open with joy. My heart was racing like crazy, and I was simply amazed at what had happened. She opened her eyes! Then I realized she was back when she looked at me and said in a weak but clear voice, "Rosie." I was overwhelmed and crying with gratitude. *Oh my God, thank you, thank you, thank you.*

The word spread quickly to our family, to our friends, and to the staff about what the Great Physician had done. I believe all of us got the message that day about who has the ultimate power. I believe we all understood that humans are limited in their knowledge. We had all witnessed the hand of God as he healed my sister's mind and body.

Shortly after she woke up from the coma, Retta was moved to a rehab floor, where she had therapy every day. Her progress was so nice to witness. So many people scratched their heads, so to speak, as they realized all that had taken place.

The next time I saw the doctor, he apologetically said to me, "I don't understand."

I looked at him, smiled, and said, "*I* understand, and it's all OK now."

He went on to tell me that he was going to consult with several doctors to study what had happened. That is exactly what he did.

At both hospitals, her case was one that was used to teach medical students.

"Just as she walked into the hospital, she will walk out." That is exactly what happened. With a smile on her face, and even though she had to hold onto a walker for a while, my sister walked out of the hospital. She is still walking, still talking, and still smiling every time I see her. How amazing what God has done for my sister!

Following His Instructions

Early in my career, Fred and I had realized it was time to end our marriage. Our priorities in life were different, and certainly our expectations of each other were unacceptable. We had tried for two years to make it work. Then circumstances enabled us to walk away and agree to just be friends. Still a young woman and desiring to be married, I was receptive to meeting my future husband when the time was right.

I met him.

Buford and I had each been married before, and each of us had two children. We discovered each other through his sister, who lived in the apartment above me and had witnessed my daily routine as a mother who was a hard worker devoted to her children, her job, and her church. We assumed we would make a good family because we agreed on some things we thought were important to have in a lasting relationship. We were Christians involved in ministry and raising our children with good moral standards. We felt that with what we had in common and our desire to join our families together, we should get married. Nothing fancy. So, we did, with a very small, private ceremony in the pastor's office.

We also agreed to have a child. But after four years of trying, I was unable to conceive. We were puzzled as to why I wasn't getting pregnant, so we decided to look into it. We went to the doctor for an assessment.

The doctor listened to our concerns, ordered some lab tests, and decided the best course of action would be to admit me to the hospital for further testing. Within a few days, I was hospitalized and had surgery so the physician could examine my reproductive system. *I'm glad I'm here so we can fix this problem,* I thought. Afterward, the doctor stood beside the bed with a disappointed look on his face. I thought to myself, *I'm afraid we can't fix this problem.*

"We took a look at your fallopian tubes and discovered that both are blocked," the doctor said. "The condition you have is called tubal factor infertility. That means it is impossible for you to get pregnant unless you have surgery."

My husband and I looked at each other, trying to take in what he had just said. We had questions.

"So, you're saying there is absolutely no way she can get pregnant?" Buford asked.

"That is exactly what I am saying," the doctor replied.

"Impossible?" I asked in confusion and disbelief. *I have two other children; how can that be?* "Oh no, that's bad news," I said. But in the next breath, I resigned myself to the fact that I couldn't have another child. *OK, since we already have two children each, together that makes four. I should just be satisfied that they are healthy and give up on getting pregnant,* I thought.

"But if you two really want to try to have a baby, there is a procedure we can do where a special device is inserted in each tube. However, if you decide to do it, I have to tell you: there is only a twenty percent chance it will work," the physician explained.

"There's only a twenty percent chance it will work?" I said in disbelief.

I looked at the doctor and back at my husband, who shook his head and blurted out, "No, absolutely not!"

At that moment and without hesitation, each of us rejected the idea of surgery. We decided to concentrate on getting me well and back on my feet, and we headed off with a new reality. *God knows what he's doing. We don't, so I'm gonna let it go.*

The following Sunday, Buford and I went to church, and while we said we were OK with the information we had received, we found ourselves seeking advice from a mature lady whom we esteemed as wise.

"Hi, Mrs. Lacy," Buford said. "Rosie went to the hospital and had surgery to find out why she hasn't been able to get pregnant. Unfortunately, the doctors found the problem and told us that the only way for us to have a baby would be for her to have surgery, and then there would be only a twenty percent chance that it would work."

We could see the wheels turning in Mrs. Lacy's head as she looked up and then back at us with a smile on her face. She said, "So, *the doctor* said you can't get pregnant unless you have surgery, right?"

"Yes, ma'am, that is what he said," I responded.

"OK, I have a question for both of you. Do you *really want* to have a baby?"

"Yes," we both said at the same time.

"Now then, listen to me," she replied. She paused for a few seconds and inhaled a deep breath as if to gather her thoughts and determine exactly how to tell us what to do. Then she looked at each of us as if looking into our very souls. She said, "If you really want a baby, then go home, get down on your knees, and ask God to give you a baby, and he will do it." She said that with such incredible confidence, it made me shiver at the faith she had in the Great Physician.

Buford and I looked at her, stood in agreement, and said, "That is exactly what we will do."

"You know he can do what the doctors can't do. His plan is final," Mrs. Lacy added, encouraging us to have faith in him. We believed her and did exactly as she said.

We went home, got down on our knees, held hands, and prayed, asking God to make it happen according to his plan for our request and for his glory. Then we got up and agreed to let go, to let God take care of it, and to accept whatever happened.

We went on about our usual activities—work, church, and so on. We were prepared to accept things as they were. But things would change.

I had told my best friend, Natalie, about it because I always wanted her to know what was happening with me. She, like most of my family and friends, had resigned herself to the fact that I wasn't going to have another baby. At that point, it was really no big deal. Complaining about my situation made no sense to me, so I stopped complaining.

Within a matter of a few weeks, Natalie and I went to the annual American Royal festivities. It was a great day, perfect sunshiny weather, and we had a great time. But after a while, as we walked along enjoying the festivities, things changed abruptly. I didn't want to spoil our fun, but I felt really sick. *What is wrong with me? I feel awful, but I don't want to go home. And I don't want to tell Natalie and spoil our fun. What should I do?* Finally I had to tell her. I thought I was going to pass out. It didn't feel extremely hot or extremely humid, so I figured there was something terribly wrong with me.

Right away, I told her what I thought, even though they were crazy thoughts. That's what you do with a best friend. "Natalie, if I didn't know any better, I would swear I am pregnant."

She looked at me, laughed, and said, "Girl, don't let nobody hear you say that. They will definitely think you're crazy."

We both remembered what the doctor had said and figured it was all in my head, and I did start to feel better. So we dismissed the notion of my being pregnant and continued to have fun at the event.

Even though Natalie and I thought nothing was wrong with me other than perhaps the hot, humid weather making me feel sick, or something I ate, both of us were a little curious.

"You know, you can take a urine sample to the lab Monday and find out for sure if you're in doubt," she said as if she were having second thoughts, yet more as if she were sympathizing with me.

Although the feeling passed, I knew that something was going on in my body that needed to be checked.

When I got to work that Monday, the first thing I did was to take my urine sample to the lab. I needed some closure so I could move on. I was not anxious about the results. I just wanted to know if by some miracle I could be pregnant.

When I returned to the lab to get the results, the technician beamed at me and said, "I checked it three times and, without a doubt, you are pregnant."

I stood motionless for a moment as I reflected on Mrs. Lacy's confidence when she had defied modern medicine and pointed us to the miraculous power of our Father. I smiled at the thought and said to myself, *Thank you. Thank you very much!* She had been right. Our Father's plans are final. I was pregnant without surgery, against all odds.

Nine months later, I woke up on June 19 at about 6:00 a.m. My water broke. I was not having any pain at all. I saw my husband off to work and nonchalantly continued working around the house. Occasionally, I had some pain but was certain there wasn't any big problem. After all, this was actually my due date, and I said to myself, *Nobody has her baby on the actual due date. But just to be sure, I will contact the office when they open.*

When I called the doctor's office, I explained what had happened and told them what the problem was. I said, "My water broke at about six this morning, but I'm not having much pain at all. I know I'm not in labor, but I just wanted to let you know what's going on."

"You need to get to the hospital right away. You *are* in labor." The nurse set me straight.

I immediately got myself ready for our child to be born.

Twelve hours later, my bouncing baby boy was born. He looked healthy and feisty, with beautiful, slightly wavy hair. As I held him, I promised that I would always love him and try to help him have a great life. As I gazed at his little face, he smiled at me as if he understood my heartfelt words.

Brian was a happy-go-lucky boy who grew up with Christian morals and did an excellent job in school. He started playing the trombone in fifth grade (first chair) and was in the marching band. He excelled in every subject.

When Brian became a man, he too entered the medical field.

As a clinical instructor at Heritage College, his primary responsibility is to equip people to become medical assistants, nurses, technologists, and whatever area of medicine they choose. As a man, his goal is to take his life experiences and use them collectively to become whatever God wants him to become.

Testing Times

One stipulation of being selected as a trainee-to-be and EEG technician was the completion of my GED by the end of training, which seemed reasonable enough at the time. I had to be a high school graduate or have passed the GED exam. In compliance with the mandate, my coworker and I went to class every Friday to prepare for the GED test. This was included in the training package deal. Trying to juggle being a good mother, starting a new career, and being a high school student was very hard. But dwelling on it would only cripple me. My primary objective was to focus on my goals.

And with such a big difference in responsibility, fulfilling the goal of a "good wife" was a major challenge. My normal routine was to ride the bus back and forth to work every day. Generally, I had to transfer twice, which meant I was on two buses going to work and two buses coming home. This was especially hard when it was freezing cold outside. I remember days when I was so cold I cried on the inside. I felt hopeless. I watched as people drove by in their comfortable cars. I absolutely hated the rain, ice, sleet, and snow. But I had no choice but to take the bus.

What added to my feeling of hopelessness was the fact that unlike me, my husband, Buford, had a brand new, comfortable car. It would have been nice to at least discuss driving me to or from work. But no, the arrangement was that he drove his comfortable car while I took the bus.

When I finally arrived at home each night, I had to revert to my role as a "submissive woman." It was my job to not only cook dinner but also to serve him by fixing his plate and taking it to him as he sat waiting. Resentment would sometimes build up inside me. I kept thinking to myself, *The food is ready. Why can't he fix his own plate? After all, I work five days a week like he does, but I have to come home and do another full-time job while he watches television. That ain't right.* I wouldn't ever say this out loud. Early on, I had learned the hard way that it was best to keep my mouth shut. The goal was to try to do the right thing, to take the bitter with the sweet. At home with my husband, the bitter was unpalatable at times. Yet, I felt I had no choice but to grin and bear it.

It was also my responsibility to make sure the kids were taken care of, which included their laundry, bathing, and helping with school assignments. It was not only my duty but my pleasure because they were my young children. They needed me to nurture them, to hear them, and to protect them. I absolutely had to end each night knowing that they came first in my world. And even my career decisions set the standard for them to follow. In the academic world, step by step, that was happening.

However, as a spouse, my insecurity had me set up to be passive—to be an enabler. Only, I didn't realize it at the time. My need to have a husband clouded my judgment. Whether God had chosen him for me was not the issue in my immature mind. So, although I was going nowhere in this relationship, I was struggling to hang on.

Hanging on is what I did. After all, I had taken vows, and my plan was to stick to those vows.

In addition to loving on my children, I kept an immaculate house. And I thought that was great. I didn't realize how my past had affected me in that way, but it had. In fact, I was a perfectionist. I wanted—no, *needed*—my husband to help. But clearly that was not his job, and he wasn't going to do it. I felt so alone in my marriage. I would focus on the blessing in being in the position as his wife because God had allowed it to be so. That got me through it until he opened the door for change.

One thing Buford took care of was the physical discipline. I suppose to him that was the manly thing to do. I absolutely could not spank my children. I *couldn't* do it no matter what. The trauma of being beaten as a child to supposedly teach right from wrong forever haunted me. That was obvious. I did just the opposite, talking to them and loving on them.

Once again it was time to stop worrying, whining, and struggling with all the stuff in my head. I had to figure it all out. My first thought was to put my GED on hold because I was overwhelmed with taking care of two small children, making sure they were doing well in school, working a full-time job, and being a wife to a man who didn't help me with chores. It was easy to put the GED on the back burner for a while. However, when I realized that doing nothing about it was like regressing, I devised a plan that would be more time consuming but better for me in more ways than one.

The training to become an EEG technician alone was overwhelming. Still, I needed to give it my all. So, when the training was over, I had not taken the GED test. Faced with the issue of noncompliance, I had to make some major decisions.

The day after the basic training was over, I marched right into the personnel office and sat down with the personnel director. I had to get it off my chest. "Mr. Mackenzie, my plan was to take the GED test and pass it by now, but that didn't happen. I haven't taken the test. I realized how difficult the training was and how important it was for me to place priority on fully understanding what I needed to know to be a great technician. I will complete the GED someday soon, but I wanted to complete my EEG technician training first…"

Mr. Mackenzie appeared pleased with my honesty and rationale, and said, "I want you to know, I have received a lot of positive feedback about you. You've done a great job as an EEG technician and have passed every test with flying colors." That made me very happy, but what he said next stunned me. "You know, passing that test isn't going to make you a *better* technician. So, don't worry about getting your GED because your job is not in jeopardy—not at all."

"OK, thank you," I said. I stood up and walked toward the door. Mr. Mackenzie stood up and thanked me for coming in to talk to him. I left knowing I could and would fulfill this requirement for the job—no matter what he said.

I left with mixed emotions. *I'm doing a really good job. I knew I would. But why is he acting like it's no big deal to get my GED? Well, it may be OK with him, but it is* not *OK with me.* Yes, indeed, I was proud of my accomplishments and glad about his confidence in my abilities. But a high school diploma or GED was the requirement for the job. I had to have it. Not getting it would have been unfair to my patients. That was my belief. Just as important was the fact that I would have been living a lie *and* holding myself back from achieving more complex goals in the future. I was cognizant of all of that.

Therefore, taking the steps to get my GED was of the utmost importance to me. I had to do it. I found the perfect place to go for class. There were teachers who volunteered their time, had a well-organized curriculum, and were excited about teaching people who really wanted to learn. After I visited the school, which was just a room in the basement of a bank, I knew I was in the right place. There was one big problem. The bus lines didn't stop there, and it would have been about a one-mile walk to the closest bus stop.

I had a few choices. I could do exactly what Mr. Mackenzie suggested and just forget about it. I could go back to the place we attended classes during training, which didn't seem as efficient.

Or, I could figure out a way to find the best class location and find a way to get to class. I chose the latter, which involved several more steps.

By now, I was sick and tired of having to take the bus or walk everywhere I had to go or wait around to find somebody with a car who was willing to give me a ride. Even though I was officially an EEG technician and was proud of my accomplishments, I was also a high school dropout. I felt so empty inside, so ashamed. That was a fact I could not deny. I had to figure out a plan to change my situation, a plan to take and pass the GED test.

OK, the first thing I need to do is learn how to drive. That's what I need to focus on right now, I thought.

You're probably saying to yourself, I don't get the connection. What in the world does learning to drive have to do with the GED test?

Actually, I was consciously implementing what would ultimately become my strategy to achieve all my academic goals. I thought of each objective, literally listed out each step, and searched within for creative ways to complete each task successfully. Always cognizant of the reality of failing, my thoughts were, *If I fail, I will pick myself up and try again and again until I get the job done. And I will not ever look at myself as a failure because if you say you can or if you say you can't, you're right. I will say I can.*

The current goal: pass the driver's test. The first step: obtain and study the state driver's manual for driving practice test questions. I took the bus downtown to get the manual. I studied, and when I felt ready to take the test, I took it and passed. I completed that within the next week. However, I wanted to wait until I had a car for part two, the driving part, which I could take after passing the written exam. But there was one problem, a big problem. I started to think it through. *I don't have a car to take the driver's test, and Buford probably won't help me. That's all right. I will figure out a way. Yes, I will.*

So, there I was. Decisions made. The "what" and "where" questions were answered. But how to make it all happen was a dilemma. Yes, I had decided to take the GED, and yes, I had decided on the best places to prepare for it. I couldn't figure out a way to pass the driver's test. I couldn't drive—duh. Yes, that was a big problem. Consequently, night and day, I found myself worrying about this test before me. Finally, I decided, *I just need to take time to make this happen.*

Taking and passing the GED test—yes, that was my goal. For starters, there were several things I had to do that some people might have deemed as unrelated. First, I focused on the primary mission before me: to have the flexibility to get to class anytime or anywhere, I *needed* a driver's license. Therefore, I had to learn how to drive. At some point, I would need to purchase a car. But buying a car was not an urgent matter. Finally, the complex part would be going to school faithfully, learning the subjects like the back of my hand, and passing all the tests. But I needed to be able to drive.

Why was I in this predicament? No one in our household had ever driven a car. My grandfather walked back and forth to work. My grandmother, mother, and older siblings never drove a car. All of us would walk, take the bus or a cab, or depend on other people to give us a ride wherever we had to go. The only close family member who had a car when I was growing up was my father, but he was rarely around. Driving or purchasing my own car had not been a priority. Not at all.

Public transportation was available to some alternative school sites, but not all of them. Of course, I couldn't count on anyone to consistently drive me to and from classes. I didn't have any-one I could depend on all the time but myself. Initially, I took the bus and began classes. A fellow student told me about some different places offering more classes and a more structured test-ing system. Of course, I wanted to attend where I could become prepared with the best knowledge in the least amount of time. That was very important. So, becoming independent was urgent. I was certain about that point and was bound and determined to make it happen.

Barbara, a beautiful Negro lady about four years older than I, was my very good friend. She and I had a lot in common. We had worked with each other at the last upscale restaurant and were social buddies away from work. As a very close friend and confidant, she knew my situation and was willing to help me out. After I told her how desperate I was to get my driver's license, she volunteered to teach me how to drive. Oh, what a brave friend!

I'll never forget the first time I got behind the wheel of her car. But before I go on, I have a confession to make. I hesitated about sharing this because it's so embarrassing. But I decided to do it because the principle may reveal a truth in your life as it did in mine, which ultimately helped me. Accept the whole truth about the issue. Here we go:

One day, she had given me a ride home from work and surprised me with a question. "Would you like to drive?"

"What? Would I like to do what?" I responded.

"Girl, I know how bad you wanna learn how to drive, and I know Buford ain't gonna teach you. So do you wanna practice or not?"

I said, "Yeah!" My heart was beating ninety miles an hour, but I was not gonna say no to this opportunity.

"It'll be so cool having you teach me. Thanks!"

Ooo-wee, I thought. I was so excited!

Barbara pulled over, parked her black Chevrolet Impala, got out of the driver's seat, and went around the car to sit in the passenger's seat. Now I was in the driver's seat and feeling on top of the world. I adjusted the seat and mirrors as she instructed me.

I was positioned and ready to drive, and it was time for me to take over. I was ready to listen carefully and pay attention to everything Barbara told me to do. After all, she knew how to drive. I didn't. And she was willing to help me out. I was extremely grateful to her. So far, we were off to a good start.

But her attitude changed abruptly when she realized that I didn't know the basics about driving. There we were on a two-way street, and there was lots of room for me to drive, which was great. I felt comfortable at first. But that changed when I began wandering into the left lane. She yelled, "Stay on your side!"

I was startled by her yelling at me, and I was also confused by what she said. So, I paused for a few seconds, tried to regroup, and then said, "Which side is my side?"

The look on her face was one of total frustration. She was angry, not at me but at the situation, and yelled back in response to my ridiculous question, "Fool, it's the right side!" I could see her shaking her head side to side and snickering, as if to say, *What in the world have I gotten myself into?*

Can you believe I thought it was OK to drive on the left side of the street? I mean, everybody knows what side of the street to drive on. Today I would say, that is what you call ignorance—a lack of knowledge about something you have never learned for one reason or another. Think about it. When you don't know something, you are ignorant about it. I was determined to change my state of ignorance in every area of my life when I was confronted with issues. That was my fundamental goal. I realized that we were all in the same boat when it comes to ignorance. That is because nobody knows everything about anything—nobody! A novel thought.

After Barbara pointed out which side of the road people drive on and started breathing again, she advised me to take it slow and gave me some other pointers about driving. After driving for less than five minutes, we changed places. She took over and just talked to me in a very sympathetic manner.

With friends like Barbara, I had hopes for a brighter future. Even after that incident, she was there for me, ready and willing to help me out. That's what friends are for, and I needed a friend like her who was willing to go the extra mile to help me, literally.

But she didn't stop there. No, she didn't. Barbara had offered to take me downtown to the driver's examination station to let me take the road test in her car after I practiced a little more. I had already gotten the driver handbook about a week before. I aced the written test and was so proud of myself.

But the actual road test was a different story. I was extremely apprehensive about it and absolutely sure I would *not* pass. With only minutes of real practice with my friend Barbara, I found myself with the overwhelming desire to try it just to see what the test would be like. *Surely I can learn a little more and be further ahead with this process. I'm going for it, ready or not,* I thought. Yes, I had decided to take my friend up on another offer to help me out.

I called her up. "Hello, Barbara. Guess what? I'm ready. I want to try to take the driver's test *today.*"

"Today? You want to take the driver's test today?"

"Yes, I do. I'm ready to go for it."

"But you don't know how to drive."

"I know. But I might learn something that might help me pass the test when I take it the next time." I was ready to take the next step.

"OK. I'll come pick you up."

Barbara was at my place in no time, and we were on our way. While I was riding downtown, my mind was in overdrive: *What in the world am I doing? I don't know how to drive. But I never will if I don't try. I have to get my driver's license so I can learn how to drive and get a car. That's it—I have to try. Today is the day to at least try. If I don't pass, oh well. At least I can say I tried. What do I have to lose? Nothing,* I thought and tried to calm myself in preparation for the test.

I knew I wasn't ready, having been behind the wheel of a car only that one time. Still, I thought that somehow I could pass the test or at least have some real-life practice in preparation for the next time. What in the world was I thinking? I wasn't actually thinking—I must have been daydreaming, but I kept dreaming anyway.

Road Test Rage

Barbara drove right to the Department of Motor Vehicles (DMV), parked the car in position for me to drive it, and we went inside to sit down and wait for me to finish. Fortunately, no appointment was necessary to take the operator's license test.

Inside, a young woman greeted me as I approached the desk and asked me what I needed. I told her. She completed the necessary paperwork, took my money, and gave me a receipt. Then she instructed me to go outside to my car while she notified the administrator, who apparently knew I was ready to take the driver's test.

I was so nervous when he approached my friend's car; my knees were shaking. He was a tall, thin, middle-aged Negro man with short black hair. He walked to the front of the car and gave me the pretest examination.

"Turn your left front signal on," he said.

What is he talking about? I thought. I had to think really fast. *I know about the turn signal. Is that what he's talking about?—calling it "front signal"? I'll try that.*

I turned my left turn signal on, and then he said, "Now turn on your right front signal." *OK, I got it right. Good job, Rosie.*

He went to the back of the car and asked me to do pretty much the same thing but with the "rear signals."

Then he said, "Step on your brakes." *Yeah, I know how to do that,* I said to myself confidently. *Aren't front and rear signals turned on the same?* I didn't have a clue what he meant by distinguishing one from the other, but I learned in a matter of seconds after doing it right.

Of course, his job was to make sure all the signal lights were working properly before we could drive off. In the first place, that was the law. And more important, it was a safety issue. Only, I hadn't figured all that out yet. I was uninformed about cars and preoccupied with fear.

Then he opened the door, sat in the passenger's seat, and told me to "go ahead."

"Which way?" I asked.

No answer. He didn't respond. *Why won't he tell me?* I thought and paused for a few seconds. Then I looked straight ahead and noticed the one-way street sign. *Oh my, how embarrassing!* Once again I felt stupid. I was very nervous.

He just looked at me with a frown on his face, as if to say, *Stupid girl. This is not going to be fun.* I don't know what he was thinking, but it sure felt like he had already assumed I was going to fail. I was sure of that.

The one-way street took us south, so I made a left turn as the arrows indicated. He had me drive a couple of blocks. Then he told me to turn left to go down a hill, where he instructed me to make a right turn next. I remembered that it was important to drive slowly and carefully, so I decided to be extra cautious before making the right turn.

Even though there wasn't a stop sign, I stopped because I thought that was the smart thing to do. It was almost as if I was thinking like a child, walking across the street, rehearsing that rhyme in my mind: *stop, look, and listen before you cross the street. Use your eyes, use your ears, and then you use your feet.*

The tester looked at me and said irately, "Why did you stop?"

Oops, I made another mistake. But what did I do wrong this time? I wanted to give him an answer fast, so I told him, "I wanted to be careful, and my husband told me to always stop before making a turn."

He said, "Nah! That is wrong, and your husband ain't here!" He continued mumbling things like, "This is ridiculous" and "I am so sick of these women telling me what their husbands said."

I accepted his scolding graciously and simply said, "OK, you're right."

He was clearly angry but instructed me to keep driving and make another right turn so I could try it again. I was grateful for another opportunity but was almost certain he would not pass me after that first big mistake. *This time, I'm just gonna keep going and not stop. I have to do it right this time,* I told myself. But the retry was so much worse than the first time because I was afraid of messing up again.

We were headed down a steep hill. Since I didn't want to make the same mistake of stopping, I didn't even slow down. I attempted to turn right once I'd made it to the intersection, but I started losing control, heading straight for the cars parked on the left side of the street. I was all over the place. It was horrible—horrible! My heart was racing so fast, I thought

I would pass out. I said to myself, *Uh-oh! You idiot! You don't know how to drive. What in the world were you thinking?* I wanted to cry, but I didn't want him to think I was looking for sympathy. I was definitely ready for my punishment. That is what I deserved.

Once the car was safely stopped and we were assured that we were alive and hadn't run into anyone or anything, he started swearing at me like a sailor. He yelled, "*You* don't know how to drive! You almost killed us! Get this car back to the garage right now, right now!"

He continued to mumble, cussing again and again. He was so angry with me, and rightfully so. Out of the corner of my eye, I could see him shaking his head and moving restlessly in the passenger's seat as if he was furious. "You could have killed us. You don't know how to drive. You stupid woman!" Shaken by the dangerous situation I had caused, he couldn't let it go and continued cussing and yelling at me.

"Sorry," I said softly and sincerely. He didn't respond.

I'm in sooo much trouble. My dream to get my driver's license has turned into a nightmare. I saw him writing on a pad while I held back my tears. *I'm getting what I deserve. I have nothing else to say to defend myself. I was so wrong. That's the bottom line. I'll do it right the next time,* I thought. *I'll practice and practice until I get it right, and then I will take the test again.*

I drove back cautiously and very slowly to the garage, which gave him a little time to calm down and collect himself. His silence brought some comfort to my guilty soul. I think he was just happy to be alive and was ready to put an end to the entire ghastly ordeal.

After a little while, he spoke to me calmly. "You don't know how to drive at all, do you?"

"No, sir, I don't," I confessed.

"So why do you want to drive?"

"Well, I want to go to school," I responded.

"You want to go to school?" he repeated as if seeking to be sure of what I had said.

"Yes, and I need to drive so I can get a car, go to class, and get my GED."

He was silent. As I continued toward the garage, he began writing again.

Before we returned to the driver examination station, he asked me to do one more thing: parallel park. I had never done that before. I was honest and told him that. He said to go ahead and give it a try. I did my very best but ended up about a mile from the curb. He looked at me squarely, shook his head, and wrote something on the paper.

I knew what was coming, and I braced myself. *I failed.*

But that's not what he told me. He said, "You don't know how to drive, young lady."

I nodded my head in agreement. I wanted to say, *We both know that, so let's just end this.* But I held my tongue and waited for him to tell me what a bad thing I had done by taking a chance like this and how we could have had a serious accident. *How stupid of me,* I thought.

"But I'm going to pass you because of your attitude."

Did I hear him right? Sounded like he said he's going to pass me.

He continued, "I like your attitude. You didn't play that race card stuff with me like lots of women do when I have to fail them. So, I'm going to help you out because you're a nice person and need help."

"Thank you so very much. Thank you," I responded humbly. I really wanted to cry.

He's gonna pass me. Oh my God, thank you, thank you! I thought. I couldn't believe what I was hearing.

"But since you can't drive, I'm going to have to give you a really low score," he said.

"OK." *That doesn't matter to me at all. Low score or not, I get my license.* I certainly didn't care about the score of seventy-two, just two points above the minimum. I was just thrilled that he was going to pass me.

Before we got out of the car, he stopped, looked into my eyes, and said, "This is what you need to do. Go home and practice going back and forth to the grocery store or just practice in a vacant lot every day until you learn how to drive, OK?"

"Yes, sir, I will. Thank you very much."

Then he gave me a "passed" note and told me where to take it. After he gave me the note, I thanked him heartily for being so lenient and understanding.

That day, I learned an invaluable lesson on my journey: my honesty and sincere attitude must have softened his heart. Life is always much harder when you lie. I had to hold my peace and not fight back in a hostile manner, especially when I was clearly wrong. When I came across an abrasive spirit, I had to maintain a meek and humble spirit myself. Only then would I be victorious—maybe not in that moment but definitely in the end.

Many years later, I memorized a Bible verse that comes in handy during similar situations. Psalm 119:165 reads, "Great peace have they which love thy law: and nothing shall offend them." When I am sure of my motives, actions, and reactions, I am not offended by the actions of other people.

Yes, I got my driver's license that day. Something within was urging me to go for it, even though it seemed to be an impossible endeavor, even though the odds were totally against me. Something within empowered me to focus on the mission and not the moment. Something within me was afraid but at the same time determined enough to try.

Bubbling with joy, I hurried home and told my husband everything that had happened. Another surprise—he let me use his car to practice. Right away, I did what the administrator suggested. I drove around the parking lot at the store close to our house, at the park, and anywhere where there wasn't much traffic. Now with my first goal, a major venture, completed and my second goal, a difficult yet short-term endeavor, behind me, I was ready to buy myself a car.

I'm ready to be independent. I hate waiting for other people to give me a ride. I hate taking the bus—sometimes two buses when I have to transfer. Oh, and when it's bitter cold and people pass by me in their warm cars, that's just awful. I need a car, and I need it now. I'm ready to buy a car now.

Reality settled in as I thought about my next short-term goal: to buy a car. Cars cost so much money. What was I thinking? Duh—apparently, I wasn't thinking. Making only one dollar and ninety-one cents per hour, I had very little money left over to purchase a car. And since getting a car was a major priority, and there were lots of good deals advertised here, there, and everywhere, I knew one car had my name on it. I mean, after all, it was the right time, and I was ready to move forward immediately. With that tunnel-vision mentality, I found my first car. I wanted a yellow Volkswagen. It was a lemon—that I remember clearly!

When I did the math, there wasn't enough money for a good car at the time. So, I spent fifty dollars on a "good used car," as the salesman told me, convincing me that I was getting a good bargain. I believed him. Yes, I did believe him just because he had said it. After all, it was a good deal—only fifty dollars.

It started up just fine, and I was thrilled as I drove home. *My first car—this is great!* But soon, very soon, I realized I got what I paid for because once I parked the car in front of the apartment, the motor died. "What an idiot I am. Why did I believe that man? This car is a lemon!" I said to my friends. *What a foolish thing to do. Oh, but this too shall pass, and I will never make* that *mistake again.*

Yes, *that* mistake was obvious—so obvious that I don't need to explain all the deceptive details. Because of that mistake, suffice it to say, my plans were on hold, and rightfully so. So much for getting a car to drive to school! It wasn't the right time. Therefore, I had to rest satisfied in the Providence I had been given—my legs to walk and enough money to ride the bus to the places I had to go. I was content with that.

A couple of years later, my eyes were set on buying a car that was almost new with a new car warranty on it. *I'm not going to make that mistake again. This time I'm going to a company that will give me a warranty and stand behind it, a company I can trust such as Ford Motors,* I thought. In time, my perspective changed. I didn't have tunnel vision purchasing a car anymore. My salary had increased to about two dollars and fifty cents an hour, and being frugal and intelligent had become my new way of life. I had started a savings account through the credit union, set a budget to save up for a down payment, and in general was a very good steward of my finances. My wants list became second to my needs list. Many times, the wants list was not even on the back burner. I completely dismissed my desire.

Purchasing the bare necessities was my objective, and I was at peace with that. None of that shopping for things such as clothing, even used clothing. After all, I figured, as long as I had soap and water, I could wear clean clothes. So, it didn't matter that I had only two outfits for church and only two uniforms for work. I washed clothes by hand every day and didn't mind. Occasionally, on very rare occasions, I would treat myself to something new such as my favorite lipstick or a pair of twenty-nine-cent earrings to add a new accessory to my wardrobe.

After patiently waiting, thinking about my needs, my resources, and how badly I wanted to drive a car, I was ready to make a grown-up decision. After I found my first drivable car, a Ford Pinto, and drove it home, I drove it for nine years without any major problems. Standing in the frigid cold to take the bus became a thing of the past. A life of independence became my tunnel vision; good judgment became my focus; and tenacity became my plan of action.

GED Test Dilemma

I had an insatiable desire to learn and continued to study for the high school equivalency exam. Before I started the training to be a technician, my test scores had shown my education level was in the upper range of eighth grade. That was very depressing to me, but I refused to sit on the pity pot. When I got up, it would pay off. What a difference education makes for most people. The only option for me was to forge ahead to reach my primary goal of passing the GED test.

Each week and with each new subject, I was focused just as I would have been as if I were in high school. I was so excited about learning the things I had missed by dropping out of school. I got my chance to study each high school subject according to each grade requirement: social studies, mathematics, English, history, and science. With each subject, I received excellent grades.

After I had passed each subject and was ready to take the test, I took the pretest again to determine if I was eligible to take the exam. The first time I had tried before the training, I wasn't even close to being ready. But this time, my score was equivalent to that of a freshman in college. I had worked hard, and it had paid off. I was ready!

I was prepared for the two-day exam. It would take about eight hours of testing each day. The first day, I realized the task before me was huge. I found myself letting my mind wander from passing the exam to thinking about how hard it was. *Wow, this is so hard. I believe the average high school graduate couldn't just come in here and pass this test. Some of them would fail for sure.* The second day was just as difficult. I had to keep reminding myself that I was prepared and ready to prove it.

I completed the test, and four weeks later, I received my GED certificate. I ran through the house up and down the hall, yelling out, "I did it! I did it!" No one had pressured me; I had done it on my own. It was as if I had just received a PhD. I couldn't stop crying. I was thankful and wanted to talk to my Father about answering my prayers, so I just walked up and down the hall from the living room to the bedroom, back and forth, saying aloud, "Thank you, thank you, thank you!" I had completed my high school equivalency exam and was so very proud of it! I had done the right thing.

My husband and children looked at me with blank, nonchalant expressions. They obviously didn't think it was that big of a deal. No, it was just another day to them. Oh, but to me, it was *not* just another day. To me it was not just a test. It was so much more. To me, it was freedom from the bondage of the past; it was freedom from living a lie when asked, "What was the requirement for you to get this job?" My patients deserved to know the truth that I had not fulfilled all the requirements. So, with this behind me, the door opened to a world of opportunities.

For days, I smiled brightly at the thought of what I would accomplish with that tangible, authentic verification of my achievement. *Now, when my patients ask me what it took for me to get the job, I can include the GED, knowing I have it. Oh, what a relief!*

As glad as I was to reach this goal, there was a void in my life that I could not deny no matter how hard I tried. I regretted not being able to have a real graduation ceremony like those students who stayed in school. Every time I thought about this, I wanted to cry. Then I remembered that many of the high school dropouts didn't *want* to go to school in the first place. That is why they had dropped out. That wasn't the case with me, so that was enough to pacify me most of the time. On the other hand, there was still that emptiness that I had never had formal classes in high school. I had never walked across the stage with my class to receive my diploma.

For years, I had dreams about being in the classroom, seeing the teachers, the chalkboard, and students. I finally realized the problem. Since I had never had a graduation ceremony, had never walked across the stage to receive the honor that most students received, I was not satisfied. Even though I had come to terms with the fact that it wasn't my fault, I was still sad about it. Most kids who dropped out of school wanted to do so. Not me—I didn't *want* to drop out; since I made a mistake, I was not allowed back in public school. I had no other choice.

❖ ❖ ❖

National Certification

Becoming a registered EEG technologist was my next goal. What a big goal it was! In the '70s, this goal was comparable to a nurse's aide becoming a registered nurse. My comments to people were, "I really want to take the test since I enjoyed being an EEG technician, and if I'm going to make a career doing this job, I might as well go to the top to become a board-certified technologist." That goal was shot down by those who thought I was not being realistic, facing defeat with my eyes wide open but my mind closed to accepting the reality of life. Some people suggested that I had lost my mind to even consider such a difficult task.

"Girl, what in the world are you thinking?"

"You will *never* be able to pass a test like that."

"I mean, you are smart, but you are not *that* smart."

"No way. I mean, come on now, let's be real; the pass rate is a very small percentage. Most people aren't passing the test."

"Listen girl, I have a question for you: Do you know anybody black who has their EEG registry? No, you don't. So, tell me this. Why are you putting yourself through all that hard work for nothing?"

I'll never forget what one friend said about me and what I was trying to do: "I mean, you don't get it, girl. White people are smarter than us. I don't think you understand that. Now, listen to me for a minute. If by some miracle you pass the written exam, which you said is two hundred fifty questions, you will not pass the second part, the four-part oral exam. Let me tell you why... because when they see your face, it's over. They ain't gonna pass you."

I believed what all the naysayers told me for years and years. Then finally the light bulb came on, and I saw the truth clearly. I stopped listening to them, stopped believing the self-crippling lies I had convinced myself were the truth, and decided to go for it the same way I was told "how to eat an elephant—one bite at a time." Even though I didn't realize it then, their opinions were now silenced as I was suddenly aware that they also had issues to deal with and goals they hoped to achieve. Absolutely every one of the naysayers was a closet dreamer him- or herself.

These people needed to focus on themselves. And I needed to be clear about myself—my goals, objectives, and abilities— to achieve whatever any person, any woman, could achieve. Without judging the naysayers, I stopped listening to them and began listening to that inner voice speaking loudly within my heart, my mind, and my soul. I didn't want to hurt their feelings or have them turn against me. But now I came to believe him instead of them.

Some of those conversations—those words of disbelief and hopelessness—are clear in my mind to this very day. I struggled to hide the way I truly felt. I wanted these people to like me, to accept me. I kept some things to myself and expressed what was safe. But I will share with you some of what I said compared to what I was really thinking.

"Who do you think you are?" the naysayers would say.

"I'm just me. That's all." *I am a hardworking person. What's it to you?*

"What are you trying to prove to people and why?"

"Nothing." *I'm not trying to prove anything to anybody. I can and will prove that I can do anything I decide is possible. If it can be done, whatever it happens to be, I can do it. These are my goals and no one else's.*

"Don't you understand that you are black and that white people are smarter than black people? That is a fact!"

"I don't believe that." *Are you serious? They're smarter because they're white? No, no, a thousand times no—that is not a fact. People are people, period. Your points are wrong. They make no sense at all. What planet did you come from? That is just stupid!* (I definitely didn't say that to the naysayers.)

"Well, you're just an average person; you're not as smart as they are."

"OK, I just want to try, and if I mess up, then I'll try again," I would answer meekly. *Whatever! That's your opinion. Everybody has his or her opinion, and that's OK. One thing I know for sure is that I am highly motivated. That's the most important part of being smart—being willing to work hard and study.*

Giggling and smiling at me, one friend reminded me of her opinion about what I was doing. "Listen, girl, if you pass the written test, it will be a miracle. You might be able to do that, but I doubt it very seriously. But you definitely won't pass the oral exam. I mean, when they see you are black, you won't have a chance. Don't you understand? *They* don't want to help *us*?"

"I know lots of white people are prejudiced. I get that. But that point is not important to me right now and what I'm trying to do." *Oh my, that's what my mother told me. I remember she said, "White people just don't like colored people." She was sincere, but she was wrong. I absolutely know that some white people are prejudiced. That is a fact. But I absolutely refuse to believe that all white people are prejudiced. That is ridiculous. I don't believe that.*

"OK, just go on and do your thing, girl. By the way, who are you going to study with? There ain't nobody black to study with. Oh yeah, I forgot, you feel comfortable hanging out with white people." *(Snickers.)*

"I don't know how I'm going to get it done, but I have to figure out a way." *I'm going to study with people who are willing to study with me. And I like hanging out with people who like hanging out with me. I really don't care about the color of their skin.*

"You just refuse to believe we have been and still are being discriminated against."

"No, I get that." *It is not true that I refuse to believe that. I know for a fact we are being discriminated against. Do you think I'm deaf, dumb, and blind? I get that. I also know that an "all of us versus all of them" attitude is totally the wrong way of thinking. All people have been discriminated against. I mean, white people were discriminated against when only minorities were allowed to go through the training to be EEG technicians. I understand that was because of affirmative action. I have truly been blessed to have this opportunity. The fact remains; they were discriminated against, plain and simple. That's a fact. Bet you haven't thought about that. Not only that, but who's doing the math to determine who has been discriminated against more? I have nothing else to say because you are going to believe what you want to believe. I'm not mad at you for your beliefs. But my beliefs are different because I am different. All of us vary in our beliefs—it's called life.*

Yes, all of us are different in some ways when we compare ourselves to other people. So, you see, the problem of comparing will always lead us to a place of discontentment. My question is this: Who wants to live in a place like that? It is not a peaceful place to live.

I decided to ignore the naysayers. For far too many years, I ignored what *I* truly believed. I accepted it as fact when my family and friends said to me, "You can't do that." I believed them, or at least I wanted to make them think I believed them. Finally, the time came when I stopped trying to defend myself and turned my mind in another direction. "Actions speak louder than words" became my mind-set.

To that end, night and day, I studied to prepare for another major project. The prerequisites for taking my national board exams were that I had to record one thousand EEG tests by myself, and I had to have a letter of recommendation from a qualified physician. At a rate of doing four patients a day, it took me years to complete the task. The good part was that I was gaining tons of knowledge as I scrutinized each test to give my technical opinion. Every procedure was an opportunity to learn more and more. I was motivated to give it my all, and that is what I did.

I passed the exam. Truthfully, I didn't pass the first time. As tempted as I am to not mention that part, the conviction of integrity rings loud in my ears. I failed by a very small number *and* by what I thought was an unfair process, but I failed nonetheless. I passed all three sections—yes, all three sections—but I missed the overall total by two points! I thought that was absolutely ridiculous. I mean, I would have taken it better if I had failed a section. Twenty-eight points were required to pass one part of the exam, and that is exactly what I got—no more. I could go on and on, but that would get me nowhere. Complaining about the process isn't going to change the facts. The process was the same for all people.

After receiving the "We regret to inform you…" letter, the first order of business was to get off the pity pot. So, I changed my attitude: *nothing beats a fail but a try, and when you do the best you can, that is good enough. I have not failed. I'm just heading toward my goal and understanding what is expected of me. That is a good thing.* That is what I told myself, and that is what enabled me to go forward no matter how hard it was. I focused on the end results and had confidence in my ability to complete the task in the midst of the problems.

Yet, without a doubt, I had some concerns. I'm not going to deny it. I refused to be ensnared by the narrow-mindedness of prejudiced people or, dare I say, ignorant people, black and white. Yes, there were white people willing and able to study with me. White people wanted to help me, and there were some white people who said yes to me and gave me a passing score when I clearly proved myself.

Prove myself is what I had to do. I knew I would pass the written exam the second time. Having to delay it six more months was an opportunity to learn more, especially in my weak areas. That is exactly what I needed to do, to learn more about electronics—not my passion but a necessary component to understanding how the equipment works.

Finally, it was time to take the test again, and of course it was somewhat different—different in big ways. Fifty more questions were added, and the passing score jumped from 75 percent to 80 percent. *Seriously?* Not to worry; I was prepared for that. My objective was to learn one hundred percent, not just enough to regurgitate the answers but rather to fully understand it all. I studied with that goal in mind, and when I received the letter in the mail four weeks later, it paid off. The letter read, "Congratulations on passing the written exam to become a registered EEG technologist. You are now qualified to take part two of the exam."

What a major accomplishment! I was almost a registered EEG technologist. The earlier "failure" meant nothing negative to me. Remember, *nothing beats a fail but a try.* As I reflected on what I'd done and the road ahead, I kept thinking to myself, *I'm almost there.*

However, the road ahead was full of detours and DO NOT ENTER signs. First of all, in the midst of my trying to become registered, we were moving to another city because my husband had a new job opportunity that was extremely important to him—not to me. But being the submissive woman I was, I had no choice in the matter. I had to leave my mentors, my accountability team— my foundation. That was my predicament.

I don't know how I'm going to finish this, but I know I can and will get it done. Somehow, some way, I'll do it. Oh, but since we're moving to Rockville, I don't know anybody there to study with. It's going to be tough. Nobody there is registered like here. Oh my gosh, that's really going to be a problem.

Out of the blue, I recalled a conversation I'd had with Darren, a white man who was taking his written test when I was taking mine. We met before the test started and shared with each other where we were from and how apprehensive we were about the entire registry process. He and I, as well as the other technicians, were in accord about one point: we were all afraid of failing.

"Would you like to get together to prepare for the orals?" I asked.

"No, not really," the man answered immediately.

I felt rejected and simply said, "OK," and left him alone. *Wow, what an attitude. He wants nothing to do with me. That hurts.*

Our paths would cross again and again, though I didn't know it at the time. My friends would say he was smarter because of the color of his skin. And if he was smarter, why in the world would he need somebody like me to help him?

He didn't want to study with me, and he let me know it. After all, what was I going to teach him? However, I wanted to study with him because I understood I could learn from him or anybody regardless of who he or she was. And, by the same token, I understood I could teach him something if he could swallow his pride and let me. That wasn't going to happen, and I accepted his decision at face value. There was nothing else I could do.

It could have been a win-win situation, so the rejection hurt in more ways than one. And I would have done everything I could have in order to help him. I would have gladly received his critique. The rejection was all too familiar to me. And it hurt a lot. That's life. I had to press on.

No matter who you are or no matter what you know or don't know, *if* you have the right attitude, you can learn from *and* you can teach other people. Even the most gifted people on the face of the earth are not all knowing. They're not. Only God is all knowing. By the same token, the average person can teach principles that will expand your knowledge like you wouldn't believe, *if* you really learn to listen—listen not only to what is being said but also to what is *not* being said. Silence is truly golden at times. Yes, you read it right: *listen to what is* not *being said.*

Some people tell you what they want you to know and omit what they don't want you to know. Perhaps they are embarrassed about the truth and want you to esteem them higher than they esteem themselves. Maybe they want to make sure you don't have power over them by knowing more than they do, and therefore they deliberately withhold information. That is a natural fact—not to use against others but to empower yourself.

You can learn from people who don't like you, people who hate the ground you walk on. I know that firsthand. But I won't take time to spell out all the negative details. There's no point in doing that. Suffice it to say, since I've learned from both people who wanted to help me and people who wanted to hold me back, you can, too. It doesn't matter who they are. It doesn't matter what their IQ is. It doesn't matter what their motives are. And it certainly doesn't matter what skin covering they were born in.

❖ ❖ ❖

Moving On

"Life becomes harder for us when we live for others, but it also becomes richer and happier."
—*Albert Schweitzer*

He Saw the Light

When I was a teenager, my father left home in search of "greener grass." Searching for that better life was a new beginning with new opportunities for happiness. He found what he was looking for, but it didn't last long. Within a few years, it was the beginning of the end for my daddy. What an end it was!

He became seriously ill and was diagnosed with terminal cancer years before he told me about it. When he realized it was just a matter of time, he decided to come home to the veterans' hospital where he was close to his family. In his final weeks, I spoke with him about his life and his relationship with the Lord Jesus Christ as his Savior. I asked him if he understood what I was saying and if he was certain of his eternal life. I remember that he looked into my eyes, and without hesitation, he said, "I have no doubt where I'm going." He said he had repented, that his life had changed, and he would never be the same again. I was confident of his answer, and I rested satisfied that he was coherent and ready to meet God face to face.

In fact, I believed his cognitive skills were completely intact. When he was in the hospital, he told me I was his beneficiary and gave me a long-distance telephone number to call so I could get his insurance policy. He was very specific. He said, "Call my girl-friend Sharon because she knows where everything is." I had met Sharon only briefly when I visited Daddy. I wasn't excited about calling her, but I had to do what Daddy told me to do. After all, he was on his deathbed, and we both knew it.

"Call her *tonight* because they will bury me, and you will never see the money." He was adamant that I do exactly what he told me to do.

"As soon as I get home, I will call her," I assured him. As awkward as it felt to oblige something so self-serving at his death-bed, I could tell it was of grave importance and perhaps my last chance to connect with my daddy.

I called the number he gave me, and it was the correct number. I know because Sharon answered. However, what she said didn't line up with what I had been told. She said she didn't know what Daddy was talking about. I wasn't surprised. *She will cash in that policy under my name and keep it for herself, but God knows and sees.* I did not attempt to point out that I knew she was lying, nor did I try to get the money. It wasn't important to me.

I told my father what Sharon had said, and he appeared distraught. He told me to call her again. She was clear in what she told me, and I was clear in my opinion. Therefore, I decided to leave it in the hands of God, who knows all things. I did not call her again. I wasn't worried about the money because I figured God would take care of me, my father, and the whole situation.

Daddy died on June 25, 1974, at the age of fifty-one. The last time I saw him was on that day in the Veterans' Administration Hospital where I walked in and found him dead.

I walked into the room, pulled back the curtain, and beheld something that was simply divine, something I had never seen in my life. The most amazing, exciting, and happy smile lit up his face as if he had absolutely been taken into heaven instantly. "Look at that smile on his face!" I said to Buford.

I stared at my daddy, frozen in awe of what I could see but, more important, of what I knew in my heart had happened to him.

God had received him. His mercy had freed my father of all his sins, pain, and suffering. His eyes were opened wide, and his eyebrows rose as if he had seen God before he passed over. His temporal time had been completed, and his new life had just begun. That look is indelibly imprinted in my brain, my mind. In that moment, I'm certain he saw THE LIGHT of glory!

Big Moves

There I was, now fatherless and moving to Rockville. Make no mistake; the last thing I wanted to do was move out of town. Leaving the comfort of our home, the convenience of my family, the security of my job, and the safety of my neighborhood was not appealing to me at all. After all, I had lived in one city all my life. It was all I had ever known. Even though it wasn't the best place to live, I was content where I was. It was the first place I had made my grand appearance, where I learned how to walk, talk, play, climb the career ladder, and evolve from a young, self-doubting ghetto girl into an ambitious adult focused on reaching every goal.

Most of my family lived here, and I had absolutely no desire to leave them. My mother usually lived within walking distance, and when that wasn't the case, I could certainly get to her house by taking a bus. The friends I grew up with were here. No, no, no, I didn't want to leave, but resisting would get me nowhere. So, I put my two cents in, asserted my opinion, and started making plans to leave. It didn't take me long to realize my opinion was only that and would not change my husband's plans.

Buford had goals and dreams that were very important to him. *He sees things differently. That's a fact.* The twists and turns of life were about to take on a new meaning. I had to be ready for whatever was going to happen because I had no earthly idea what to expect in this new place. Furthermore, I didn't have a choice in the matter as the wife, who was supposed to be obedient no matter what. Buford would say, "A good wife is submissive to her husband." Being content with the good, bad, or indifferent; rolling with the punches; going with the flow; and going along for the ride was my resolve. And what a ride it was.

The few things that I'd heard about this place were not pleasing to my ears. A friend said, "You know there are only two percent black people living in Rockville."

I replied, "Only two percent! Oh my, that's really different from what we're used to. Is that good or bad?"

"Well," my friend said, "some things about it are good from what I hear. The crime rate is very low. That's a good thing. In fact, that's great. Schools for the kids are somewhat segregated but basically very good schools."

I would figure out a way to take care of that situation, no problem. I would simply live in whatever area had the best schools. That took care of that dilemma. But in some ways, living in Rockville was bad. I was told, "There aren't many black people there, and the ones who have lived there move when they grow up." They want the chance to get away from where they were the minority. These are the facts and concerns when being a minority is the essence of who you are, I concluded.

We had rubbed elbows with people who had accepted us and worked in a culture where people treated us like family. We had lived during the time of overt discrimination based on skin color. Our skin color dictated where we went to school, where we ate, and where we sat on the bus. It was a daunting time. Now, things were much better for most of us. These memories are forever ingrained, though life is different now in so many ways.

Really, the truth was I just didn't want to move. It wasn't my choice or my children's choice. We were OK living in a nice ranch-style home. Things were just fine in our little world. We had made the best of our situations. In our little world, things were pretty good. The kids and I were comfortable. Buford was not. It was his choice to leave the comfort of a nice home for greener pastures. He wanted to fulfill *his* goals and objectives. Since we were his family, we had no recourse but to follow him.

Buford had found a small church in need of a pastor, which was a golden opportunity for him.

What about us? I thought. *I have a really good job, an awesome career with a once-in-a-lifetime opportunity in the medical field. I feel really good about myself for the first time ever. Why, oh why do we have to leave all of what we have to go to this tiny church just so he can become a pastor? Why can't he do that here so I don't have to give up everything I've worked so hard for?* I thought about all of the pros for him and the cons for me. The scales were not even close to being balanced. Yet, I remained passive when speaking to him since he had made up his mind, and there was no changing it.

There I was, ten years on my job, three years after being in a supervisory position, working with a board-certified neurologist, Dr. Abernathy, and it was time to move—time to leave an awesome job and an incredible calling I had so appreciated. It was an awful position to be in. I was an adult, yet as voiceless as a child forced to give up the toys that made me so happy. It was very hard, but I had lived through hard times before and had learned how to survive. This time would be no different.

It occurred to me that I was being selfish and self-centered. Even though I felt justified in my thoughts, the facts weren't going to change. So, as it was when I was a child, I had to change my thinking. The game of survival kicked in once again. I had played this game countless times before.

I remember meeting that man, Darren, from Rockville who was also seeking national certification as a registered EEG technologist. Now both of us had passed the written EEG exam and were apprehensive about taking the orals. I had a solution to our predicament: "Let's study together." I thought it was a great idea. He, however, as I mentioned before, did not want to study with me.

Once again, I found myself with that self-defeating attitude. *I'm alone for sure with no one in this city to help me because no one in this city is board-certified in EEG—no technologists, no physicians. What do I do now? I feel as if I'm out in the middle of the ocean again, wondering how in the world I got here. All that matters is that I'm here. I have two choices: sink or swim. I think I'll swim.*

Swimming was not what I did at first. Instead, I cried, moaned, and groaned as I wandered in the wilderness of frustration and doubt. I did not go forward. No, not at all. I was stuck in doubt. I thought, *No, I can't do this part by myself. It's way too hard. I know I made it through the written exam, but as they told me, this part is different. Yes, it is. Why am I trying to fool myself? I remember Mama said, "White people don't like colored people." Yes, I remember.* The messages from the past spoke to me, telling me to change the way I was thinking. That "woe is me" victim mentality showed its ugly face. Worse than that, I believed it—for a little while. Thankfully, I didn't stay in that frame of mind very long.

Instead, I stopped wandering in the wilderness of doubt. I decided to rise to the challenge with a positive attitude. Once again, I stood firmly, abiding in the truth that would never let me down. That was a good thing because I was at a place where I came to learn another invaluable lesson about tenacity. My friend Lessie, who lived in Rockville, used to say, "If it is going to be, it is up to me." She was talking about losing weight—physical issues. I was thinking about having a can-do way of thinking.

Since quitting is not an option, and since a registered EEG technologist is what I'm going to be, it is up to me to make it happen. Yes, it would be easier if I had help, but I don't have anyone to help me. So, I can and I will do this all by myself, I thought.

Looking on the bright side became my focus. I said to myself, *Get yourself together and don't worry about the future. First of all, the future is not promised to me. All I have is right now. The past is history, gone forever, never to return exactly the same again. The future will take care of itself. What I have to do is trust God to take care of me and the kids. I know he can and will do that no matter where we live and no matter what we are doing. I really believe we will be just fine. After all, I know who is really in control.*

I heard the messages loud and clear from within and prepared myself for the next chapter of my life. However, the journey ahead was much different from what either Buford or I expected.

It was in Rockville that another pivotal message was delivered to me. It came from an unlikely source. Jackie, my coworker at the hospital, was the first person who found my life's journey to be interesting enough to share and help other people. While taking a lunch break in the cafeteria that day and having one of our many thought-provoking conversations, Jackie said, "Wow! You really ought to write a book about your life. It's really fascinating." Then she said with a big smile on her face, "I'm so glad you trained me and I got a chance to know you."

"Thank you, Jackie. I will write that book someday," I responded.

Jackie's idea was just a passing thought, but actually, writing a book was another thing I believed I couldn't do. As with becoming board-certified, I had believed that only smart people who were not just intelligent but *super* intelligent were the people who wrote books. I didn't have any friends, relatives, or acquaintances who had written books. It would take years for me to understand that, as with everything else in life, average people like me can do extraordinary things when they are passionate about what they're doing.

Once again, I remembered what I had been told, both the bad and the good. Before I left the hospital, Dr. Abernathy had told me that when I worked as an EEG technologist in Rockville, I would find out something very interesting and challenging. He said, "You will have a better understanding about EEGs than anyone in that city."

I was accustomed to working with a registered technologist, a brilliant, board-certified neurologist, knowledgeable peers, and a system of accountability conducive to ongoing learning. I held leaders in high regard and felt that one never learns above their teachers. Therefore, the teachers in my life became the standard by which I measured my potential. According to Dr.

Abernathy, it was conceivable that I was going to be a leader without a leader. This was a first in my career. Looking forward to those challenges, I forged ahead.

The Food Plant

Rockville was a very nice city to live in. Compared to home, its reputation was impeccable, with a low crime rate, definitely enough to pacify me. Finding a job would be a piece of cake, or so I thought. I was certain that with my qualifications, I would get an EEG technician job instantly—but that didn't happen. I was wrong. There were no openings in either of the two main hospitals, and they certainly wouldn't fire their technicians just to hire me, even if I *had* already passed part one of the national certification exam.

I waited for a few months, which seemed like an eternity. I was concerned that things weren't happening the way I had envisioned. Finally, I resolved to accept the state I was in. After all, I couldn't change the situation. I thought to myself, *I just need to keep busy and find a job to make some money.*

One day, I had a bright idea. *People say, "It's not what you know but who you know." That is a true statement. I know somebody who can help me out. There is a very nice man in our church who is also a foreman at a food manufacturing plant.* I would take a chance and talk to him about helping me get a job. *I'm a little bit afraid, but he will either say yes or no, and I will be OK with it.*

The following Sunday, I saw him at church. When the service was over, I decided to go for it and pop the question.

"Harold, I was wondering if there is any way possible that you could get me a job at the plant where you work."

He paused briefly and looked a little bit surprised. "What would you like to do—work days in the production department running the lines or work nights in the sanitation department cleaning the plant?" he asked.

"Which do you think will be better for me?" I asked.

"Probably sanitation—it doesn't require any long training; plus, you'll make more money. It's easier, but it's really your decision."

Working the lines sounds tough. Working nights doesn't sound so good because I've never worked nights. But more money sounds great and it's a job, so I'm grateful for either. I need to decide right now, I thought. Harold was being so kind and, after all, I had asked him about a job and didn't want to back out now.

"So, the question for you is, are you OK with working sanitation at night?"

Of course I am. I don't dare say no. "Yes, I am. I think that will be better than learning how to work on the lines."

In a very kind tone, Harold said, "OK, come in tomorrow, and I'll see what I can do."

I was there on time and prepared for an interview and a long, drawn-out process with lots of red tape. But that didn't happen. Harold had set the stage. All I had to do was fill out a few forms, and I was hired.

At first, I worked nights. That's the shift Harold worked on. I say "worked." Actually, he was the boss, so he did very little manual work. It was comforting knowing he was both my spiritual brother and my boss. But after a short time, I learned to work the line on both shifts. Then I had a different boss.

I embraced challenges to stretch myself and prove that I could do anything I decided to do. If it was humanly possible for someone to do something, then I could do it. "Hard" was not a plausible reason to take the easy route, not for long. "Easy" was not the better choice for me.

I recognized that this was a good opportunity to stop, look, and listen to what was going on in my little world. That I couldn't get a job in the field of my training was a problem. I looked around, and the doors had been closed to my career. I listened to that voice within saying, "Don't worry." In my heart, I sensed that he was saying to me, "I've got you covered. When you don't know what to do and you don't know how to do it, just trust me."

I had an opportunity to pause and accept another promise of Providence. I had an opportunity to accept him at his word.

Interestingly, I would make more money working at a food manufacturing plant than at any other job I'd held before, and a nice raise would be in my check in just a few months. *Wow, this is a lot of money I'm making. I like this part,* I thought. Yes, the job was great as far as money was concerned. I loved the big paycheck. But my passion was still neurology. No amount of money was ever going to change that. I had to be honest with everybody about my feelings and about my allegiance—or rather the lack of allegiance to the plant.

The day I filled out the application and was hired, I felt obligated to be upfront about my intentions, goals, and objectives. I told my employer that if and when there was a job opening in one of the hospitals, I would give my two-week notice immediately, even if I had just been working a matter of a few days. I was candid with them and wanted to give them the option of hiring me or not. I did need a job. But more importantly, I *needed* to do what I had been called to do in Rockville. I was absolutely certain of that.

Dressed in my uniform and wearing my hairnet, I was ready to go to work. Harold gave me a tour of the plant, introduced me to lots of people, and gave me a list of the places I was to clean during my shift. He showed me where to get my supplies and explained the rules of the company, such as breaks and lunchtime. Literally within less than an hour, I knew everything I needed to know about the job and was busy getting my work done.

Working at the plant was an easy job, especially on the night shift—a piece of cake. In the sanitation department job, I had eight hours to clean the offices, the ladies' restrooms, and the cafeteria. Basically I emptied the trash, dusted the areas, cleaned ashtrays, and swept and mopped the floors. I took my time cleaning each area because it really took only about half the shift to complete the job. It was so easy to do. At times, I felt as if I were cheating the company and would just go over the same things again and again to look busy. My boss knew exactly what I was responsible for and only expected me to do my job, nothing more. I didn't complain about having it easy and getting a big check for it.

Then I decided to go to days. Working the day shift was quite different. It was fast-paced with ten times as many people occupying the rooms I had been accustomed to cleaning at night. It was interesting how different the atmosphere was between days and nights. There were huge, complex processing machines all over the plant. There was a loud symphony of nonstop production noises—clicking of connectors, movement of belts, shouts to keep the process running smoothly, and even louder shouts to abort production when something went wrong. There was also the ongoing chatter of all the employees.

I worked on the line, which rotated in about six different positions. Unlike cleaning the rooms, I had to be trained for the production position. Things moved really fast on the line, and a moment's hesitation was a really big deal! It could affect the whole production process, costing the company lots of money and making the veteran employees very angry if the line went down. I had to keep focused. Until I was able to joke around and work at the same time, I worked like a well-oiled robot. It was intense at first. However, it was challenging, and soon it was a lot of fun. I was promoted again and proved that I was up for the task before me.

Finally, after several months of working there, I received a call about a job opening in one of the hospitals. I was so excited about getting my career going again. It was a coincidence that Darren, the man with whom I had taken my written exam, was the supervisor. I was a little hesitant because of my gut feeling, but I decided to focus on the blessing to have a job as a technician.

The very next day, I went to the department to talk to the technician. I went to the human resources department, filled out the necessary paperwork, and was set to go. When I officially received the call to offer me the job, I instantly said yes. Yes, instantly. I didn't ask a lot of questions. I just heard, "We want you, and we need your help." Even though my salary was going to be several dollars less an hour than at the food plant, I was ready for that. In the first place, I had a job, and second, I was going to make about the same amount I had made before I moved. So, with that being said, I went back to the initial plan to work on my career in Rockville. *Finally, it's really happening!* I was grateful for the job.

As promised, I gave Harold verbal notice to terminate my employment, and he was gracious to do so without question. It was an amicable situation. As I recall, I was allowed to leave without giving a two-week notice. That Friday was my last day, and I was ready to report to work for the EEG position that Monday. I was so excited—excited about having found a job, excited about the things I learned and the money I made from working at the plant, but ecstatic that I was moving on. I could see the light at the end of the tunnel, and it was beautiful! I said to myself again, *It's not what you know; it's who you know, and I am so glad to know Harold because he's got my back. He helped me get the job.*

Bait and Switch

It was my first day at work, a new beginning for me in my career. It was a new start after I had been so concerned about never being able to get another job, another opportunity like I'd had before I moved. As I had expected, a door would open. I would walk through it and embrace the opportunity to start over once again. A brand new day had arrived, and I was receptive to learning from all the awesome things I thought were in store for me.

I met the two people working in the lab, Darren and Janice. They were the supervisor and the technician, respectively. I was so excited that day when I walked into the EEG lab. I arrived early, wanting to get to know my new coworkers, familiarize myself with the lab, and begin working in this awesome career with people who wanted and needed my help. My attitude was upbeat, my language optimistic, and my mind set to do great things.

However, in contrast, Darren's expressions were subdued, which concerned me. Janice had two roles—the secretary and the technician. She was very pleasant as she smiled at me and expressed how happy she was to have me become a part of the team. Sensing her approval was a refreshing feeling. Yet, I also sensed that something seemed disingenuous, even in her politeness. It was hard to put it all together. Maybe she was trying to balance things out in favor of working with me and, at the same time, maintain loyalty to Darren. I was sure something was wrong. I struggled to overlook it but honestly could not deny that sixth sense. However, there were two more things I knew for sure: I wanted the job, and I wanted them to want me as a coworker.

Desiring to get off to a good start, I quickly convinced myself that my perception must have been wrong. *Surely they are glad I'm here. After all, Darren offered me the job,* I thought. *He knows my work history and the experience I'm bringing to the EEG lab. I have so much to offer. That's why he wanted me, right?*

I wasn't seeing this from a prideful perspective but rather from a servant-leader position, one that I felt blessed to be in. They could take full advantage of my knowledge, experience, and certification and become registered themselves. Furthermore, the other hospital in Rockville was in competition. I would give my all to the hospital where I worked.

I realized my perceptions were right on target. Darren did indeed have ulterior motives for hiring me. He wasn't interested in having me as an employee but rather to simply take advantage of what I knew. When my suspicions were confirmed, I thought about our previous conversations. Since we both had passed part one of the board certification exam, as I told you before, I wanted to study with him for the four-part oral exam, which was the more difficult portion. Without batting an eye, he had quickly rejected my offer, which I had questioned for only a moment. But that was history, and I wanted to keep it there. I had thought to myself, *Why doesn't he want to study with me? After all, two heads are truly better than one. What he doesn't know, I will know, and vice versa,* I thought. I understood and resolved to study hard and pass the test all by myself.

Yes, indeed, I remembered all that as I stood talking to this man who had blatantly rejected my offer to work with him before. Now, here we were again. Darren reached out to me to hire me to work with him. As a half-full, optimistic thinker, that was all positive. So, I wasn't going to hold his past opinions about me against him. *It's a brand new day!* That was the message I was holding on to.

Darren had offered me a salary much lower than I was making at the plant, but that was OK with me. After all, I anticipated making less money as a technologist in a local hospital than working in a food manufacturing plant. So, that wasn't a problem—not at all. But he never told me exactly what I would make. Since I was satisfied with the range he had quoted me, I trusted him at his word. I wanted to believe him. I really wanted to believe that what I saw when I arrived was true, not just my hopeful imagination. With all my heart, I wanted to believe he cared about me as a human being, a human being who could be a part of his team. I was hoping he had come to the conclusion that having me as part of his team would be good for all concerned. For sure, I knew it would be an answer to my prayer to find a job in my field in Rockville. Reaching that goal meant the world to me.

Maybe he really doesn't want me because I'm a female, a black female. Maybe something is lurking in the background that I don't know about, and he is looking at me as different. I can't think like that because that's probably not the truth, and I am most likely reading into things. It will be just fine. I'll wait and see.

Looking on the bright side was my strength, being a positive person and seeing the cup as half full. That was what I had always done. That was the way I survived. I had never truly come to grips with how hard it had been. Never had I completely understood the horrific pain of rejection and separatism. I didn't want to understand it because it was wrong, as wrong as two left shoes.

It never made sense to me—never. Still, I was in denial. *Surely everything will work out fine* was my resolution, and so I ignored the voice of negativity screaming at me: "They don't want you working with them!" So, I lifted up my bowed-down head and remained positive and focused.

The problem was that there was nothing in writing for me as a new employee. *Hmm?* Thinking it was a complete oversight on Darren's part, I asked him about my salary.

"Darren, we haven't talked about exactly how much my hourly wage will be or done any official paperwork for my employment." That seemed very strange, but I tried to dismiss it.

He said, "I'll talk to you about that later." *What? Why can't he tell me now? It's just the two of us here.* There was something wrong with that picture, but I attributed it to his being so excited about the new position and did indeed dismiss it as an oversight. I gave him the benefit of the doubt, sensing I was wrong for having brought it up.

Within minutes, there was an overt distraction. Darren started quizzing me about a lot of things I knew from my experience. He wanted all kinds of details that would empower him and the lab. It was as if he was trying to get everything he could out of me the very first day, the first hour of my employment.

Even though I was a brand new employee, Darren had not given me an orientation to the hospital—where the patient rooms were located, the intensive care units, the cafeteria, or anything like that. As I recall, I wasn't sure if there was a lounge where we took breaks, a locker to store my purse, or other associates in the hospital we would interact with on a daily basis. None of the fundamental parts of the system appeared to be a priority. Finding out what I knew and how I could teach the two of them was the only priority. I was absolutely sure of that by now. I couldn't continue to deny something that was crystal clear.

I decided to teach them all I knew with the hope that they would want more and, as a result, decide that having a good person working with them who was also knowledgeable about EEGs would be a good thing. I figured they would look at it as a positive two-way street for both sides to travel.

Right away, Darren had me do the first patient. I didn't even know what the schedule was for the day. I didn't even know the patient was on the way to the lab until he appeared and Darren said, "Your first patient is on the way. I want to talk to you about how you're going to do the procedure. I know you do it differently than we do."

I explained how to do what is called a 10/20 measurement system of the head, a detailed process used to determine correct placements of electrodes.

Darren also drilled me about all kinds of hypothetical technical situations, hanging on to my every word as if he were a human tape recorder. "I heard you've been doing EEGs for ten years. I have lots of questions, things we can learn from you."

He asked me several more questions:

"I want you to teach us how to do the five measurement steps. Can you do that?

"What about the other procedures such as photic stimulation? [This is a test with bright flashing lights over the eyes, which can trigger seizure activity.]

"Do you do photic stimulation on all your patients? Explain that to me.

"How about hyperventilation? [This is an overbreathing procedure that can also trigger certain types of seizures and can reveal areas where there is a lack of adequate blood flow to the brain.] What is your experience with hyperventilation?

"Do you have the patients do it for three minutes or five minutes?

"How do you determine who needs to have it and who doesn't?

"Do you get sleep studies on your patients or just wake studies?

"By the way, have you noticed a difference in the brain activity when they are asleep? I've heard that doing the EEG while the patients are awake is enough.

"What is your experience with finding abnormalities in sleep as opposed to being wake?

"What about your relationship with the neurologists? Tell me about how you guys worked together."

Wow, he has lots of questions. They are obviously ready for change, and that is exciting to me! I am here to help them, and I'm going to give it my all. In fact, I'm going to teach them according to ASET (the American Society of Electroneurodiagnostic Technologists). Even if they don't believe me at first, I will prove it to them—everything I know— and I am adamant about following the governing body with national guidelines. I'll show them all the details. Then they will believe me, and it will be just fine. That is what I thought and what I held on to as I decided to ignore what I suspected in terms of their motives.

It was as if I had been hired not as a working technician but as a technical consultant, hired to teach every single thing I had learned in ten years working under a board-certified neurologist. While I was willing to share what I knew, it was impossible for me to do that in the first day, much less the first hour. Darren didn't want to talk about the salary he had promised me, show me where the patient rooms were, or anything a new employee would want and need to know.

I felt totally bewildered and didn't know what I should do. I had already left my other job. I went ahead and worked with the patients scheduled for testing that day, did my best, and explained all my steps to both of them. Janice didn't have much to say, which was interesting. I began to "hear" what she wasn't saying.

Throughout the day, I kept thinking, *Something is wrong with this picture. I'm not exactly sure what, but something is seriously wrong.* I couldn't deny it any longer. I decided to take off my passive hat and have a candid talk with Darren at the end of the shift.

I said, "So what are you paying me? What is my hourly wage?"

Darren responded with a figure far less than his verbal promise. Almost in tears, I proceeded to tell him how he had made me feel all day, to which he scoffed and said, "Oh well, it's too late now. You already quit your other job."

I was frozen with anger. I was livid! I felt like a used toy, some object to be played with and then tossed away in a sea of forgetfulness. *You are an awful person. You are rude. You are a manipulating con man.* I'd been conned before.

I didn't reply to Darren out loud about feeling used like a nobody, a person less than human. I thought to myself, *Oh my God, what have I gotten myself into this time? Now I have no place to work.*

No, I did not beg Darren to accept me. I absolutely expected he would laugh in my face again and reject my request to become his partner rather than his competition. No, I did not try to explain how much I could help them and the hospital because I got the real message. *He* didn't want *me* to be a part of his team. No, he did not. Finally, I saw the whole picture, and I had to face the fact that I had made a big mistake. Instead of trying to change Darren, I realized I had to change me.

That is what I did, but the old records kept playing in my mind. "Rosie, remember, white people just don't like colored people" resonated in my heart. I remembered hearing my mother saying that but kept trying to make myself believe that wasn't the reason I had been rejected. Realizing I was lying to myself, I paused to analyze all that had taken place, and I could not deny the facts. *Is that what this is all about?* I asked myself. *I want to say no, but if I'm honest, I do believe that is exactly what this is all about.*

I calmly acquiesced, said my good-byes, and walked out the door. I refused to be taken advantage of no matter what the cost, and I decided that I would not come back the next day, job or no job, career or no career. I would not be a slave to the master of deception, no matter who he or she was and no matter what I had to give up.

I found myself in need of grace and mercy. Once again, he showered me with mercy and forgiveness. He showed me exactly what to do—to let go and let God take care of me. And I did.

As soon as I got home, I called Harold at the plant. I explained how the supervisor of the EEG lab had deceived me. Then I asked if I could have my job back. And he said, "Yes, come in tomorrow morning on the day shift, and you will work in production."

Wow! Somebody was watching over me. I knew it!

So, I got my job back and worked at the plant for about six months until the door was open for me to work at another hospital in Rockville. This time, the entire hiring process was as different as night and day—very professional, structured, and acceptable.

The door at the first hospital had been closed because what was behind it would pull me down and never lift me up. It would have lowered my self-esteem. So, what the enemy meant for evil, my Father meant for good and opened my eyes to the truth, removing me from the grips of one who intended no good for me. Now something different was on the horizon, and I was about to add an invaluable chapter to my life story.

The Real Deal

Initially, when I applied at another hospital, I was told there were no openings. I was disappointed, but I understood they weren't going to give me a job just because I wanted one. Nevertheless, the application was there. They were impressed with my skills, but they couldn't hire me because they had two full-time technicians.

Then things changed. One of the technicians quit, and the stage was set to hire me. When the lady from the human resources department called, I was ecstatic! Once again, I notified my supervisor of my intentions to quit. And once again, he was very supportive of my decision to continue my career. Harold said, "I hope things work out this time because I know how important this is to you. Let me know if you need a reference from me. And if it doesn't work out, you can always come back."

"Oh, Harold, I appreciate this so much. You have been a great help. I want you to know that I will never forget all that you have done for me." With tears almost streaming down my face and appreciation making my heart pound, I looked into his eyes and said, "Thank you. Thank you very much!"

For some reason, I felt that my working at the plant was over. Lots of memories flooded my mind—most of them good, especially the money. It was easy money. It was lots of fun and challenging at times working on the production lines with such diverse people. It was like a melting pot, a homogeneous group of human beings who were not repelled by their ethnicity but rather excited about their humanity. It felt great! We were all blended together for a common cause. We were like family, like friends, and that was right up my alley. I absolutely loved that part. I was quick to call home and share with my family and friends how awesome working at the plant was for me.

Now I had to focus on what was ahead, on leaving what was good for what would be the best of the three places I worked. I was called to a career that was more important, and I had to leave temporal pleasures behind to work for the prize of the higher calling that began when I was nineteen.

My first interview was with Joyce Williams, a hospital administrator. She was a tall, attractive, and delightful lady with ivory skin. I felt totally comfortable with her. My immediate perception was that she felt totally comfortable with me also. She didn't appear to have any concerns about the color of my skin, none at all.

Her mannerisms and tone of voice seemed to underscore her honest and straightforward words. There were several points she expressed that I heard loud and clear. I've never forgotten what she said. Right there in her plush executive office, as she sat across from me, we had an open and thought-provoking conversation. She got to the main points right away. She said, "We have never had someone like you—someone with your experience, someone who is willing to go for the challenge to make a change and to show us exactly how to change the things we are doing wrong. It won't be an easy job—not at all—because there will be some physicians who will not want to change. So, my question is, are you OK with that? Are you willing to accept the challenge, Rosie?" I remember those words as if it were yesterday.

I hung on to every single word. More important, I felt a sense of honesty and calm from Joyce. She wanted change not for selfish reasons but for the patients' sake. Her motives were crystal clear. *Wow! This is really happening,* I thought. So, before I started talking about all the details, I simply said, "Yes, I'm willing to take on the challenge. Thank you."

We talked about salary, which was less than what I had made at the plant but more than I'd made before I moved to Rockville. So far, everything seemed to be going just fine. *It took a whole year working at the plant to start my career again. Now is the time to get back into my career; I know it!*

We were off to a great start. Joyce called Pamela, the EEG technician, to her office to introduce me. She smiled at me and said, "Hello, it's really nice to be meeting you."

I believe you mean that. "Thank you. It's great to be here," I responded.

Pamela took me to her EEG lab, a very small room, and introduced me to other associates in the area. They were like her, kind and unpretentious. She explained to me all the pertinent details about the hospital, the department, and the physicians. The best thing is that they seemed very excited also. I was confident that they wanted me on their team.

Once I started working, I learned that Pamela was receptive to learning a different system, one that complied with national regulations. "I'm so glad you're here," she said. "I can't wait for you to teach me how to do EEGs the right way. I know we haven't been doing everything right, but that's the way I was trained, and that's what the doctors have wanted us to do," she said.

"You know, we have to do what we are told. We're technicians, and they are the physicians. You have no choice in the matter," I responded.

"They said we have to use the O'Leary Montages, which is something another physician discovered a long time ago. This way, we can get more patients done."

"Well, I can change some of the ways I test my patients, but there are some things I can't do differently with a clear conscience."

"I'm eager to learn and grateful that you're here to help us," Pamela responded softly.

We continued talking about how things were done and the reasons why some things should be done differently. Pamela accepted my rationale, but when deciding between what she was accustomed to doing for the neurologists and doing what *I* deemed best, her decision was clear. She had to obey the doctor's orders, which I understood completely.

I silently appealed to a higher court, to my Father, who could see the big picture. Only he could see everything, no one else. Only he could help me to stand my ground without hostility, negativity, or prejudice. Only he could empower me with knowledge and wisdom and still keep me humble as I tried to prove my points. My sincere motive was to help all humanity with the knowledge I had been given. So, I rested in his Providence and his promises to do what only he could and would do.

Pamela and I maintained a great relationship as coworkers in the EEG lab. I was very comfortable there and, as a result, I rested satisfied that I was in a good and healthy work family.

Not to worry—I had not forgotten those people who did not want me around. I didn't have blinders on. I didn't have to work with them like I worked with Pamela. So, I tried to remain focused on what was and not dwell on what was not, particularly what and who I would not change.

However, my time with Pamela was not long. Unfortunately, she had a back injury and had to stop working. For a time, I was in a very difficult situation, having to carry the weight of the lab all on my shoulders. Although it was tough at times, I came to the place where I realized my limitations and asserted that to Clyde, my supervisor.

As in all situations in life, "doors open and doors close." "The rain falls on the just and the unjust." "You have to take the bitter with the sweet"—all those things. I got the message and looked for "the light at the end of the tunnel." I found it.

The light was bright. The light was understandable. The light revealed that Pamela wasn't coming back. She wasn't coming back, and that was a fact I had to accept no matter how difficult it was to lose her, the delightful lady willing to befriend me, a person I needed and who also needed me. It was over. She had not given notice, but I could see the handwriting on the wall. Her time with me as a coworker was coming to an end. I needed to understand that and keep my eyes and ears open to exactly how to go forward.

To start, I needed to train someone to replace Pamela. At first I thought to myself, *Replacing Pamela is not going to be easy— not at all. I have no idea how I'm going to do it. I know for sure I can't work in this department all by myself with the way I want to do EEGs.*

I had forgotten the promises I had heard deep within. As I reminisced, I understood once again that things would work out just fine. In fact, the task before me was not difficult at all, not even a little bit. In fact, I remembered the perfect candidate—Jackie had been lurking in the background, waiting for an opportunity to learn. She was just as kind as Pamela and very inquisitive about my job.

When I first met Jackie, she worked as a transporter. Her job at that time was to go get the patients from their rooms and take them to departments such as the EEG lab. Then, after the tests were completed, she returned the patients to their room.

Jackie wore a striking smile and emanated confidence. Day after day, she stopped by, even when she wasn't transporting patients. We always had an upbeat chat. I found her enthusiastic personality quite interesting. I was aware that although she wore a different covering, she accepted me just because I was more like her than unlike her. Oh, how refreshing it was to meet Jackie!

It was apparent from all of her questions that she was clearly fascinated with EEG technology. Then one day, without hesitation, she popped the big question: "Do you think I can learn to be an EEG technician?"

"Of course you can," I responded. "I would be absolutely thrilled to teach you. You have the most important thing you need to learn everything you need to know and become certified if that is what you want to do. Your attitude is great! So, as long as you are motivated and really want to learn, the sky is the limit for you."

Jackie decided to go for it. Consequently, she got the job and became a suitable replacement for Pamela.

By the time she was trained, we had moved to a different area of the hospital because the lab had expanded. The original lab with one EEG machine had been transformed to a neurology suite with two individual labs and a reading area for the physicians as well as a waiting room. In addition to doing routine EEGs, we would eventually add other tests such as evoked potentials—a neurological test to check auditory, visual, and somatosensory pathways to the brain—and ERGs to check for diseases of the eyes.

When Jackie heard about and witnessed my experience on this journey, coupled with what she learned as we worked together, she was on top of the world. And after she saw the transformation in that hospital—all the changes that had taken place since I had started—she reminded me of what she had said. "You should write a book about your life someday. Seriously, you should."

"Someday I will," I responded.

Father, thank you for Jackie and for letting me see through her what you are telling me to do. I've been checking out what she has to say. Now I see it clearly.

Without a doubt, I had done the right thing by accepting the job. What I didn't know was all that the position would entail. There were high expectations but often low gratitude, especially from a couple of the neurologists. I remembered trying to plead my case with them for change. They resisted.

"Let me prove my recommendations from ASET [American Society of Electroneurodiagnostic Technologists] how to perform EEGs correctly. Don't believe me; believe them. Allow me to model this lab accordingly," I pleaded respectfully. "I want what's best for the patients. I'm not looking for brownie points or a bigger paycheck. You're not going to pay me more money for caring. This is not about me. Can't you see that? I want things to change because I care about these patients," I insisted.

The negative responses ranged from turned heads walking away to "*Hell* no! Not on my patients!" I realized it was still an uphill battle, but I was there to climb up the hill of resistance until we reached the top, with clarity and excitement about the changes. The problems were denial, rejection, and—I hesitate to say it—ignorance.

Being honest with ourselves is so important. It is important because the truth will set us free from ignorance. And the fact is, absolutely *all* of us are ignorant of countless things. As I said, it is worth repeating: absolutely *nobody* knows everything about anything. Absolutely nobody!

OK, time to get off that soapbox and back to the situation between me and those who fought against me. Although it was very hard at times, I was happy with every patient I was able to touch in ways over and beyond the call of duty. I loved it.

Some of the physicians were genuinely receptive to my critique and accepted my proposals. Others were at least willing to give me an opportunity to prove myself. It was great to have their support. After all, they had been working for many years doing things quite differently. Then I showed up and made trouble, even if my intentions were good.

Usually, I did the tests on one of the neurologist's patients per his required protocol. But on this and other occasions, I had to cross the line. I justified it by doing the test the way he wanted it done and then adding more to it. Based on the patient's history and previous EEG, I would feel very strongly about my decision. The additional information changed at times based on the additional procedures that ultimately helped the patient. It made perfect sense to me. If I had been in the patient's shoes, I would have wanted it that way.

However, one day, I went too far—according to Dr. Kaplan, a neurologist. He ripped me apart for doing what I deemed would help the patient. Literally, he left me a nasty note. He wrote, "Don't you ever let my patients sleep during the EEG!"

"Why not? Some of them need to sleep during the test," I explained to Jackie. They really do in order for us to find out if they have certain kinds of seizures. If we get a normal EEG and the patient did not drift off to sleep, he or she may need to be on medication. But with a normal EEG, we don't have definitive information. That's a fact.

Oh my God, please take care of these patients. Please help me stay here until somebody comes along whom they will believe.

After that, I worked hard simply doing as I was told, but I decided to find other ways to "cross the line" for the sake of the patients who truly needed it. Crossing the line is exactly what I did in a way, I prayed, that was acceptable to the same neurologist who acted as if he hated every idea just because it came from me. I had a plan. I would not give up. I *could not* give up.

First of all, I did the test according to his standards, and it revealed no abnormality—a normal EEG. Since the test was perfectly normal while the patient was awake, I recorded the test exactly as I was told.

Then the possibility of hurting instead of helping the patient plagued my conscience. I decided to wait for the patient to go to sleep and risk being yelled at, cussed out, hated, or even fired. The patients never knew how much I cared or how much I risked for them. I had to live with my actions, and I was going to make a difference, plain and simple. That's what I was born to do.

One day, I purposely instructed a patient to sleep during the recording, and when he did, the seizure activity—an epileptiform discharge coming from his brain—was blatant. *Blatant,* I tell you. Undeniably abnormal! I had crossed the line, and yet I was totally at peace about it. I wasn't at all concerned about facing the physician's wrath. I simply did what I had to do. Whatever happened would happen. *What will he say about my helping the patient the way I did? Can he really be mad at me? Will I be in trouble? I don't think so, but truly I don't care. I remember why I was hired. So, I don't think they will fire me,* I thought.

This time, the doctor's response was verbal, but it was positive. He walked into a room right outside the lab to read the EEG, began turning the pages, and was surprised at what he saw. He started talking loudly to himself, but loud enough so that I could hear him.

I smiled to myself, very happy at his initial response.

"Look at that!" he said out loud to himself. "There are abnormalities during sleep. It was perfectly normal while he was awake!" Then he walked into the room where I was, looked at me with a big grin on his face, and said, "Wow! That's great! From now on, get sleep on all my patients who have seizures. I mean it was as different as night and day," he said, as if in a state of shock—and as if he had never heard that before.

"Yes, I noticed that," I said humbly as I shouted within, *Yes, I told you so! Just think of all the patients who have been misdiagnosed because of pride!*

My credibility hit the ceiling! It was apparent to most of the staff. *I'm so glad they are coming around, finally, but some of them are still not accepting some of the changes I know are really important.*

It would take years before things would totally change in accordance with national guidelines. In the meantime, my colleagues from back home asked me how I could work in a lab that was not following national standards. My response was twofold: "I like to eat, so I need a job and, more importantly, there hasn't been anyone to fight for change on the patients' behalf." I truly believed this was the reason for my living in Rockville. It wasn't a coincidence.

When I told Joyce, she applauded my persistence. And she always appeared delighted to be my friend. I said to her, "I believe one of these days, the right person will come along who agrees with me, a person they trust. I don't know how long it will take—it could be five years—but I honestly believe that things will change one day when he starts to work here and witnesses what I've been talking about."

That's just the way it happened. Remarkably, it was five years from the time I was hired until that day, that pivotal point in time.

I was in the lab alone on that Saturday. What I had waited for, what I had hoped for, and what I had literally prayed for finally happened. Dr. Quigley walked into the lab and said, "So you're the registered tech they've been talking about." I didn't respond for a few seconds but rather listened to what he had to say. "Let me see the records."

"OK, come right back here," I said as I took him to where the tracings were stored.

He walked in, looked into the lab, and looked at the recordings. Then he looked at the equipment as if a thousand ideas were running through his mind. "Tell me what's going on," he said. "How were you taught to do EEGs?"

I hurried to gather all types of evidence to prove my points. I showed all of it to him. After all, he was the man I had been waiting for—for five years! He was amazed at the current and potential problems. We talked about what resources we would need to adhere to national guidelines and to gauge competency in the neurology lab. He talked as if the two of us would become a team to completely transform the department. He said he was delighted to support me as the technologist. Together, we provided textbook studies and were essentially given a blank check to buy new machines, new supplies, and expand our services to include ERG (electroretinogram), a test to diagnose eye diseases such as retinitis pigmentosa; cognitive P300s, an auditory test to check for comprehension; and evoked potentials, the test to examine auditory, visual, and somatosensory pathways. It was amazing! I felt as if my mission here had finally been accomplished.

But what was unfolding behind the scenes was disheartening.

One day, I received a call from Tom, who worked in a different department. He was amazed at what I was doing, how the lab had changed, and he wanted to talk with me about it. I agreed because that's what I was there for, to empower others with my knowledge. He was in awe of the neurodiagnostic position and all that was involved. I had no problem telling him about it all, but I did have a problem with what he said to me the next time he came into the lab.

"You are a valuable commodity," he said. *Commodity! What in the world did he call me? He said exactly what he meant to say.* That made me sound as if I were not even human—just something to be used rather than a valued part of the team. I felt sick in my gut, which was speaking to me loud and clear. Something was wrong.

After talking with me, he apparently spoke with my boss, Clyde, and the two of them formulated a plan that would end my journey there at the hospital. A few days later, Clyde walked in the lab and announced to me with a smile on his face, "We have some positive changes going on around here. Tom is the supervisor now, and I want you to train him to do everything you do." *How can he be the supervisor when supervising is my overall job description? I am responsible for the lab's operations. How, when did that change?* I was furious! I can't honestly remember exactly what I said. Suffice it to say, he found out I wasn't pleased. I told him how unfair it was.

Clyde pretended to be a little concerned about my reaction. But he said he had already approved the position and was hoping that I would work with Tom to help him out. I could not and would not hold back what I really felt about this horrible thing they had done. They wanted to get what the "commodity" had without any regard to the commodity's feelings. I had a deep desire to work together as a team. After all, for five years, my responsibility was to take charge of the entire department. I was the one who weathered the storms. I was the one who worked with the physician to completely transform the department to be second to none in the country, even better than the lab I'd come from. I had accomplished that, and Tom knew it. He described me as a commodity, took my job, and got the supervisor's pay and title for what I had worked to master with torment, sweat, and tears. How unfair—so I thought.

Some people who heard what happened said, "That is wrong. I wouldn't teach him anything."

But what I said to Clyde, the department director, right then and there after his grand announcement was, "You can force me to train him, but you cannot make me think this is right because it clearly isn't." He did not respond. He just looked at me with defiance. Then, I had to say exactly what was on my mind. "I've already been doing the job for five years without the title or the money, so why don't you make *me* the supervisor?"

I could tell he was ready for that question because he did not hesitate to answer. "You don't have a college degree. Tom does," he said flippantly.

I was angry but held myself together. I had made history in the hospital and in the city as the only registered EEG technologist ever, helping set up a neuroscience lab second to none I had ever seen. Tom didn't have any of my skills, just a BA degree. I vowed to never be in that position again. He—*they*—had the ammo to fight me and win. And I knew it.

I learned a lot that day. It is better to have and not need than to need and not have. Because I didn't have a degree, Clyde and Tom had an excuse to concoct and get away with this scheme. I had grounds to fight for the position that should've been mine, but the truth is that I really didn't want the title. It was clearly time for me to return to my hometown. Despite the bittersweet ending to my time there, I was thankful to have been able to make a difference in the lives of those who would now have access to better neurodiagnostic procedures and never know how it came about.

Within a few months, much had changed in my life, both at home and at work. Another mission accomplished. It was time to go home. I wasn't going to rock the boat no matter what weapon I had to do it with and no matter what my friends suggested I do.

One thing I have to add—one very important, positive thing—is that the physicians who had been against me in the beginning made a one-hundred-eighty-degree turn. They were all on my side. They wanted me to stay. In fact, the one I least expected asked me a question: "What will it take to get you to stay?"

I made sure Tom was trained and equipped to supervise the lab. I had no regrets because I did an awesome job. The facts proved that. One more thing: Clyde said he would replace me only with a board-certified technologist. So, the lab was now following the standards set by ASET.

Mission accomplished!

My Plan vs. God's Plan

My plan was to learn from my mistake of being unequally yoked with a nonbeliever—to choose a Christian man. That made perfect sense to me. However, it was not wise to believe that just because he was a Christian, he was the man God chose for me to marry. And just because he saw me as a suitable lady, that I was the wife God wanted for him. What we wanted to accomplish was different from that which would be grounded in matrimonial unity. But that thought never entered my mind as I was captivated by the idea of finding happiness. You see, I was starving for love. So, I didn't understand where that desperation would lead me. My perception of happiness overshadowed my reasoning.

Therefore, my fourteen-year marriage came to an end. It was a hard pill to swallow—initially. Buford and I had "irreconcilable differences" that severed our relationship. That was a fact; that was the bottom line. Understanding God's mercy and grace was exactly what I focused on. Then, I was equipped to accept the consequences of my predicament with dignity.

I survived the dissolution of the relationship remembering God's promises: "All things work together for the good for them that love the Lord." Several things became apparent to me: not only did God know the details of the past; he knew the details of the future. With new insight, it was time for me to press on.

I understood that like lots of marriages, we had bumps in the road. The bumps in the road had been set up by Satan for *his* plan. As I quote from the Bible so often, "We are not dealing with flesh and blood but with powers and principalities."

You see, those whom God has joined together for *his* plan and *his* glory cannot be separated. No, not anyone, not for any reason. I decided not to compare who was more at fault but instead to "trust the Lord with all [my] heart and lean not unto my own understanding." I remembered that "all have sinned and fall short of the glory of God" and that "his mercies are new every morning." So, by the grace of God, both of us had an opportunity to let the past stay there, and trust God with the future.

God's plan was to bring me to repentance. I had been distracted. My thoughts had pulled me down in the dump of depression. I felt the need to completely change my life—to stop trying to live such a pious life and just focus on having a good time. That is what I did. I convinced myself it was OK to have a drink every Friday—to drown away my misery, to hang out with a new set of friends, and to have a boyfriend just because, after all, I was a woman. That worked for a little while. Then I found myself making one mistake after another. I couldn't live with what I was doing any longer. I had sinned against my Father and was deeply ashamed.

I fell on my knees before the Lord, confessed my sins to him, and asked him to forgive me and show me how to trust him in my weakness. Finally, I was very clear in my request that I needed a husband. God was very clear in the response. *Yes, you do need a husband,* I heard in my heart. He told me clearly and exactly where he was.

I was ready to wait for the man God had chosen for me, no matter how long it would take. I was no longer content with doing what I knew displeased God. No longer did I justify my desire to find happiness in a bottle or a man. Instead, I found happiness as I visualized my Father looking at me walking in his way. What a future life it was to behold.

About a month later, I decided it was time to go back home, just to visit. That was my thought at the time—nothing more. I packed my suitcase, and my son and I left Rockville. I was very nervous because I had never driven for hours on the highway. Yet, I realized it was time for me to step out of my comfort zone, time to visit my family and friends.

We arrived without any problems and went directly to Mama's house. It was so nice to be at home, to cry on her shoulder, and be comforted by her love in person. "God's gonna take care of you, Rosie. I know he will. I've been praying for you, and I promise you everything will be all right."

"I know it. Thank you, Mama."

It was not only her words. It was her eyes, which connected with mine. I could see the love radiating from her. By now we had an amazing relationship. It was great being at home. We just sat around talking and loving on each other.

I had one more day to be home. I was torn between going to church the next day with Mama or going back to the church I had attended about fifteen years ago. We agreed I should go back to my old church.

I didn't tell anyone I was coming; I just showed up. As I walked upstairs to the sanctuary, the music was playing, and people were gathering for worship service. It was so refreshing to be with them. I loved it! I knew what to expect.

However, I became a bit distracted by a new church member I hadn't seen before. I tried to figure out who he was. *Who is he? He looks like Betty and Ada. He sure is busy. He's checking the microphones. Now he's at the pulpit talking to the choir director. He seems really nice. Who is he?* I was genuinely curious about him but didn't know why.

He stood out as the only person I saw doing all of that. The other church members were in their places, so to speak. The choir was in the back, ready to come in. The ministers were in their positions, and all the church members were sitting, waiting for services to start. He looked like a real servant, going about helping others.

It just so happened that there was going to be the monthly "Mates and Dates" gathering the same day. What a coincidence. The meeting was going to be at my friend Sharon's home. She and others invited me to come out for a time of fellowship. I accepted. I figured it would be an opportunity to hang out with my friends from church a little longer. I was totally on board with that.

When I got there, I heard laughter; it was sweet music to my ears. Right in the dining room, they were playing cards. Really focused on the game, they didn't stop to talk to me a lot. I understood. So, I chatted for just a few minutes. Then I moseyed to the back room where my girlfriend and her husband were talking. I joined the conversation, catching up on the latest gossip. I told them about my job and my new life as a single woman. I needed to get a lot off my chest while I was there. So I did.

Then he showed up, the man I had admired at church. He introduced himself to me, and instantly my opinion was confirmed. He was a nice man. Not only that, but I learned he was my friends'—Betty and Ada's—brother. I had never met him before because he was living in California when I was a member of the church.

He sat down and we had such a good talk. I gave him my undivided attention as he quickly appeared to play the role of an insightful counselor. He listened politely as I told him about my divorce and my desire to live a godly life as a single woman.

It didn't take long for him to sum up what he sensed, assert his opinion, and tell me how to take care of myself. "You have a gullible personality, so you should be careful. You could get hurt." He told me he had been married, had two sons, and was focused on his job, volunteering as a leader with inner-city children and, most important, being a leader in the church. I was hanging on every word.

What a nice man.

I drove home thinking more about this man whom I thought could become like a big brother to me. Somehow, I knew I could trust him. Our spiritual and moral connection was obvious; we were compatible. He admonished me to protect my mind from distractions and told me how he was doing that in his single life. *What a nice man I can trust, with no strings attached.*

We exchanged phone numbers so we could keep in touch with each other. Since it was my first time driving on the highway for hours, I agreed to call him to let him know I had arrived safely. The conversation was brief but very pleasant. I had time to take it all in because there were no expectations beyond friendship between us.

Then, one day I began to see that we were friends in the areas that matter the most. Our core values were the same. Mostly, we were servant leaders wanting to please God. When I realized that, I called him again. Then he called me. Finally, we could see this as a new chapter in our lives. We talked for hours. We could already see the so-called coincidences unfolding one at a time. I remembered what God had told me. His message was detailed; it was clear. He told me where my husband was. Now, I knew *who* he was. And I understood completely why he was chosen for me.

That was God's plan for David and me—holy matrimony, as ordained by God.

College Experience

After I married David Hill, he supported and encouraged me in everything I had dreamed of doing. I wanted to attend college, and that is exactly what I did. Attending community college was great! Some of the classes were fairly easy, while others were overwhelming—a huge challenge. All of the classes equipped me with knowledge, fueling my desire to learn more and to apply what I learned to help others and to dream bigger dreams.

I had been dreaming about going back to school for many years. Apparently, going back to school must have been in the back of my mind. I had a second chance, and I was in total control of achieving academic excellence. I studied to that end.

The dream of walking across the stage along with my classmates was about to become a reality. Getting that GED in the mail was one of the best tokens of accomplishment I had ever received. I was delighted when I got it. However, this time, I would receive a college degree—in person, personally handed to me—when my name was called. That dream was about to become a reality.

What a huge opportunity before me to graduate from college. I was so excited! I hadn't graduated from high school—no proms, no homecoming dances, or any of that fun stuff. But this was a brand new day in my life. I had worked hard and was very proud of what I accomplished. Education was freedom from ignorance; that was very important to me.

It's frustrating when people are ignorant and don't get the help they need. I remember when my grandfather was having difficulty walking. My grandmother wasn't at all concerned that he had a problem. I told her he needed to get to the hospital and see a doctor. Once again, I was criticized for thinking that I knew so much from listening to all "those people."

"Buster [my grandfather's nickname] will be just fine. He just needs to have his toenails cut. That's his problem," my grandmother said. Seriously, that is what she said; that is what she believed. A few weeks later, my grandfather was in the hospital. He died. I have several other stories just like that, things I have witnessed personally. Ignorance can be detrimental—even deadly.

The next step on my journey toward academic achievement was to get a bachelor's degree. I didn't want the degree just to have another set of letters behind my name, but rather to prepare myself for the future. That's exactly what I did. I received an associate of arts degree at a community college. A few years later, it was time for me to receive another degree.

I walked across the stage, totally excited to receive my bachelor of science degree in organization management and leadership

(OML). What a relief to know that my past mistakes were not a prerequisite for failure in the future. Oh, how content I was to know I wasn't going to major in a life of horrific mistakes. I knew God had chosen me to be a vessel of honor.

One step at a time, I completed every task I deemed important. It took a long time. I wasn't in a hurry. I had an agenda that required diligence—to really learn. While getting excellent grades was important, learning excellent skills for life-changing reasons was more important. Integrity and tenacity was the name of my game. And I set out to win each time, competing with no one but myself. I had clearly been selected to be in this field of medicine, and I was going to continue pursuing excellence.

One year, I was at another crossroads regarding college. I questioned whether or not to get a master's degree. That would take only one year. Or, I could get a biblical certificate. That would take four years. At first it was a no-brainer, but I began to have second thoughts.

I asked David what I should do. Almost as if he knew what I was thinking, he suggested that I go to the four-year school for a biblical certificate. And then he said, "I don't know what took you so long." He graduated from the same school about ten years before I thought of attending. And since we were both active leaders in the church, he could see the reason I should invest my time in eternal endeavors. He was very supportive.

Four years later, I graduated and received the Christian Leadership Award.

Real-Life Connections

*"God allows us to experience the low points of life in order to
teach us lessons that we could learn in no other way."*
—C. S. Lewis

The Girl in the Wheelchair

Early in my career, an incident at work caused me to really think outside the box. The day started out like every other day in the EEG lab. Orders came down, patients came to the department, and we completed their tests. That day, an order came from the psychiatric unit. We tested patients from that unit frequently. But this patient was different. And I was the technician selected to do the test. I would find out it was no coincidence at all.

The patient entered the department in a wheelchair. I received her and was handed her chart. I wheeled her past the secretary into the lab. She wore ivory skin, was petite with straight brown hair, and was twenty-one years old, I believe. She was single and had a son. *She's kinda like me, young and has a child…She's still single; I'm here to help her.*

"Hello, I need you to come over here and lie down on this exam table so I can do your test. First of all, I want you to know that the test doesn't hurt at all. I'll explain everything to you as we go."

The patient did not make eye contact with me. She did not respond. She remained in the wheelchair and said nothing.

"I need you to get out of your wheelchair and come over here with your head on this pillow so I can do your test," I repeated politely because perhaps she hadn't understood me. I gave her the benefit of the doubt.

Again, she did not respond.

Then I explained how her doctor wanted us to do the EEG so he could help her. I told her I wanted to get the information that he needed so *I* could help her. I continued speaking to her politely and more professionally.

She still did not respond.

I had to make a decision. *I've tried to get her to cooperate. She won't do it. And I can't force her. I'm done.*

I walked out of the room, went to talk to the secretary, and told her about the situation. "I can't do the EEG. She won't cooperate. Please tell her nurse and send her back to her room."

Soon the patient was taken back to the unit. The physician was notified and understood that we were unable to do the test. All that information was documented. Everyone agreed that there was nothing left for us to do.

I realized that this patient had issues. I could certainly relate to her because I had issues, too. However, one of her issues was different from mine. Her boyfriend had broken up with her. I could relate to that. She did not want to live without him. I couldn't relate to that. In fact, she'd cut her wrist—attempted suicide. At twenty-one, she was so depressed, she wanted to end her life. I couldn't relate to that. I never wanted to kill myself because a man didn't want me, no matter how depressed I was. That was the epitome of low self-esteem.

What kind of jerk is he? I thought. Then I realized *he* was not the patient; she was. What he did, why he did it, and whether he was a nice guy or a bum was not my concern. I had never met him—didn't know him. However, she was my patient. I was concerned about what she had done, why she did it, and how I could help her. I realized that the psychiatrist was responsible for her care—not me. However, I still wanted to do whatever I was able to do to help her.

She was my patient, had been assigned to me, and yet I could not help her. I had proven that. My goal was to do the best I could do with all my patients, understanding that my best would always be good enough. That was my attitude with her. But deep down within, I was not content to just dismiss this patient. "I can't do it" is what I had said, yet I began searching for answers, a way to get it done. *If she won't let me, I can't force her,* I thought, trying to convince myself. But I couldn't— wouldn't—let it go.

The next day, I went to my supervisor and asked, "Will you let me try one more time?"

With a confused look on her face, she said, "What will you do different from what you did yesterday?"

"I don't know. I just wanna try."

I had no idea what I would do or how I would do it—no idea. But I had to try something different. Of course, I knew I could pray, which I did.

My supervisor looked at me again as if she wanted to drill me about the patient, but she didn't ask me any more questions. She just said, "Yes, you can try again."

When the patient arrived the second time, I wheeled her into the lab, but this time, I closed the door. I just wanted to talk to her. I had no idea what I was going to say. I would have to figure that out.

Instead of standing in front of her, I sat on the examination table and looked at her, trying to figure out what I would say. She was looking down at the floor. I wanted her to lift her head up and look at me so I could connect with her.

I started talking. "I read your chart, and I know what you did and why you did it. I want you to know his mama ain't the only one who has a son. (It wasn't the way I typically spoke to patients, but that's what came out naturally.) "I understand how hard it is on us girls when we want a man who doesn't want us," I added. "That's happened to me. I know how you feel."

She said nothing. It wasn't working, but I wasn't done.

"I know you have a little boy. He needs you. The truth is, I don't know anything about your son. Not really. But I would bet he is healthy. I'll bet he has eyes to see, ears to hear, legs and feet to walk on. I'll bet he is not sick, not disabled. I have no way of knowing, but I just feel I'm right about that. But as healthy as he probably is, he needs you. He depends on you to take care of him. He is only a child, and *you* are his mother. What do you think would happen to him if you had killed yourself? Now your boyfriend, he would go on about his business and find another young lady to take your place in a heartbeat. Not your son—he has only one mother. He would suffer beyond measure without you. Do you want that for your son?"

She began to cry.

I'm reaching her, I thought.

I continued talking. "I don't know where you live, but I'll bet you and your son have a roof over your heads, a place to call home. The way I see it, you have *so* much to live for. So, why would you worry about hanging on to somebody you love who doesn't love you, who doesn't want you? I don't understand that."

The tears were streaming down her face faster, but still she did not speak.

"I don't know exactly how to say this, so I'll just say it. [I paused briefly.] I don't know you, but I love you. I do love you because you are my sister in a way. *In God's family.* I really want to help you just as much as I would help someone in my own family. *You* deserve better, and your son needs you to get help. Please, let me help you?"

She began crying like a baby. This time, she responded. She looked up at me, got up from the wheelchair, and said, "Tell me what you want me to do. I'll do it."

I completed the patient's EEG test that day. Her test was normal. And everything went well. My parting words were, "I will never forget you. I'm sure you will never forget me."

She gave me a big hug and said, "You're right. I will never forget you."

When she returned to the psychiatric unit, the nurse called the department, talking about the change in her. Now she was cooperating with them for all the other tests she had refused.

The nurse called my supervisor and asked, "What happened in the EEG lab?"

My boss told her that somehow I had convinced her to undergo the test. My thought was, *That was an assignment. God's business happened in the EEG lab.*

The Sorry Woman

"**Y**our patient is here," the transporter announced as she wheeled a middle-aged, pleasant-looking lady into my lab. She was the picture of class. Her skin was ivory, her makeup refined, and her hair a beautiful gray. It was short and curled; it looked as if she had come to the hospital straight from the beauty shop. (I didn't want to mess up her hair.) My impression was that she was clearly a beautiful lady—only, that impression would change when our conversation revealed something ugly inside her beautiful exterior.

"Hi, my name is Rosie. I'm going to put electrodes on your head because I will monitor your brain activity in surgery." I continued to explain the process of making marks on her head and attaching electrodes with glue to provide perfect contact and therefore a reliable study.

The patient interrupted me. "You're gonna do it?" she asked with a frown.

Oh my—there's something wrong with this picture.

"Yes. I have worked with your doctor for many years. We're a great team." *I know what she's thinking. How do I handle this? Be very nice and reassuring. You know what to do.* I looked at her with a bright, sincere smile and said, "We will take good care of you. I promise."

She looked at me, frowned again, rolled her eyes, and just sat there with a look of defiance.

She really doesn't want me to work with her. OK, I just have to get this done.

I proceeded as if it were a normal procedure with a pleasant patient. "I'll need you to come over to this cart and put your head on this pillow. Are you able to walk all right?"

With that, the frown on her face turned to a blatant grimace as she got out of the wheelchair and followed my instructions. She looked like she was furious. With the most pleasant voice, I pretended to deny what I was feeling (that she was prejudiced!) and began to explain every detail of the recording process. I continued with my role in the operating room and how many years I had been working at the hospital. Most important, I emphasized how the surgeon and I had a great working relationship.

I hope that makes her feel better, I thought. *Doesn't she understand that I wouldn't be allowed in the operating room if I hadn't proven myself? What is her deal? It doesn't matter. She is my patient, and I am here to help her. I will treat her like family because that's what I do.*

I continued to prepare her, explaining how I would record her brain activity in the operating room. After the setup was completed, she was put on a cart and transferred to the holding area for assessment and final preparation for surgery. Finally, she was transferred to the operating room. I was there when they brought her in, ready to focus and use my skills to help her.

The patient was transferred from a cart to the surgical table. As the anesthesiologist and nurses were doing their jobs, I went over to attach the electrode connector and start the recording process. Of course, I wore a surgical mask, but she recognized me, and what she said hurt me to my core.

"Oh, it's *you!*" she scoffed.

Oh my God! I haven't done anything wrong. I just tried to bend over backward to get her to trust me. Why doesn't she trust me? Why won't she trust the doctor, the hospital? What's wrong with her? She's about to have an operation. She needs to have a positive attitude with everyone— including me. I wanted to cry for her—*and* for me because this was ugly.

What if something bad happens and I'm the one who has to help her? Then what? I hesitated as I rejected that hostile thought. *I am a woman of integrity and will do all I can to help her. That is what I do.*

Finally, we came to the critical part of the case. My experience and expertise were needed most when her carotid artery was clamped to remove the plaque. I had obtained a baseline recording of her EEG in my lab and in the operating room with continuous recording. Everyone in the room was prepared for changes that would require the placement of a bypass shunt.

Most often, there isn't a need for shunting, so I was prepared for smooth sailing without any problems. But that's not what happened. The patient's brain was not handling the clamping process and thus began to change. One side of her brain was slow, like it was deprived of oxygen.

Immediately, I spoke up loud and clear and was delighted that I had an opportunity to help her. I smiled with relief as the bypass shunt was placed, her brain activity returned to normal, and she was clearly doing well. No longer did I care about her attitude toward me. I focused on what I could do for her. The operation went well, and so it was well with my soul.

I returned to my department and prepared to see the patient one last time in the recovery room. The last phase was to remove the electrodes. The truth: I was delighted she was OK, but I didn't want to see her frown at me again—didn't want it at all. So, I had attitude. *I'm ready to be done with her.*

I went to her bedside, explained in a pleasant and professional manner the process of removing the electrodes, and told her what she should expect when she shampooed her hair. She did not respond. *OK,* I thought.

After I finished rubbing her scalp with a solvent and removing the electrodes, I said, "Good luck to you," and walked away. I was done.

But she wasn't. Just as I was leaving, she said, "Hey, come here."

I went back, looked at her, and just listened. She grabbed my hand and said, "I'm sorry about the way I treated you. That was wrong." She looked as if she wanted to cry. For sure, tears welled up in my eyes as I thought of how painful that was for me but how God had clearly taught both of us a lesson I believed we would not forget.

As I held her hand, I just smiled while I held back the tears and said, "It's all right. Take care."

Full of joy, I walked away. I thought about how something or someone in her past must have hurt her, and she judged me to be like "them." This day was different. I don't believe it was just a coincidence. I believe that I had witnessed it all as another tool for the mission God had set for me.

The Man Who Loved, Loved, Loved Me

These kinds of "assignments" occurred more times than I can remember. Years later, it was time to do an EEG on another patient. Only, it wasn't just "another patient." I have done thousands of patients over forty years in my career. Each of them has been different in one way or another. *We are all a little different in one way or another.* This patient was unique in a way I never could have imagined. I was surprised, to say the least.

When this pleasant man, about ten years my senior, arrived in our department, I greeted him, told him my name, and asked him to tell me his name. I had read the physician's orders on the chart and found all the pertinent information. Now ready to start the test, I wheeled him back to my lab.

I prepared him for the recording by thoroughly explaining the procedure and applying electrodes to his head. Then he started talking to me about a lot of interesting issues. I was quite interested in what he was saying. It was obvious he felt comfortable talking to me, which was great. But I had to end the conversation when it was time to start phase two, the recording portion of the EEG. He was supposed to keep his eyes closed, keep movements to a minimum, and remain quiet unless he deemed it urgent to speak.

While I was recording, I thought about what he had said, how he appeared somewhat tentative about one subject, as if trying to see if I would be receptive to what he had to say. I have found when something out of the norm happens in my life, it happens for a reason bigger than I am. Basically, I figured that what he had to say was for both of us. He had a message to deliver, and I had a message to hear.

I completed his test, removed the electrodes and conductive paste from his scalp, and sent for a transporter to return him to his room. We waited together.

Finally, there was time to listen to what he had to say. He had my undivided attention as he told me more of his story. "I died twice," he began. He explained in detail how he had died. "I saw people frantically working with me, trying to bring me back," he continued. "I could see what my wife was going through. I wanted to assure her that everything was OK. I saw light, and it was very peaceful."

He saw light. He saw his wife. The only thing that he wanted to change was to let her know he was OK.

I was eager to hear his story, so I did not interrupt. When he stopped talking, I asked him what he thought it all meant. He then told me he was a Christian and began to talk to me about his faith and another subject I am passionate about: racial discrimination. I told him that I was also a Christian, but I had not shared my passion about humanity with him. Yet, he clearly wanted to share his passion with me. What he said *and* what he did next blew me away.

Lying on the cart, he lifted his head, gazed into my eyes, and grabbed my hands, holding them firmly. He started talking to me about something different from his near-death experiences. And while he was talking so passionately, I thought to myself, *I wish I could get a picture of this: the look on his face and the unity of a sister and brother who are so different yet so much alike. I wish I could capture this moment because this is beautiful!*

As he held my hands in his hands, he said something loud and clear: "I *love* you." He gripped more and said it again. "I *love* you." A third time, and even more emphatically, he said, *"I love you!"*

Wow—what? But I could hear him loud and clear. His face was sincere, and so was his grip.

It was time for him to go. The transporter was at the door, but my patient was on a roll, and I was eager to hear the entire story he had clearly been sent to share with me. As the transporter waited, he continued, "You know, there is no difference between me and you—no difference. We are the same. We have the *same* DNA. I've just been bleached out a little bit, but we are the same inside. We have the same DNA," he repeated several times, at least three.

"You know, I just don't understand why people are so prejudiced," he continued. "I don't get that. And instead of things getting better, they're getting worse. It is awful how prejudiced people are who discriminate against others just because of the color of their skin." He talked about several situations he deemed to be racist problems. He went on to say even more. "Sure, I've done some bad things. You've done some bad things. But we all came from the same place."

What does he mean, "We all came from the same place"? What does he mean, "We all have the same DNA"? No, we don't. We all have different DNA, I thought. I had to let him go. But as it turned out, he was a volunteer at the hospital and I would see him in passing again.

As I pondered what this patient had told me, I realized what he was talking about. First, we were from the human race. Period. He and I spoke the same language. The passion he had for racial equality and his disdain for racism, regardless of whom it was against, was amazing. From what he told me about his life, I could see that he was my brother. Based on how God works in my life, I know it was not a coincidence that he just happened to share his story with me. I will never forget him. I thank God for sending him to let me know I'm on the right track in my quest to write this story. I pray you get the message as you continue to read.

Yes, we have the same DNA from God, who created DNA.

However, I decided to do more research. This is what I found: "We all have DNA with the same structure, but there are slight variations in our DNA that make us unique."

What is God's DNA? DNA, in layman's terms, is the "blueprint" of inherited genetic molecular material for our unique identities. Our DNA comes from the combination of genes contributed by each of our biological parents. When there is a question regarding a child's parentage, a paternity test, using blood samples from one or both parents, is taken. The result of this test undeniably reveals a child's biological parents through their similar DNA structure.

Humans can reproduce only human life, but the Holy Spirit gives new life from heaven. When we received the gift of eternal life through our acceptance of Jesus Christ as our Lord and Savior, God breathed new life into us, bringing a spiritual birth. At that moment, we received heavenly DNA into our souls in the form of the Holy Spirit. Now we possess two sets of DNA—one physical set from our earthly parents and one spiritual from our heavenly parent.

With God's DNA inside of us, the divine life of God grows. Now, we are radically different from the rest of the world. We are all part of a distinct race. We resemble our heavenly Father as evidenced by our new Christ-like attitudes, motivations, perspectives, desires, goals, and godly value system. We have a deep desire to be a blessing to others as God has been a blessing to us.

After our spiritual births, we are connected eternally to God in such a way that no matter what happens in our futures, our heavenly genetic link to him will not be broken. How can this be? Think about this:

Is it scientifically possible to remove the DNA connection we have with our earthly parents? No, because new scientific breakthroughs in molecular research have proven DNA can't be completely removed or dramatically altered due to its complex structure.

Is it spiritually possible to remove God's DNA from our souls once we are born again? No. We are linked eternally to him in such a way that no matter what happens in our futures, our heavenly genetic link to God can't be broken.

In other words, we won't lose or cut our eternal link with God. But we can break our relationship with him. How? By turning our backs on him in rebellion, similar to what sons or daughters do when they choose to disown their birth family. They may never see their family again, but whatever they do or wherever they go, it will never change the fact they have a DNA connection to their biological parents. They are still family members, if only through their shared DNA.

So, if we ever think we've done something to lose eternal life and our spiritual position as a member of God's family, we need to ask ourselves this question: How can I undo my spiritual DNA or my spiritual birth or my salvation? The answer is, *I can't. You can't. We can't.* We all have the same DNA.[1]

In this chapter I've shared three real-life connections I will never forget. What an awesome picture revealing what matters the most in life—love. Of all we do and of all we have in life, the best gift we have is the present. We have received unconditional love; and each day, we have the opportunity to give the gift of love to others.

"And now abideth faith, hope, charity, these three; but the greatest of these is charity" (I Corinthians 13:13).

---

[1] Excerpts taken from Kathleen Brown's "God's DNA the Holy Spirit." For more information, please visit www.spiritualsurvivor.org.

Covering the Past

*"Those who are lifting the world upward and onward
are those who encourage more than criticize."*
—*Elizabeth Harrison*

In the Beginning

In the beginning, God decided that two women should become friends. We were totally different in so many ways but so alike in more important ones.

You know, I can't even remember the first time I was introduced to or recognized Rosie. We had both been going to the same church for a long time before we ever connected. I remember seeing her and her husband, David, around the church. David had a BBQ restaurant, and I had even eaten there on several occasions. Rosie, I remember, always had a smile on her face and just seemed to be real, and although I didn't really know her, I admired her from afar.

One summer, I decided to take the summer off from teaching summer school. I just "happened" to have been on several trips to teach discipleship in the past. The person who was supposed to go on a discipleship trip to Dallas, Texas, just "happened" to end up with a conflict and had to cancel. Another person on the team just "happened" to call me and see if I would be willing to go on the trip with less than two weeks' notice. I just "happened" to have that time totally free and to have the money for the trip. That is how it all really started. Coincidence? I think not.

When the trip started, all I knew was that I was going to Dallas. I knew how many people were going and what lessons I was responsible for teaching. When you travel for several hours in a van pre-iPod era, you either sit in silence or you end up chatting with those you are traveling with. So, of course, the conversations commenced.

I think we were about halfway to Dallas. Rosie and I had been talking about the trip, when she pointed out that we were going to a "black church." Now, let me explain something and be totally honest. I was TOTALLY unnerved, and here is why: I am a nearly six-feet-tall, blond-haired white girl who had never stepped foot in a "black church" and knew that the culture of the church was going to be different from what I was used to. Being a very organized, analytical type, I don't always deal with the unknown so well. Yep, I know…and don't worry; God has definitely dealt with me in this area. I like to know what to expect so I am prepared, and I generally do have a plan A, B, and C.

The issue wasn't that the church was black. It could have been a church predominately made up of Latinos or Russians, and I would have had the same angst in my gut. I had all of four hours to mentally prepare for something different with an unknown element. The last thing I wanted was to do something wrong or embarrass the church I was representing on this trip. Apparently, Rosie picked up on my emotional distress pretty quickly (since faking my emotions is not a strong suit of mine). "Krista, just stay close to me, do what I do, stand when I stand, clap when I clap. You will be fine." Those words immediately put me at ease, and I then stuck to her like glue for the entire trip.

Rosie may have eventually regretted those words or thought I wouldn't take them literally, but I did. If she would have literally run away, I would have chased her down at that point. But if you haven't figured it out by now, let me explain. Rosie is a five-feet-tall black woman who is twenty years my senior. So, I knew if I followed her directions, I would be fine…and I was. Of course, during this time on the trip, we learned many things about each other. It is hard not to learn about someone when you are making sure you are stuck to her like glue! Rosie gained even more of my respect when, at one point during the trip, one of our members was having "the crankies." We were all kind of tired of it and just wished the person would be quiet. Rosie finally spoke up, and I remember thinking, *Uh-oh, how is this going to play out?*

Rosie ever so gently worded it in a way that let the person know that it was time to stop complaining and at the same time did not embarrass the person. That skill…I was in awe of. I even thought to myself, *If that were me that she had just said that to, I think I would have hugged her and thanked her for the gentle rebuke.* I was so impressed! At this point in my career, I was a teacher working with the emotionally disturbed population at the high-school level, so any time a person can correct with that kind of grace, I take note of it!

On the drive back home, I asked Rosie about her salvation. She then began laying out her testimony. I was enthralled for hours. In my day, especially in my field of work, I had heard it all. I have worked with many drug abusers, mentally disturbed clients, and abused children in every way imaginable, BUT I had never known someone who had been raised in that kind of environment, had gone through the abuse she had, AND had pulled it together—had gotten her education, had a very good job, was happily married and, most importantly, was saved and living a righteous life. I remember thinking, *None of us has an excuse to not do what is right. If Rosie can make it through all of that and be the Christian she is with such a positive spirit, there is just no reason for me to ever complain or choose to do what is not right!* It was one of those moments in life when you KNOW God is saying, "Take note—I am teaching you something right now," and you know you had better follow directions.

Once we returned from the trip, "life" happened, and we all got back into our normal routines. But something was different. Now, at this point, Rosie and I were not the best of friends, nor did we start hanging out together after this, but we did talk more when we ran into each other, and I knew this had all happened for a reason. As time went on, there were many things that I noticed about Dave and Rosie. At this time, I was one of the leaders for discipleship at my church, and I was in charge of matching up ladies who wanted to go through our discipleship ministry with ladies who were willing to be the disciples. Dave and Rosie had always been involved in this ministry, and I KNEW that if you were discipled by them, you were a very blessed person. As a person who had a leadership role in this area, I always knew I could count on them to communicate any issues. They were responsible and always followed through.

A few years had passed since our Dallas discipleship trip when Rosie had taken me under her wing. Rosie was in Shepherd School (our church's four-year Bible institute), and she was getting ready to do her dissertation. Rosie told me that she was going to do hers on neurotheology, which she explained was the mind–spirit connection. Rosie is a neurodiagnostic technologist at a large local hospital. She has been studying the brain most of her entire adult life and sees the spiritual connection between our brain and how we choose to handle emotional issues, specifically forgiveness. Part of the findings in her dissertation would be based on information she was collecting via surveys she would distribute to people about their forgiveness issues. She asked me if I would be willing to pass some out to people I knew and then get them back to her. I told her I would be happy to do this for her. This is where part two of our relationship really took off.

After getting the surveys back to Rosie, and in the process of writing her dissertation, she sent me a copy for my feedback. Honestly, I can't remember if I just offered to edit or if she asked me, but as a teacher and someone who had taught English for several years, I was EXCITED to use this knowledge in a way to glorify God. Who would have thought you could use your skills in English for that? So the editing began. I don't know if Rosie knew what she was in for. I edited wording, spelling, and grammar. You name it; I was on it. There were lots of e-mails back and forth. Once the edits were done, she turned it in and, of course, she earned an A. She had done her research, and it was a topic that no one we know personally had tackled in this manner from the neurological standpoint.

Rosie and Dave saw this information as a tool to minister to others. It was very clear that many people were in bondage to unforgiveness and bitterness. They were allowing it to take root and stunt their spiritual growth. There was a true need to educate people as to how they could be free from this, IF they chose to take those biblical steps. From this came the Fruit of Forgiveness ministry.

Rosie took the material from her dissertation and created two things: a workbook that could be used by people on a personal level and a book that expounded on her dissertation, encompassing all of that material, her findings and research, and medical information about the brain and how it functions in relationship to our emotions. As this process was beginning, I began helping with the editing process again. There were day-long conferences at which I was allowed to help present. After each one, I would always identify ways to make something sound better, a little clearer, and so on. I don't think that process ever ends. It is the teacher in me.

During the last years since writing her dissertation, Rosie and I have really developed our bond. She and I enjoy exercise, and we started going for walks occasionally versus going out to eat. I love the walks. We are guaranteed at least an hour and a half of uninterrupted time to talk. God is always the focus of those conversations. Even if we are encountering trials, our talk always comes back around to how to deal with it as God would want us to. We have never been the type of friends who just tells each other what we think the other wants to hear. One thing I love about our relationship is that we can totally disagree about something and never have an ill feeling toward the other person. We are always willing to listen to the other's feedback and consider it. I love the fact that when you look at our upbringings and look at us physically, we are about as opposite as you can get, but it just doesn't matter because our foundation is the same...our love for God and his Word.

We joke about how God just made us friends…and he did! We couldn't have planned this if we wanted to. We aren't the type of women who have to talk on the phone every day. In fact, we might not talk for a couple of weeks, but that is OK; we are totally secure in our friendship with each other. When we attended the same church, we didn't have to sit together or make a point to talk or fear that the other person's feelings were hurt.

There were many times throughout all of the edits when Rosie would bounce an idea off me, and my response would be in total alignment with the direction that she saw God leading her. Other times, I could point out something from my perspective that she had not even considered. I love that she is always honest with me and has my best "God-interest" at heart.

Our relationship is like a puzzle. There are many pieces that fit together, but they are put into place one piece at a time. You know when you start a puzzle and you see all of the pieces, and you KNOW they go together but you aren't sure how? Well, that is how I have felt since I got in that van with Rosie and headed to Dallas. I saw one piece fit into place and thought, *Hmm, how is this going to look when it is completed?*

You know, I am sure that it is still not complete. Maybe in this lifetime, the puzzle will never have every piece in place, but the edges are done, and most of the pieces are in place. I see the big picture, and I know that it is beautiful. Maybe I can't see every detail, but that is OK because God knows exactly what it will look like when it is complete. What I do know is that as each piece continues to go into its special spot, our friendship deepens, and that is a good thing!

Do I think that our friendship is perfect? I know better than that; there isn't one that is. Any relationship worth having has trials and obstacles, but it also has joy and peace. Each trial and obstacle, when overcome, brings more of that joy and peace we long for. I sit back, and I see the trials in life and the many circumstances that had to happen in order for Rosie's and my relationship to have even formed in the first place, let alone continue as it has. And I am in awe of God…of his perfect timing, of his perfect love for us, and for his many blessings…one of which I call Rosie!

—Krista Connell

My New Friend

David and I had participated in many discipleship confer-ences—local, out of town, and even out of the country. One particular trip stands out among the best—the Dallas conference. With each conference, there were many things that happened to the members of the church to rejoice about and learn from. I had no idea that when I agreed to be a part of the team, a myriad of changes would happen in my life just because of one friendship God had ordered for me. Her name is Krista.

What we had in common was what God had called us to do together as friends, only we didn't realize that at the time. He was unfolding his plan for our friendship before our eyes. There were no holds barred in our conversation. Krista seemed delighted, which made me feel receptively delighted.

When I look back at our relationship, I agree with Krista. Our friendship has been like a puzzle that has now developed into a beautiful picture. As we have "put together" the insight of diversity, the story has revealed a picture that many people never see, never understand because of deception, of tunnel vision. We understand how life's trials can completely change to joy as we focus on our Father. When that happens, the picture of God's Providence becomes crystal clear.

Yes, it was many years ago, but that memory is with me forever. There was a time when I wanted to choose my own friends, but such friendships were forbidden because of the color of their skin. Seriously. I found that quite disturbing but did not want to rock the boat. That is the way I thought when I was a child. I am an adult now and will not allow that to happen.

The friendship between Krista and me completely rectified what had been taken away from me when I was a child. Not only is it resolved, but it is healed. Without a doubt, our relationship was a divine intervention. It has fueled my mind and my heart with tangible proof of my passion about humanity, prejudice, and the proof of how much our Father loves us equally. Although our coverings are different, God made us friends. He made us friends not only for personal reasons but also to reveal the tapestry of his humanity. This brings him glory!

Forgiveness

It is wonderful to look at the past and see healing. I recall the day of the carnival when I was just a little girl. I was so angry about being hurt so badly just because I wanted to have fun with my friend. I held on to these grudges for so many years.

Then one day, I repented about my thoughts against Sam—perhaps he had been abused in the same way he had hurt me. Yet, at the same time, I felt justified in my thoughts. Then my mind traveled down a different road—a hostile road. *I want to get back at him. Cancer isn't enough. I want to hurt him myself. I want to make him pay for what he did to me,* I raged inside. He died about a year later. He was gone forever, and I never had a chance to make him pay for what he had done to me. I was angry!

After a while, I realized there was another problem—not with him but with me. Even though he had hurt me, just how much I hated him really bothered me. Something about hating him was as wrong as what he had done to me. And deep inside, I knew it.

I was trying to be a positive person, trying to put this all behind me. Still, I couldn't put my finger on exactly *why* I couldn't just forget about it. After all, he was dead, physically out of my life forever. But emotionally, he held on to me through my conflicting hatred and guilt.

I tried to tell myself that life goes on. I had to let go of the past and move on. But that wasn't happening, and I wasn't able to make it happen—not at all.

Many years had gone by, and I had become a devoted leader in my church in Rockville. Teaching Sunday school was one of my responsibilities. I loved to teach, and the members appreciated all the lessons I taught the children. Actually, I felt teaching was my innate gift. I loved to study and learn creative ways to get biblical points across. It brought joy to my heart to realize that I could help people understand the Bible so they could live happier lives.

One day, I was preparing a message titled "Forgiveness" to present at my church. I was to present it at a special evening service. As I contemplated what I would say, my own unresolved forgiveness issues surfaced. Suddenly I realized I was not practicing what I was about to teach. I felt like a hypocrite.

How can I honestly and effectively teach the congregation when hostile feelings litter my heart? I can't do it.

My conscience troubled me. I couldn't rest. I knew I was wrong. But I didn't know how to ignore what was troubling me deep within. I felt trapped, entangled in hatred. I remembered vividly how he had hurt me. I couldn't shake it off. It was like emotional warfare, an internal losing battle. I kept fighting my feelings and looking for ways to forgive and forget only to remember and hate again.

It was wrong to hate anyone, for any reason; I understood that. Trying to make myself stop hating him was quite a different story. I could not just say, "I forgive you," and have it happen like magic. I tried to convince myself that forgiving was the right thing to do. However, that didn't work—not in words and certainly not in deeds. Spiritual warfare is what was really happening. I had to change the way I was thinking. But I had no idea *how* to forgive. After several days of talking about it with my friends, I realized exactly what the problem was.

I had to cry out to God to show me how to do what was unnatural, what I was unable to do on my own. I had to understand that there was only one way I could do that, only one way I could end the struggle. I had already tried to simply dismiss the whole thing and hope everything would be all right, but something within me wouldn't let me rest until I learned and did the right thing: forgive the unforgivable. How was I supposed to love and not hate? How could I change the way I was thinking and feeling? It took months for me to stop harboring the bitterness. But I did stop. Starting with the truth of God's word and mandates about forgiveness, I began to pray about the application of the messages found in the Bible. The solution at that time was healing.

Pleasing my Father by forgiving those people I came in contact with who had hurt me and living a life of integrity—becoming a living Epistle to be read by people everywhere—became my objective. I knew that for certain. Determined to resolve the conflict within, I endeavored to figure out how to do the right thing.

That is exactly what I did! And this is the story of how it happened.

"Please, God," I asked. "Help me understand why this happened to me. I am so sorry for my vengeful desires. I want to learn how to forgive him." Daily, I prayed for God to help me, and he did. He showed me that my anger wasn't hurting the man who hurt me. It was hurting *me*. I had no peace—just guilt, shame, and displeasure, knowing that that was just a step along the way. Then, one day, I got it! I understood exactly what I needed to do.

I decided to go back there, back to the house where it had all happened—not literally to the house but to all the details of that day in my memory and thoughts. I would go back there with a new attitude. That was the plan. My goal was to revisit that day from God's point of view.

Using my mind to recreate the situation, I went back. This time, I could see the situation with transformed vision. As I prayed, I felt myself returning to that old house emotionally and spiritually. I visualized myself in that very room and at the spot where I was hurt so badly. As I recalled that evening, I could see my mama's boyfriend hurting me just as it had happened that day. Oh, how it hurt to relive that day! I was furious at how he had hurt me physically and emotionally and how he had gotten away with it. That was hard, very hard—at the beginning.

It was easy to remember what he had done and what my mama had done and had not done. What was missing was the *why* and *who* behind all the hostility, violence, and pain. That was the missing link I needed to put this behind me at last and to close the door on what continued to hurt me years afterward. I finally understood *my* problem.

I had the final piece of the puzzle. Now I knew that I had been divinely enlightened. I understood that I had what I needed to be victorious in this situation: a brain with indelible memories and an insatiable desire to change—but this time to change for the right reason. I realized, in essence, I could rewrite the script. *What a powerful idea!*

As I share this story of my journey and path to healing through forgiveness, Job comes to mind. What trials he went through as a blameless and upright man! "There was a man in the land of Uz, whose name was Job; and that man was perfect and upright, and one that feared God, and eschewed evil." (Job 1:1).

Job's suffering was much worse than mine. Yet, what stands out to me is why he suffered. It was Satan's scheme that God permitted. As if losing all his possessions and his family weren't enough, he had another problem. Job's friends turned their backs on him and accused him of lying about why he was going through a horrific time of trials in his life. He didn't know all the details and was defensive about it. He didn't realize that what had happened to him was Satan's scheme that God permitted. As Job continued to try to fight his own battle, his friends continued to falsely accuse him of having some unconfessed sin. Finally, when he turned to God for answers, his life changed. He learned how to forgive when he stopped believing the deceptive messages from Satan, the father of lies. Then he could hear and trust the messages from God. Then he was empowered with the sovereign message from the Creator of the universe.

Job repented about his attitude. And *after* he repented about *his* actions and reactions, God dealt with his friends who had falsely accused him of some secret sin in his life. After all Job had been through, losing everything he had, he changed his mind. He took his eyes off himself and, as I would sum it up, decided to rewrite the script.

Job 42:10 reads, "And the lord turned the captivity of Job when he prayed for his friends; also the lord gave Job twice as much as he had before." Wow! Job must have been compassionate and merciful toward his friends. Then he repented. After repentance and forgiveness came restoration. That was the turning point at which God restored everything he had lost.

I hadn't done that. No mercy came from my heart for Sam, who was a human being whom God loved so much that he sent his son to die for him. I extended no mercy or grace to Sam, only justice and revenge. Not understanding God's plan for my life had been hindering me from knowing how to forgive according to his standards.

My eyes opened to see the truth. I prayed, "God, help me. Please help me understand what I'm supposed to do when I return to that room where I was hurt so badly." Then, with my mind's eye, I looked up and saw Jesus Christ standing there above us in the kitchen. There was a sad look upon his face, an expression of love and empathy in his eyes as they followed Sam's, Mama's, and my actions. To my surprise, he did not feel sad only for me but for each of us involved in this incident. I had been enlightened; I had a new way of thinking.

At that very moment, I stopped focusing on the incident, on what had happened to me in the kitchen that day. Instead, I reflected on what had happened to Jesus Christ as he was dying on the cross, the ultimate in unjust, unfair treatment. In my heart, I heard him pray to God about the men who were crucifying him on the cross: "Father, forgive them, for they know not what they do" (Luke 23:34). He said that about his enemies as they were trying to destroy him. This intentional act is what I heard in my heart about Mama and her boyfriend: *Forgive them, for they knew not what they were doing to an innocent little girl. Satan was trying to destroy all of us.*

I understand why this happened to me, I asserted within as a sense of unequivocal calm and peace enveloped me. *Mama and Sam could not understand the magnitude of the pain that I felt and would continue to experience. They did not have serenity and love deep within their hearts if they could hurt me that way. People who are destructive within reflect destruction. People who are serene within reflect seren-ity,* I thought. I had acquired a forgiveness tool—a different perspective.

I knew what I needed to do, and I understood exactly how I needed to do it. I needed to pray and trust God's clear direc-tion. I was ready to share this divine message with anyone and everyone God had prepared to hear it. I was ready to forgive and not feel like a phony. I was determined to help the people in my church and everywhere to see the light of God shining through Satan's darkness.

I have been asked if Sam ever apologized for hurting me. The answer to that question is no. But, you see, that was not *my* issue—not at all. My issue was that I had been disobedient by har-boring grudges and trying to justify my actions, pretending that it was OK. It was not OK. Now I could see mercy and grace per-sonified in not just this situation but in all forgiveness situations. It's one thing to read the Bible. It's another thing to obey the Word, to surrender to God, and to follow his plan. I wanted to please him by refusing to fight with the weapons of vengeance. The Word of God became my defense and offense—the Word is often referred to as the "Sword of the Spirit," which seems like an appropriate analogy. I realized that he knew it and that he enabled me to do through him what was impossible for me to do on my own—forgive those I considered unforgivable.

I was now prepared for the next step in the forgiveness process. I was in denial and still angry with my mama. I felt disappointed by her allowing me to suffer at the hands of her boyfriend. I real-ized that I needed to forgive her completely. I had been telling myself a half-truth about her, which I realized was a whole lie. I had to get it right. God heard the prayers of my heart, and again his wisdom became clear to me. So, I rested, knowing what had to be done. He already had plans for when, where, and how my mama and I could find forgiveness.

Shortly after realizing I had not forgiven her completely, Mama and I had a conversation that freed her of guilt and helped me to forgive her with all my heart, mind, and soul. She spoke first to my daughter, who was in the car with me and had been complaining about me. Mama said to her, "What if you had the kind of mother your mother had? *Your* mother is totally different. She gives you everything you need and takes care of you. What if you had a mother who was always gone, or whenever you did see her, she was drunk? You had better appreciate your mother, girl!" Full of anxiety and with tears streaming down her face, my mama said she had made many mistakes, some of which she could never erase.

Mama paused, turned around, looked at me, and said, "You're a good mother, Rosie—so different from me. I raised you kids the way I was raised. I did the best I could." She sobbed with tears rolling down her cheeks, her eyes red, and her countenance distorted.

I fought back the tears as she went on and on confessing and apologizing. I managed to touch her on the shoulder and waited to comfort her and ease her pain. Her honesty touched my heart and gave me the peace God wanted for me. I understood clearly that she needed to get a great deal of guilt off her chest to find peace within. When she stopped sobbing, I looked into her eyes and said, "It's all right, Mama. It's all right." The process of forgiveness for this hurt was complete.

Happiness hardly describes what I felt. What peace—what an awesome sense of relief! The pain of bitterness was over, and it was the first day of the rest of our lives together as friends.

Yes, friends. I released my mama from guilt that day. She was forgiven at that very moment, and she knew it. There was no turning back. I had learned the meaning of compassion, and it was pure joy!

I have often wondered how she must have felt. I ponder how she must have been agonizing within over all the things she had done that had affected my life. Now she had opportunities to tell me she loved me, knowing that I could echo those words back and mean them.

It had taken about twenty years for me to forgive Sam completely. I began to understand that God was and is no respecter of persons. "Then Peter opened his mouth, and said, Of a truth I perceive that God is no respecter of persons" (Acts 10:34).

The passion to forgive ignited a mission within me to stand up against the deceiver and stand out as an obedient servant of God. When I now think of that day when I was disappointed, brokenhearted, and wounded, I realize that I was not the only victim. Each of us had been deceived, hurt by an enemy who was not flesh and blood. Although each of us was hurting for different reasons, each of us also needed to rest in the loving arms of God. Not one of us was wise enough to understand that at the time.

I will never know what Mama and Sam were thinking to spark the abuse—never. I do know that *I* was hurt. But I also know that my mama and I enjoyed a good relationship from the day she apologized until the day she died. From what I knew of Sam, he never changed, which saddens me. You see, if he died without knowing Christ as his Savior, he is in hell, and forgiveness is out of his reach forever. That is a pain I wish for no one.

I remember hearing Mama say to Sam years before that horrible day, "You're a fool, and you will never change because a wise man will change, but a fool will never change." Her words to him were powerful and perhaps more profound than she could have known. "The fool hath said in his heart, There is no God" (Psalm 14:1). Flesh and blood did not reveal that to my mama. God did.

Sam's destiny and his repentance were not in my control. Forgiving him *was.* I understood it! Once blinded by the deceiver, the eyes of my heart were opened to the truth, and thus I understand that forgiveness is a commandment, a mandate from God.

Period. Following Christ as a Christian, I needed to understand what it meant to be Christ-like and forgive as he forgave.

Yes, I had been trapped in the bondage of unforgiveness, but now the chains of the bondage were broken. I was truly free to love the unlovable, not by my own strength but by the power of the Lord Jesus Christ, by his saving grace—for Christ's sake and to bring him glory.

As a new person empowered with wisdom from God, I decided to change the way I was thinking. My attitude became, "I have learned, in whatsoever state I am, therewith to be content" (Philippians 4:11). To fulfill my calling as a Christian—to live in forgiveness—is my insatiable desire. Here are a few more scriptures I carry in my heart to please God:

Know truth: "And ye shall know the truth, and the truth shall make you free" (John 8:32).

Embrace the Word: "Sanctify them through thy truth: thy word is truth" (John 17:17).

Obey my Father: "But I say unto you, Love your enemies, bless them that hate you, and pray for them which despitefully use you, and persecute you: That ye may be the children of your Father which is in heaven: for he maketh his sun to rise on the evil and on the good, and sendeth rain on the just and the unjust. For if ye love them which love you, what reward have ye" (Matthew 5:44–48).

I am certain that one day long ago, Sam wounded my body, but it was not possible for him to wound my soul. It was sealed, protected by my Abba Father, the Lord and Savior Jesus Christ. I did not realize it at the time, but God was teaching me about grace, preparing me for the future. He had a plan for that day. God knew that experiencing this hurt would allow me to help countless people for the sake of Jesus Christ's life. Jesus shed his blood as the ultimate act of forgiveness—the price he paid to redeem everyone who receives him.

❖ ❖ ❖

Color of Tears

When I was a little girl, Mama had convinced herself and tried to convince me that "white people don't like colored people." With the exception of some people, like people she worked with or had business relationships with, she suggested that they had hidden agendas. It didn't make any difference to her who they were—medical professionals, teachers, even pastors. She assumed they didn't care about her. She clung to her old attitude, at times refusing to go to a doctor because, as she told me, "Those white people just want my money. They don't care 'bout me. They don't mean me no good."

I told Mama that to say that *all* of them are horrible people was just not true. To me, thinking like that was unreasonable. It made no sense. Of course, I was careful with the words I used so as not to upset her. I explained how that was no more a fact than to say *all* black people would do the opposite—love her and strive to protect her.

Although I tried to convince her, the negative messages from her past must have been more powerful than my logic. She clung to her beliefs nearly all of her life. She seemed blinded by the facts of life that enslaved her mind. She was clinging to a misunderstanding.

My mother couldn't look beyond the faults of the white race to see the emotional scars of discrimination. To her, "we" were victims, and "they" were responsible, even though most of them were not alive and certainly were not responsible for the blatant racist acts that had happened in the past. Back then, she didn't see the picture of humanity that all people had in common. That would change.

Finally, while she was sick in the hospital in her final days of life, she got the message! Her attitude abruptly changed. One day out of the blue, without anyone talking about white people, she said to me, "Oh, Rosie, *they* are *so* nice. They help me, take good care of me, and I am grateful to God for them." With tears of joy in her eyes and the brightest smile on her face, she began to say their names—the doctors, nurses, and other staff at the hospital who were taking care of her. She seemed pleased and appeared amazed to finally get the big picture.

Mama acted as if, for the very first time in her life, she understood that there were nice people of a different race who genuinely cared about her. There were people who did not judge her by what was on the outside but rather by what was on the inside. There were people whose eyes had been opened to the fact that we are one human race with the need to love and be loved unconditionally.

I was so happy to know my mother got that message, saw the truth clearly! No longer was she in the dark. I had longed for her to get to that point since I was a child. Now, I could see her change right before my eyes. It was awesome!

But within a few months, she would be in heaven. There was no way for her to turn back the clock, to redeem the years that were now history. There was no way to make right the wrong done to her. Now she wasn't able to impact our family and our friends with the same kind of deception. No, there was no going back. So, I focused on the blessing of witnessing the transformation.

Mama had spent her seventy-five years bound by prejudice and that horrific disease of bitterness. I vowed to make a difference when and wherever I could.

What a shame that my mother's life was shaped by an overt discriminatory lifestyle she was born and raised in. No doubt, her parents taught her to fight back based on how *they* were treated. I understood that clearly as a child. But I longed for my mother to look beyond the darkness of the past and to focus on the possibilities of a brand new time when change was happening all around her.

If only she could have understood this years earlier. If only she could have understood what was wrong with *her* attitude about the people she thought were her enemies. If only she could have recognized that *the enemy* was not of flesh and blood but rather of powers and principalities.

You see, the enemy was and is *the deceiver*, the father of lies, the god of this world. Mama would have been free in her relationship with God. Her life could have been much happier, much healthier.

Mama's life had been tough. It makes me sad to think of the many times she probably cried out in desperation to live a good life. Surely, and finally, that happened. Both of us were products of our environment, ignorant in many ways with so much to learn. And even though Mama and I had mended our relationship, she still had the disease of bitterness until just weeks before she died of metastatic cancer.

There are countless people living in the darkness of deception. They cry because they need to understand and they need to be understood. They need to love and to be loved. Most of all, they need mercy and grace—not because they've been good but because God alone is good. He does not discriminate among his children. He understands where painful, heartbroken tears come from—and that they are the same: colorless.

Uncovering the Coverings

*"Though no one can go back and make a brand new start, any-
one can start from now and make a brand new ending."*
—*Carl Bard*

Lifetime Dreamers

I vividly remember distinct messages from my past. There are words and phrases indelibly written in my brain. There are also unforgettable messages I heard as a child, such as "one nation under God, indivisible, with liberty and justice for all," which must have made a big impression on my developing mind. It was the official motto of the United States of America: "In God we trust." That awesome declaration has impacted me deeply. There's no doubt I have also been influenced by the civil rights movement.

I witnessed what was happening before, during, and after hearing the "I Have a Dream" speech. I believe Dr. Martin Luther King received orders from our Father. I believe God instructed Dr. King to remind the nation of the need to change the way we were thinking: We should not judge people "by the color of their skin, but by the content of their character." Only God could have called him out to impart those mountaintop messages to all races.

I had a dream, too. With the deepest of passions, I had a dream. Only a few people knew about my dream—a few family members and friends. Frustrated with what was going on, I had what I thought was a novel idea, a new approach to reach the same objective. I set out to become what I called a true minority, a person who would look beyond the skin covering and see that which is within. Speaking out against racism and making a difference in my own little world became my objective. Sharing it with the world was my ultimate goal.

Growing up in a racist society, I was disturbed by the mutual bigotry between those I knew. I could see the difference in attitudes toward people who were clearly narrow-minded and prejudiced and favored the people who looked like they look, justifying their actions both good *and* bad. However, they justified their disdain for those who were born of a different race, even when they were clearly the innocent party. It was clear that the issue was prejudice. People seemed to not understand or simply refused to live by the Golden Rule. It was something most everyone knew, but following the rule only applied in certain situations. It was an "us" versus "them" mentality.

I remember the "WHITES ONLY" and "COLORED ONLY" signs of the past. These signs revealed the blatant racism that made it hard to be accepted, to be understood, and definitely to be loved by the other race. These messages evoked fear, sadness, bitterness, and vengeful desires against people—against humanity.

Any time people are judged based on their skin covering, it is unacceptable to God. So, in order for this horrific problem plaguing our world to be recognized, understood, and rectified, we need to change the way we think.

My mission was crystal clear. Step one was to start with the one person I could control—myself. That is what I did. My goal was to become assertive in this area, albeit with a gentle spirit. Saint Francis of Assisi wrote, "Tell them. If necessary, use words." *Actions speak louder than words* became my plan to make a difference. Seeking wisdom became my prayer, searching for tools to make a difference in humanity, my passion, because I had a dream, too.

❖ ❖ ❖

The True Minorities

With my sights on bettering the human race, I thought about a minority mind-set and its impact on human-kind. I researched the lifestyles of minorities. I have included the information below.

Who are minorities, for example? I wanted to know. Right away I learned that the answer depends on who you ask. Some would say the minorities are the dark-skinned people, once called colored people, Negroes, blacks, and now African Americans. Based on countless documented facts, these people have been victims of horrific racial discrimination and hatred. Many have literally been murdered for minor mistakes simply because of the color of their skin. These people would say adamantly, "We are the minorities."

If you have read about some contemporary minorities, you might come to a different conclusion. If you live in South Africa and are white, you are considered a minority, albeit not in a negative way. This label is strictly based on population and not on lifestyle.

For example, the group called the White Minority is taking a stand not based on skin color but rather on their cause, based on their right to be different from all the other groups of people. They have what we might call a minority point of view.

If you are white, you may have been passed over and denied a job because of affirmative action. You might consider yourself a minority. After all, other people were given opportunities for higher education and therefore better jobs based on their status as a minority. Some nonminorities have described their positions as reverse discrimination. To them, *they* have been discriminated against. Therefore, they might say, "We are the minorities."

Many years ago, I came up with this idea: I wanted to become a minority among minorities. I could see how in a figurative and positive way, standing up for one's rights was not a bad thing. I even found myself so passionate about my new way of thinking that I wanted to present it to someone bigger than me. This person might see my point as plausible and want to take it to a national level. However, when I realized it was an overwhelming task, I decided to put it on the back burner.

That is what I did, for a while. But I never forgot about it. Never did I forget how important it was for me to share my heart with people about this matter. I really believed that this idea was sanctioned by my Father to benefit humankind as a whole.

The true minorities would literally become the minority of minorities in every sense of the word. They would oppose all forms of global discrimination, whether it was inflicted by those perceived as victims or perpetrators.

On a personal note, I wanted to show blacks and whites that we are all God's children, created in his image. And I wanted them to see how different their lives could become if they could see racism as an issue of narrow-mindedness. If only they could understand how to recognize the bondage of deception.

For years, I imagined pioneering an organization of people from all races, cultures, and ethnic backgrounds who would become single-minded. I envisioned the people joining this group: those who were fed up with the status quo mind-set of separatism, those who understood the pain of rejection, and those who recognized the problem associated with discrimination. People would join this group who realized the underlying problem simply based on tunnel vision, self-logic, skin pigmentation, and learned behavior.

The true minorities would not be involved in marching movements or any kind of negative protest. Instead, each of them would stand up for equality. Each member of this group would vow to our Father to stand out with a lifestyle reflecting his or her position. These people would arm themselves in prayerful protest against discrimination against humanity. A change of heart, mind, and soul in obedience to our Father would become their deepest desire. They would stand unified with the words written in the United States' Declaration of Independence:

"We hold these truths to be self-evident, *that all men are created equal,* that they are endowed by their Creator with certain unalienable Rights that among these are Life, Liberty and the pursuit of Happiness."

Oh, if people could only see how much we need each other, how all of us deal with discrimination in life. If only we could see each other the way you see us, I prayed.

Focused on Diversity

Thursday, July 18, 2012, was a very busy day. It was my day off. In addition to my routine household tasks, I had two appointments. The first appointment was to meet with my co-workers. We would all leave from the hospital to go to a five-star restaurant for some fellowship.

Two physicians had decided to treat us to an elegant lunch, showing their appreciation to us for a job well done. This was something they had done in the past and were excited about doing again.

The nurse practitioner was the liaison between the technical staff and the physicians. We could count on her to organize and determine the best time to accommodate each of us. She was both an outstanding professional and a friend to each of us.

Focused as a neurodiagnostic team, we were flexible to accommodate each other at the hospital. And yet, apart from work, we had diverse lives and different short- and long-term goals. The one thing we had in common was that we were proud to work at a hospital with an outstanding reputation to maintain excellence for our patients and associates.

Ready for a good time together, we took it all in, savoring this special occasion. The ambiance was superb, and the servers were pleasant and skillful as they took our orders and served our drinks, appetizers, scrumptious entrees, and mouthwatering, delicious desserts.

While in that small, private dining room, we also engaged in great conversation, both verbal and nonverbal. I was grateful; this was the best neuro team I had ever worked with. I silently thanked God for the food and the gift of time.

For about two hours, both the minor differences and similarities were evident. Some of us were outgoing; some were very talkative, while others were quiet, shy, and reserved. In our own way, each of us appeared excited and ready to thoroughly enjoy the fellowship and special time. And special is exactly what it was. Each of us consumed more than delicious food that day. The beauty of a new beginning with a diverse group of people was mesmerizing.

There were five women and four men: Asian American, African American, Hispanic, and Caucasian. Our backgrounds varied from blue collar to white collar, urban to suburban. Some of us were single, some of us married. We were a mix of the young, the middle-aged, and the young at heart. Some had many years of experience in the medical field. One was in training. And some had titles setting them apart as unique. The unique ones were not only physicians, but specialists. They were doctors who specialized in the treatment of epilepsy. What a melting-pot picture to behold!

Look at this, how awesome this is. It looks like everyone is taking it all in like me. For sure, each of us had a story, part of which was revealed by what we talked about that day. The sports fans weighed in on their favorite and least favorite teams, while the family-minded people talked about spouses, children, and siblings.

There was never a dull moment. Yet, with the sum of all the conversations, I also thought about the unspoken messages, the words that were buried within our hearts, minds, and souls. Without a doubt, there were some among us who were insecure, distracted, or frustrated. Others may have been anxious, but we all covered up well.

Then it happened. *Oh no, nobody's talking.* The brief silence was palpable. *Seems like we're all trying hard to break the silence. But nobody is doing it. Everyone is probably thinking about what to say. So, somebody say something—somebody,* I thought. Then one person decided to speak up. It was Yolanda, the best one for the job because that was natural for her. She asked tons of questions, which was great. Then the rest of us were off the hook.

After that brief distraction, I focused on those things we all shared that were *exactly* the same: humanity, our desire to be accepted just as we are, and our need to belong, to be understood, to understand, and to be free to live our lives in peace and harmony. What was clear to me was that we needed so much more than the very best food at the most exquisite restaurant. Not everyone there considered the group as friends—but rather just coworkers with nine-to-five relationships.

Surely in our future, each of us would see happy times and sad times, and we would cry happy tears and sad tears. I sensed that and marveled at the importance of enjoying the present time we shared together, as the human race. It was more than just a time of fellowship for me. It was more than a delicious meal in a fabulous restaurant. It was so much more than a gift of appreciation from two awesome physicians.

For me, it was a gift of time, of reflection, of hope, and of new relationships. It was a picture of the plan of our Father who loves us no matter who we are, no matter what our condition, no matter what we have done or have not done.

I think we would all agree that it was a fantastic meal. So, we left the restaurant to return to our routines. I personally left there satisfied that the luncheon gift had been given and received with much gratitude.

As I was driving home, I mentally recapped what had happened. *That was nice—really nice. Thank you for letting this lunch happen,* I said to my Father.

My second appointment for the day was to get a manicure, which I had been pampering myself with monthly. The lady who usually gave me a manicure was on vacation. So, I had the pleasure of meeting and chatting with a lady whom I had never met. I was OK with that. Unlike the luncheon, there was nobody who looked like me—their covering was ivory. It didn't matter. Not at all. Actually, I sat down eager to see what would take place as more food for thought.

We had at least an hour to be together. I decided to make the best of it. I think she had the same thought in mind as she asked me lots of open-ended questions. She asked about my family, education, job, and so on. Each question led to another question. Some questions were quite personal and hard to answer. In fact, the thought of my abuse almost brought tears to my eyes. The memories were depressing. Then, my honest answers opened up subjects about discrimination and tenacity. There wasn't a dull moment.

At times, she appeared shocked but amazed at my answers, as well as my positive attitude and long history of trying to make a difference in relationships. We talked about how crime and ignorance are color-coded at times. I took the opportunity to demonstrate how all people are basically the same, a topic I was passionate about. To have her see humanity through a different set of lenses was refreshing.

"We have all been discriminated against in one way or another…" As examples I used incidents covered by the media. Sometimes the attitude is "justice should be done." Sometimes the attitude is to have mercy on them because of the way they were raised. Many times the position a person takes changes according to the players. People speak out in protest against "them," while it becomes a moot point and is justified when it's about "us."

With well-manicured fingernails and having imparted a detailed message of humanity to her, I left there a satisfied customer. And I'm absolutely sure she heard some things that she would not soon forget. Mission accomplished, and all was in my Father's plan for the day. I would soon be reminded of our conversation.

The very next morning, the news of the Aurora massacre flooded radio and television stations. One human being with his personal story of bitterness and disappointments, who had experienced a time of darkness, had an agenda that affected the lives of countless people.

The day before was as different as day and night. But now, evil had come, and darkness shattered dreams, goals, and expectations of a better life. Violent images stained the memory portion of the victims' and their family's brains.

Not one sane person would justify the perpetrators' actions that night. The tears falling from their faces were just like the tears that have flooded my face and your face. They are colorless. And the blood that was shed was the same because as my friend Yolanda, a black woman, said, "We all bleed red."

Hurt people hurt people.

Focusing on similarities is vital to seek a life of peace. The diversity among us is a divine gift to behold.

Thank you for the time I spent with this lady, Father. Teach her what you want her to learn. That is my prayer.

"Colored People in Our Church"

In June of 2013, my husband and I had a conversation with John—a plump, middle-aged man with ivory skin and thin gray hair. We had met him about six months prior at a Fruit of Forgiveness conference held at the church he was attending at the time. It was a great conference, and many people expressed their gratitude at the blessings they received.

As we were leaving the church, John said, "I'm coming to your church one of these days."

David and I smiled and said, "That will be great. We look forward to seeing you again." We were pleasant, but, honestly, I don't think either of us believed he was coming to our church. We figured he was just being polite.

However, true to his promise, he came to our church. When I saw him, he and David had been talking. I was really happy to see him and wondered what he expected. I assumed he simply wanted to experience worshiping in a predominantly black church. While I'm not exactly sure what he expected, I am certain he was flabbergasted by what he saw.

As he stood right inside the door watching the people, the look on his face was priceless. He smiled, seemingly amazed at what he saw in the midst of diversity at its best in the church—all ethnic groups mingling together. He stood there and kept looking around as he witnessed the people coming inside for the second service and leaving the church after the first.

I stood there for a few seconds and thought, *What a blessing for him to be here today. No doubt this is another divine appointment. Thank you, God!*

"I wanna tell ya something," he said eagerly, as if he had something amazing to talk to us about. We gave him our undivided attention. "I used to go to this particular church not long ago, where some colored people started coming to visit. One lady had a problem with that. Can you believe that?"

We didn't answer but paused and waited for him to say more.

"She started talking to some of the members and said, 'Why do *they* have to come here? If *they* keep coming, I'm leaving.'"

He appeared relieved to get that off his chest. He continued. "So, they kept coming, but she stopped coming—never came back. Can you believe that?"

Again we waited and continued to listen. I'm glad we kept listening because apparently he had more to get off his chest.

"That really bothered me," was the last thing he said about that lady's attitude about people who wear a different skin cover.

Seriously, in 2013 and in the church. That's crazy, I thought. *He didn't say they were accused of doing anything wrong at all. They simply came to the church.*

"I mean, what does the color of their skin have to do with them coming to church?" he scoffed. Then he smiled, looking around in awe again at what he saw. "Now, look at this," he said. "This is the way it should be."

"Yeah, you're right. I believe this makes God happy. We are all his children. And when we judge others simply by the covering," I said, pointing to my arm, "he is not pleased."

The conversation went on and on about the problems of discrimination, especially in the church. Then, I left to talk to some other people as John and David continued conversing with each other. I loved what I saw in these brothers in Christ.

So glad he has seen this problem with the coverings people wear and the messages they believe. I know you are speaking to his heart. And I know he will share this with others. I pray they will hear him, I spoke mentally.

I'm sure you know people who go to church and perform pious rituals, yet are prejudiced against people who don't look like them. Haven't you seen people who are bound in covers of racism and narrow-mindedness? These covers mask the real issue that is not always the other person; it is egotism. They completely disregard his clear instructions to love others unconditionally—all people. What they don't understand is that we are one in the human race.

Don't let this happen to you. Don't get distracted from the truth. Don't believe a lie—that God made some people inferior to you. He didn't! Likewise, no one is superior. No one!

Nelson Mandela said, "No one is born hating another person because of the color of his skin, or his background, or his religion. People must learn to hate, and if they can learn to hate, they can be taught to love, for love comes more naturally to the human heart than its opposite."

The idea of treating church like a country club wasn't birthed in common racism. Didn't the Pharisees take issue with would-be joiners? They might as well ask, "What are those tax collectors doing here?" or "What's that Samaritan woman doing here?" The ones who ask, "Why are all these colored people in our church?" need to talk to Jesus about their problem with why those people have to come here.

You and I know what God's answer is to that question.

How is it that people who gather as the body of Christ miss the whole point? Christ condemned those who tried to outcast every last and lowest one of his beloved. If we are going to be the body of Christ, our hearts can't beat like his while we ask, "What's that sinner doing here?" How absurd that anyone who claims to be a Christian would mistake skin for sin anyway, FOR CRYING OUT LOUD!

It's Life—and We're All Living It

Recently, the stage was set for me to pause again, reflect, and engage in my position as the true minority I wanted to be. Four of my coworkers and I were having another interesting conversation. Current events—diversity, discrimination and, most importantly, God—were the topics of the hour. These were right up my alley.

Rex, a white man, and an avid book reader of both historical and contemporary events, knew a lot about this subject. About discrimination, he said, "I've read a lot about racism; in fact, I'm reading a book now, *Unforgivable Blackness*, a true story about Jack Johnson, the first black heavyweight champion of boxing in 1910. They spent years trying to find a great white hope to beat him. No one did until about 1915; it's just not right."

Susan, one of the kindest ladies I had ever worked with, witnessed inequity up close and personal. Though she and I wore different skin covering, the stench of overt prejudice was a hard pill for her to swallow, too. "The way people discriminate is absolutely ridiculous!" she said.

Ralph, a Hispanic man, said, "God divided the people and confounded the languages, so he must have been OK with the division that we have in our world. He must have had a good reason for doing it…"

"You mean in the tower of Babel found in Genesis chapter eleven," I said, "when he confounded the languages?"

He said, "Yes."

I agreed that since God had done it, there was nothing I would say against anything he did. He does all things according to his purpose. I simply said, "God knows."

Next we discussed the gay lifestyle and, in particular, whether "they" are born gay or have chosen that lifestyle. We all agreed the answer to both questions is yes.

Then somebody said, "You know what the Bible says about homosexuality?"

I chimed in, "Yes, it's a sin according to the scripture. Romans 1:26–28 spells it out clearly...Romans 1:29–32 reveals the sin issues we all have." *Good answer,* I said to myself.

I thought about gay people I know and gay people I had heard about or whom I had read about. Some of them looked like they had a physical anomaly. They looked like the gender they wanted to be, and some of them had committed suicide because they couldn't deal with the consequences of the lifestyle they had chosen.

So, I asked the next question: "Do you believe some people are born deformed?"

"Of course, the answer is yes," my coworkers replied almost in unison.

I continued, "Do you believe it's possible for some genes or chromosomes to form abnormally? For instance, there are some people born without limbs. Some people grow up to be only two or three feet tall. So, is it possible that with all the people in this world, some of them may not be gay by choice? For sure, some people choose to be gay; they *choose* to disobey God. That is an undeniable fact. But who other than God knows the heart?" I asked. "God hates sin—all sin—but he loves the sinner—all of us sinners. Remember all have sinned and fall short of the glory of God—and if you break one commandment, you have broken them all," I said.

I remembered reading in Proverbs the six things that God hates. And as I thought of myself, I declared that God sees all our sins the same and that you and I are liars (according to the Bible, God is true and every man a liar), and yet he loves us. "God forbid: yea, let God be true, but every man a liar..." (Romans 3:4).

I continued with what was on my heart about minorities. "Remember the devastation of Hurricane Katrina?" I asked.

They nodded.

"Remember how most of the victims were black people, and there was talk about how the president handled the situation, and they blamed him—accused him of not reacting quickly because they were black?" Then I added, "But did you notice all the people who came to help them at the time they were trying to rebuild? Did you see the color of their skin?"

"Most of them were white," Yolanda pointed out.

I continued, "I want people to see grace and love in me, drowning out bitterness and hatred. I hope people learn to treat others as they want to be treated. I want them to look beyond skin color."

Ralph said, "You know that's never going to change."

"You are absolutely right—not for everyone," I said. "There will be no complete peace until the Peacemaker comes. But until then, I just want to shine as a light in my own little world. If all I can do is make a dent in the change needed in this world, then that is what I want to do."

He smiled.

So, "God created man in his own image, in the image of God created he him; male and female created he them" (Genesis 1:27).

Satan covers with the bondage of deception—which leads to the bondage of ignorance—which leads to so many problems.

Living in one culture was my condition. Desiring to unite both cultures was my position, my indescribable passion. Somehow I wanted people of all races to begin to think differently and to ask themselves the questions I had presented to small groups: What color is joy and pain, a frown or a smile, sickness or health, fear, laughter, drops of blood, or floods of tears? The list goes on, for that which is in all of us desires to be loved, appreciated, and accepted as a unique person from the Creator.

No, I can't change the world. What I can do is cover my mind with the knowledge of truth and wisdom. I can do that. You can do that. The question is this: Will you do it? You can make a difference, not just in this world alone. You can affect lives for eternity.

An Issue of Blood

The Bible speaks of a woman who had an issue of blood. Her story is in the Bible for a reason, a very important reason. As I recall those ingrained messages, I can relate to her. Maybe you can, too. Apparently, her illness had been haunting; she had gone from physician to physician. But no matter where she sought treatment, no one could help her. Absolutely no one was able to rid her of that frustrating ailment—no one.

Finally, she had an idea. She heard Jesus would be coming to her vicinity. Her help was on the way. She had faith in him because she believed he had the power to heal her. After all, he had healed other people.

No doubt she was pushing her way through the crowd unapologetically. Most likely tears were falling from her eyes like buckets of water, her heart pounding in desperation to meet him. Praying silently on the way, she was probably planning to beg him for mercy. She really believed in her heart and soul that if she could get close enough to touch his garment, her issue would be over once and for all. He must have heard her prayers because she was able to be at the right place at the right time, waiting for that touch.

"And, behold, a woman, which was diseased with an issue of blood twelve years came behind him, and touched the hem of his garment" (Matthew 9:20).

When she saw him, she did not doubt. She did not hesitate. She did not think or worry about what the outcome would be. She probably had the biggest smile on her face. So, she obeyed her gut feeling, her faith in Jesus Christ. Full of bold excitement, she was ready for a divine intervention. Finally, it happened. There he was within arms' reach. Her time had come, and she was ecstatic!

She declared it to be so. "For she said within herself, If I may but touch his garment, I shall be whole" (Matthew 9:21).

Now she needed to trust and obey. Focused on the mission, she touched the hem of the garment he was wearing. I imagine that after she touched him, she stopped in that very spot—the place of healing. She probably felt an awesome sense of peace and said to herself, "I did it. And now I know I will be whole once again." Most likely she didn't see or feel an abrupt change in her body, but she felt an instant calm and peace within her heart and soul.

Of course, Jesus knew exactly what had just happened— every detail. So, he stopped at the point of healing and said, "Somebody hath touched me: for I perceive that virtue is gone out of me" (Luke 8:46). It was crowded and obvious he had been touched by somebody. Yet, he declared it to be so. He knew the whole story behind the healing.

He looked into her eyes with passionate mercy and said to her, "Daughter, be of good comfort; thy faith hath made thee whole. And the woman was made whole from that hour" (Matthew 9:22).

Her issue was an issue no more. Her Father had called her out, covered her condition with his marvelous power and used her illness to prove himself to everyone who witnessed the miracle he had performed.

Recently, in 2013, I found myself with an issue of blood. It was quite troubling. I had just left the doctor's office for my yearly physical exam. No big deal; no problems to speak of. All went well. Dr. Perry asked me all the pertinent questions, checked my heart and my blood pressure, and examined me thoroughly. Everything checked out fine. Then, he ordered routine annual procedures. Assuming all was well, he bid me farewell and reminded me to see him again in one year. I left the office feeling really good about my physical examination.

Returning to work with a smile on my face, I was focused only on the good report from my physical exam and ready to go forward with the other projects on my to-do list.

However, there was just one problem. Something was bothering me that I had just swept under the rug—completely ignored. My urine looked dark. It looked like blood was in it. But that didn't make sense to me. So, I elected to ignore it. I figured it could have been because I had started taking some different multivitamins about a week earlier. So, I stopped taking the vitamin. Yet, something didn't make sense about it. Even though I was a little concerned, I had dismissed the problem as a benign issue.

Now, a few hours after my appointment, I began to worry—really worry. I began to fret and judge myself harshly for not talking to my physician about it. *It's probably nothing serious, but why didn't I tell him? Now the office is closed. What was I thinking? I wasn't thinking; that's the problem.*

It was time to go home. So, I went to the restroom again before leaving work. There it was again. I was totally baffled now that I had a problem, was at the doctor's office, and forgot to mention it. Suddenly, I could hardly think of anything else. My thoughts were whirling in my head.

Something is wrong. It looks like there is blood in my urine, I thought. I got in my car and started driving home. Now, I was really worried and absolutely sure blood was in my urine. *Why didn't I say something to Dr. Perry? He could have at least eased my mind; but I didn't mention it at all. Why didn't I at least tell him my suspicions? Now it's the weekend,* I thought as I drove home. *By the time I get home, I will be a nervous wreck. Why in the world would I ignore a problem like that? Maybe it will be over in the morning and this will all be behind me.*

Then I stopped listening to all the negative messages in my head, pulled over, and parked my car. I took a deep breath, began to calm down, and started to focus on what to do next. *I will call Brian,* I thought. *He will know what's wrong with me.* My son, Brian, was a nurse and a teacher. With his understanding of the urinary tract system, he could explain what was going on and hopefully ease my mind.

I called him and thankfully he answered the phone quickly. I stammered on, "Brian, thank God you answered. I am worried. I had an appointment with the doctor, got blood work done and a urine sample, and I'm sure there is blood in my urine. I'm really worried." I told him every detail. Together, we had eliminated some other sources causing the bleeding.

"OK, then they will see blood if it's there. You know, it could be something as simple as an infection," he said very calmly.

I started my car and continued driving home. But now, I was really nervous. *Brian said it* could be *as simple as an infection. What if it's not an infection? Then, what is it?* I thought. He didn't say what else it could be, like cancer. I started thinking about what he didn't say. *He said it that way because he is worried about me. I can tell by his reaction,* I thought. It seemed like he was choosing his words very carefully.

As soon as I got home, I went to the restroom and confirmed my suspicions again. Then I explained everything to my husband. I didn't want to tell him over the phone. I told him what it couldn't be and got straight to the point of where I was sure the blood was coming from.

"David, I don't *think* there's blood in my urine; now, I *know* there's blood in my urine."

"You should call the doctor and tell him," he said.

"I know, but what is he going to do? It's the weekend," I responded.

"Honey, do you want me to take you to the hospital? Just let me know what you want to do."

"Nothing right now; let me sleep on it."

We were both worried.

I decided to wait one more day. Early Saturday morning, I called my doctor's office to leave a message for the on-call physician. He called back quickly, within about five minutes. I gave him the summary of my problem and told him that I had just left a urine sample there. He said, "I don't have your lab work here.

You should go to urgent care; they will take a urine sample. They can tell you if you have blood in your urine."

What? I already have the answer to that question. What about the information there in your lab? Why can't you tell me? I thought.

"OK, I'll do that. Thank you," I said politely.

But I didn't do it. No, I didn't. After all, by now I knew without a doubt it was blood. I didn't want to spend the money for somebody to tell me what was obvious. And since I had told the on-call physician that my sample was there and looked the same, I was OK for a while. *Maybe the test results will be ready by Monday.* I decided to wait until then to check with my primary physician, Dr. Perry.

When I woke up early Sunday morning, I could no longer ignore what was obviously a major concern to me and to my family. Finally, it was an urgent matter in every sense of the word.

David drove me to Urgent Care. *If something is serious and I put it off because of money, I will never forgive myself. Not only that, but the doctor told me to go to Urgent Care. I must comply with his instructions.*

We arrived at Urgent Care, checked in, paid the fee, and waited for my name to be called. When the nurse called my name, she instructed me to stop by the bathroom for a urine sample. I did what she told me to do.

Then I walked a short distance to the room where the nurse instructed me to sit on the examination table. "The doctor will be here in a few minutes." She left the room.

Within about ten minutes, he came into the room, introduced himself, and asked me a few questions. Then he said, "Are you having any pain anywhere?"

I answered no.

Then he said, "I'll have your lab results from your urine sample within a few more minutes, but I want to get a blood sample, too. In a little while, we'll be able to tell you if you have an infection. That's probably what it is; and we can give you some medicine before you leave to clear it," he said in a straightforward and optimistic tone.

Thank you. I felt so relieved to be there. *Like he said, it's probably an infection. I'm going to be just fine,* I thought.

About thirty minutes later, he returned to the room. Only this time, his countenance was not uplifting and positive. He had changed. He walked over to the chair, looked down to the floor, and then looked up and into my eyes like he had negative results.

"It's *not* an infection," he said quickly, as if it was hard for him to give me the disappointing news. So, he wanted to do it quickly and be done with it.

I sat there in bewildered silence for a few seconds. Then, I remembered exactly what Brian had said. "It could be as simple as an infection." I was devastated to learn it wasn't a simple problem like a urinary tract infection. I had told both physicians that my deceased mother had a history of bladder cancer. Now I thought the worst. *So, since it's not an infection, it's something serious. It's probably cancer like Mama had…Oh my!*

I thanked the physician, and left more concerned than ever.

I began to pray almost nonstop. I needed my Father to fix either the issue or my attitude to be content in what was happening. After all, I should learn to be content in whatever state I am in. That was God's instruction for me. I had experienced trials and tribulations in my life, but this was a new situation. Understanding that God was still in control was my resolve.

Monday morning, I called Dr. Perry's office as soon as the office opened. His nurse answered the phone. I explained all the details to her. She said, "I will talk to Dr. Perry and call you back."

Within an hour, she called me back and said, "Dr. Perry wants you to see Dr. Peters, a urologist. But since it may take a while for you to get in, he wants you to go have an ultrasound of your bladder and kidneys as soon as possible."

I thanked her, relieved at the thought of having an appointment with a urologist. A specialist could do the best tests for me to get definitive results. Still, I needed to prepare myself for bad news. The first bad news was that they didn't have an opening for me to see the urologist for about two weeks. I asked if waiting two weeks would be OK. I was assured that waiting would not change the situation.

They were able to get me in for the ultrasound the next day. *They will be able to see my bladder. That's good.*

In the ultrasound room, the technologist scanned my bladder, kidneys, and surrounding structures. Rubbing the warm gel over my belly, she could see lots of images. The physician came in and was looking at the images along with the technologist. He also scanned my belly as confirmation. They were talking to each other as they identified structures out loud. Sure of their expertise, I was content.

Then the technologist told me to drink water, empty my bladder, and return to the room for more scanning. *What a thorough test. I feel good about this test showing what's going on in my bladder,* I thought. The test was completed, and I returned to work.

Blood was still in my urine every day and every night. Every day I waited to have an all-clear sign, and I prayed for God to prepare me for whatever happened. By this time, the word was out to nearly everyone I knew—and even people I had never met. I sensed the body of Christ praying for my healing.

Again, with thoughts whirling, my attitude shifted from God healing me to my finishing what he called me to do. I said to God what I had said to him on countless occasions: "I love you like I love air." No matter what happened to me, my Father was in control.

Finally, after about three weeks from the onset of this problem, I found myself sitting there in the urologist's office. My daughter, Markela, and my husband, David, went into the examining room with me. Conclusive test results were forthcoming, and oh was I ready! By now, both my primary physician and Dr. Peters had the results of my sonogram as well as all my lab results.

Dr. Peters and his nurse had the results and were going to get more information for treatment. I was so glad to be there, so ready to get answers.

The nurse called my name, pointed to the room, and said, "Go in there and get a urine sample, place it in the container, and then wait in this room across the hall."

I followed her instructions. *Oh, the blood,* I thought. *I'm glad they can see the blood, and I will remind them this has been going on for three weeks.*

I went into the examining room and was instructed to undress from the waist down. The nurse prepped the area and explained the scope examination. Dr. Peters arrived within just a few minutes and introduced himself; he welcomed my husband and daughter to watch the entire exam. He explained the procedure before he began. However, he had more to say. I was not prepared to hear his declaration and his plans.

He said, "As you know, you have a mass in your bladder, which was found on the ultrasound test."

I didn't respond, just listened.

"So, we'll take you to surgery to remove it. Most likely, you'll be able to go home the next day."

Meanwhile, another physician seemed to be struggling, yet skillfully focused, as he was giving me some disturbing news. I continued to listen as I waited for him to finish explaining the ultrasound results and detailed plans for surgery. Though I was flabbergasted, I did not interrupt. *What? A mass?—surgery—oh no!* I didn't know the results of the ultrasound. Actually, I perceived that the results were good for some reason. So, I waited to get all the information from the specialist, Dr. Peters.

Now that I had heard everything he had to say, I was ready to speak. I said to him, "No, I didn't know I had a mass on my bladder. I waited to get the results from you." (Since he was the specialist my primary physician had referred me to see, it made sense.) He looked both surprised and somewhat embarrassed, assuming I already knew about the mass. After a few seconds of silence, he said, "Let's take a look at it."

He then had me lie on my back and position myself for the exam. He sat down on a stool in front of me and inserted the scope. The five of us could all see what he was looking at. The bright light shined on all the structures of my bladder and my kidneys. It was amazing to see! He moved the scope back and forth again and again. I couldn't see blood but wasn't sure what it might look like in that kind of light. He was very thorough indeed. My eyes followed his scope to every spot. He repeated the maneuvers again and again, left to right, right to left, up and down. There was no physical pain during the exam, but I was still anxious and curious.

Finally, he stopped, looked at me, and said, "Nothing is there; there is no blood in your bladder, no blood in your right kidney." Then he moved the scope to the left kidney and said, "There is no blood in your left kidney. There is no mass; this bladder looks good. Yes, this bladder looks good."

He removed the scope. He looked at me and my family and said, "The mass is gone—it's gone!"

I was absolutely overwhelmed with joy! I began to praise God.

The doctor walked away with a smile on his face as if he had witnessed the hand of God healing me. *Oh, he didn't say the mass wasn't there; he said the mass is gone.* I heard him and I believed him. God took care of my blood issue! And I knew it.

Dr. Peters was a Christian who was at the right place at the right time. He was leaving the next day for a mission trip. I count it an honor that before the doctor left, God had used my situation for a fresh demonstration of his awesome power. Remember, for three weeks and just minutes before the exam, there was blood in my urine. It was what they call gross hematuria. In other words, it wasn't just microscopic; it was blatantly clear to the naked eye. Now, there was no sight of blood anywhere, not in my bladder or my kidneys. *Where did it go?* I wondered.

An expert sonographer and a physician concluded that there was a mass. They captured images and had an official interpretation of the mass. The interpretation was from a different physician. So, you see, three experts had agreed there was a mass. Dr. Peters did not disagree with the findings—not at all. He simply agreed with what had happened before his eyes. He appeared amazed when he said, "The mass is gone!"

Even though all of them had ascertained it was not an infection, he had his nurse give me a pill for an infection just before I left. Then he ordered one more test—the computed tomography (CAT) scan to be done after I left his office.

After he left, his nurse confessed that she didn't want to be in the room when he gave me the "bad news" about the mass. She seemed so happy to witness it was a false positive.

I waited about a week for the CAT scan results. It was normal.

You see, like the woman in the Bible, I had an issue of blood, too. I went from physician to physician with no change in my condition. Then I came to the place of faith when I realized who was covering me, no matter what happened.

I believe he called me out to tell you about his healing power at this time in history. My Father knew I would do three things: thank him with all my heart, tell people about his mercy and grace and, most important, give him the glory, no matter what happened to my earthly body.

Calling You Out

My passion drove me to write this book and to share some real-life issues with you. I know that sometimes life's struggles are hard to deal with and that, like me, you can find life-changing messages, even in your worst times. If only you could see what is really happening. You can make a U-turn at any time. I understand. You can live a life of peace in the midst of the storms. Allow me to take you to the beginning of time, to a beautiful place where the first relationship was created.

When Adam and Eve fell into deception, they disobeyed God. Then, they realized they were naked. After that they covered themselves with fig leaves. "And the LORD God called unto Adam, and said unto him, Where art thou?" (Genesis 3:7–9).

It is in the "where are you" call that you and I have been given the mandate to listen to the voice of God. The voices influenced by the god of this world will uproot you and take you to a place of corruption. So, remember the real problem: "For we wrestle not against flesh and blood, but against principalities, against powers, against the rulers of the darkness of this world, against spiritual wickedness in high places" (Ephesians 6:12).

"Unto Adam, also and to his wife, did the LORD God make coats of skins, and clothed them" (Genesis 3:21). He covered them like he covers us when we mess up. Whether our mistakes are rooted in free will, ignorance, or deception, the lord God has covered us.

Praise the Creator for his miraculous powers. You see, he created the human body from one single cell. From that one cell, he created the human body. I read that the adult human body is made up of about sixty to ninety trillion cells. The very second you were made alive in your mother's womb until this very moment, he has been working out situations in your life, not according to your plans but according to his plans. And along the way, he has never said "oops."

I'm sure you've encountered difficulties. God knows. Maybe you are like countless people who need to stop traveling down the roads you *think* will give you everything you need. Maybe you have been making detours in your thinking based on somebody's opinion. Remember they are in the same boat you are in—Humanity 101. Everything in life happens for one of two reasons: he ordered it, or he allowed it.

Jesus Christ put on flesh and dwelled among us for thirty-three years. He left heaven and came to us as a perfect covering for our sins. Sometimes in his humanity, he was frustrated, disappointed—but never in doubt. The most difficult times I remember about him were while he was praying in Gethsemane, when Peter denied him, and when he was hanging on the cross. Can you imagine the pain he was going through? Divine yet human, "Jesus wept" (John 11:35). He cried out saying, "My God, my God, why hast thou forsaken me?" (Matthew 27:46).

He died and shed his blood so that you and I can live eternally. He loves you just as you are. Only God can cover you with a holy identity. So, when it storms, understand you are covered under the wings of the Almighty God. He can keep your mind fixed on *his* promises. He can protect you from covert deception disguised to destroy you from the inside out. He alone can give you grace and mercy, daily and eternally. So, stand strong in the power of the Word, with your heart and mind focused on Jehovah God, who is the only covering in every sense of the word—the All-knowing, Sovereign, Creator of the world.

Will YOU step out and stand under THE PERFECT COVERING?

Me and My Emerald City

One morning I woke up thinking about *The Wizard of Oz.* Out of the blue, the familiar story just popped into my head. I began thinking about Dorothy and her plight, but I didn't know why. I began to talk to myself. *Why am I thinking about this story? There is absolutely nothing I should write about the Wizard of Oz. So, why am I thinking about it so much?* Minutes later, I answered my own question. *I should write my thoughts down and walk away.* That's what I did.

Time after time, I have gotten incredible messages from basic, simple, and even what I considered silly thoughts. While thinking about this story, what I knew for sure was this: those unsolicited thoughts are for me to ponder, scrutinize and, yes, sometimes even pray about. The messages, as I began to see them here, hold basic truths about people who are in bondage. That is the truth; I had to write about it.

Dorothy was in a place of contentment. She was surrounded by people who were thriving in interpersonal loving relationships. She wore a beautiful smile. She had a good life, and it was simply wonderful to her. She wasn't focused on all the stuff around her; rather, she was focused on the people in her life. Satisfied in her life with friends and family, it was now time for a peaceable rest. Little did she know a storm was brewing, coming out of nowhere. It was coming and when it came, life would be totally different for her. Suddenly her life was turned upside down. Hurled into a different place, with a totally different life, a major struggle ensued.

Now, a stranger in a foreign land, she was terrified, vulnerable, an absolute nervous wreck. The thing that mattered the most to her was to go back home. One step at a time, she began searching for something, somebody, anybody who could help her. Surrounded by people who could see her situation clearly, she got mixed emotions. After all, their agenda was not her agenda, and she witnessed things happening that knocked her off her feet. People were laughing, playing, and enjoying themselves. They seemed happy. What was she to do? Who was she to believe when they offered her advice? How in the world could she know who to trust and what to do with all these strange people? They were so different from her family and friends back home. Nobody looked or acted exactly like her—nobody. She stood out among all of them.

What a dilemma. She decided to take a chance, trusting people to help her escape. So, she really listened and decided to do whatever they told her to do. Kind strangers told her exactly where to go, how to get there, and who to look for. The wise Wizard of Oz was the man she needed to find. That's what she was told, so she set out on a quest to find him. However, she was distracted by many things and many people. She believed what she had been told—that he could help her find her way back home. Marching ahead confidently in her actions and reactions, she would stop at nothing in her search for deliverance.

As she traveled what she thought was the road to victory, she stopped, looked, and listened to many people. Three of them had their own issues, but she could relate to them. For a while, she was satisfied in knowing she had a purpose for being in that strange place. It would be a two-way street. They could help her get back home, and she could help them overcome their weaknesses. That was enough to appease her. They became a team, searching for strength and guidance in their weaknesses and desires.

Dorothy met the evil one who was clearly trying to destroy her. She also met the beautiful one, poised and ready to deliver her from darkness to light. The difference was clear to her. Wisdom was personified, destroyed evil, and directed her to the road of hope. Yet, she was distracted and depressed. Almost everyone she met seemed to be clothed in trickery. But she wanted and needed to trust somebody to get back home.

Finally, she met the wise and powerful wizard. With great anticipation, she was sure her answers were right in front of her. She could hear him—oh, what a powerful voice he had. Surely he was a powerful man. That's what she thought. She was so excited at the very thought of what was about to happen. But it didn't happen like she thought it would. She was wrong; she had been deceived. How disappointing it was when all of his covers came off, every single one. She realized that like the other so-called nice people she met, he was an imposter. She had been encircled in earth-shattering disappointment. Now, what was she to do, and how was she to do it?

Changing her thinking became her answer, her focus, and her attitude. The tornado that uprooted her could only be calmed by something within her. Stepping out in faith, she began to see things differently. She realized that although she was unable to have prevented the storm, she did not have to stay in the midst of it and struggle needlessly. In following simple instructions, she stopped fretting about her situation. Instead, she listened and obeyed the gentle directive. Suddenly she was at home—only home had been transformed in her eyes. She was at peace like never before.

Now, I understand my reason for relaying this familiar story. I can surely relate to the principles therein. My storms had me in a different place, wandering in the confusion and doubt and believing people who were imposters. Sometimes I trusted them and doubted myself. I saw myself as a victim, a person who lacked confidence and had low self-esteem.

Can you identify with me? Look around on any given day, and you will recognize when you are wearing negative coverings. You are not alone. However, beware; you cannot change anyone but yourself. Keep your energy focused inward. Reject that glass-half-empty attitude. It will take you from the place of contentment and pull you into a place of frustration. If you understand the power you have to return to emotional well-being, you can weather any storm.

Mama Doe

Although she's been gone for many years, I am constantly reminded of the connection with my mother. The thought of our relationship together is forever embedded in my mind. It seems like the older I get and the more I pray for wisdom, the more I understand. My time with Mama is over, but memories are still fresh in my mind.

Some things, however, have slipped my mind until now. They say confession is good for the soul, and I need to confess—because I just had an eye-opener. I've told you a few awesome things about my mother—*mighty kind of me.* But I also told you many, many negative things about my mother, about all the times she would not listen to me when I was a little girl and really needed her to hear me. I told you how I just wanted to touch her, and she would push me away. I pointed out her weakness in my eyes and how she just wasn't taking care of my needs as a child. I dwelled on the details of all those issues—like a victim.

I did tell you about the pivotal times in our lives, like when she was seriously ill and almost in a diabetic coma. She accepted Jesus Christ, and it was amazing to witness God healing her heart.

I told you how God turned our lives around when she apologized about the mistakes she had made—when she repented to me. Clearly I expressed how our lives were changed forever, how when I said to her, "I love you," she would respond with "I love you more."

But I want you to know there was so much more I didn't tell you about my mother, so much I had not learned to appreciate, to understand, and to praise God for—until now. I am ready to give my mother the honor, respect, mercy, and grace she deserves.

Our relationship became like magic, like magic I tell you. A total and complete change. No longer was there any abuse. No longer was there any desire to touch her, only to have her push me away. Our hugs at the end of a visit made me melt in happiness toward my mother.

God chose her for me because we were made perfectly according to his perfect plan. Without my mother, my life would have been incomplete, impossible, because without my mother and every single thing she did—good and bad—my life would not have been the same. I judged her words of wisdom by what I thought she was *supposed* to do because of her duty—her job as a mother. I was wrong to judge her that way.

I see what she did in a completely different light through lenses of grace, gratitude, and my focusing on God's Providence. Each picture in my mind's eye reveals the most beautiful human being I have ever known—second to none.

In addition to attending church, being actively involved in the Lord's work, she worshipped at home. Every Wednesday, she had Bible study in her home. Three times a day my mother prayed—morning, noon, and night. And when she prayed, she called each of us by name. When she said, "God, take care of Rosie," she was praying to our Father in heaven on my behalf. When she said, "Protect her from hurt, harm, and danger," I was protected with power from Almighty God. With my mother covering me with prayer, I was able to endure rejection from an ex-husband, trials at my workplace, and countless other human challenges. Talking to my mother and having her as a friend, I could always lean on her shoulder for advice. And she always had my back. Oh, she wanted so much for me to be happy. That's what good mothers do—pray for their children to be happy. I could hear the disappointment in her tone whenever I was distressed. I could also see the joy on her face when I was happy. Even when talking to her on the phone about the good times, she was clearly pleased from a place deep within that I was happy.

When David came into my life, I remember how happy she was to know that I was happy, that I had finally found the right man for me because this time, I'd consulted God. When I told her all the details, she was thrilled.

When David asked me to be his wife, of course I said yes.

"But I can't marry you without your mother's permission," he had insisted. So, he called her, told her he wanted to talk to her, went over to her house, and did exactly what he said he was going to do. He asked for her permission to marry me.

"I am so happy for you two—*yes!*" she had said. She loved my husband and always said to me, "He's a good man, and he makes you happy." Even when I found fault in him, she always reminded me that he was a good man. Even in his human flaws, she could see him as a gift from God for her daughter.

I am so grateful because I realize more than ever what God did for me when he chose Mama Doe to be my mother. For the first time in my life, I see the complete plan of God as best as my human eyes can see. Unlike before, it is a beautiful thing. I see God, the Creator of time, putting our story all together just like he spoke this world into existence, created light from darkness, separated the waters—*everything* he created—and placed humankind in a perfect habitat.

Oh my God, that is what has happened to me. You placed me in the perfect habitat. You gave me the best of the best. And you started out with the woman you chose to give me life, my mother! Oh, how I missed that part of what you did for me.

Never did I focus more on your Providence through my mother—never. In my pious attitude, I always thought, *Yes, she became a Christian, but.* There had always been a "but." Although

I've been sincere in thinking that way, I've been sincerely wrong in my logic. You see, my mother has been the absolute most wonderful mother I have ever known.

The memory that lingers is the prayerful woman my mother became. Never, never, *never* in my life have I known a woman who prayed like she did.

Yes, indeed, I had the perfect mother for the perfect plan—God's plan. When Mama Doe went home to be with the Lord, she had only one thing I wanted, her Bible. When I opened it, I was speechless. I learned we had the same favorite Bible verse. It was highlighted. This is our life verse:

"Fear thou not; for I am with thee: be not dismayed; for I am thy God: I will strengthen thee; yea, I will help thee; yea, I will uphold thee with the right hand of my righteousness" (Isaiah 41:10).

God covered Mama Doe. He is still covering me.
He can cover you, too.

Doctor's Orders Completed

The year was 2002. At the end of a long day at work, my final procedure was completed, and I was locking the doors so I could clock out. When I walked out of the technologists' work room, Dr. Powell was leaving the department, too. But unlike every other day, after she closed the door, she opened it again and walked back in.

Then, looking at me with conviction in her eyes, she said something to me that caught me by surprise: "It's time to write your story." She said nothing else, but her expression implored me: "You *must* do this."

How does she know? I wondered.

Dr. Powell is a consummate board-certified neurologist. She has beautiful shoulder-length, dark brown hair and a clear, ivory complexion. She is as polished in her stylish attire as she is confident in her position. I have a deep respect for her. So, her statement made quite an impact on me. *Write my story?* I thought. *What is she talking about? How can she know? I know it's time, but where is she coming from? Why her? How did she become the messenger? Why now?*

I didn't say anything aloud until she spoke again. This time she asked me the big question: "Will you do it?"

"Yes," I replied instantly.

Although this wasn't something she and I had ever discussed, I was encouraged to write my story many years before I met her. I had agreed it was something I should do. But her saying "it's time" was just the prompt I needed.

The next day, when I saw Dr. Powell again, she said, "I told someone I convinced you to write your story," to which I simply replied, "OK."

What? She's serious about this. Who did she tell? It doesn't matter—not at all.

However, I was curious about who she told and exactly what she thought I should write about. I assumed she was thinking about my career. After all, she knew my situation before I began my career.

I had more unfinished business, and it was urgent that I speak with her. So, the next time she was in the lab, I waited for her to finish her dictation, and then I popped the question. I said, "Dr. Powell, what specifically did you want me to write about? Do you want me to write about my career?" Even though I thought that's what she meant, I still wanted to hear her say it; I needed to know for sure.

Her response came in the form of a question. "Can you remember as early as when you were four?"

I wasn't at all prepared for that question.

"Yes."

She hadn't exactly answered my question, but now I knew she was thinking I should write about much more than just my career. *Why?* I was thinking yet again. *What in the world is on her mind about me? It sounds exciting, but honestly, I'm confused.*

I had no idea what was really happening. What I did know was that I was supposed to pay attention to these messages; and I was to really listen to this messenger, in the person of Dr. Powell.

So, I started writing my story.

The next week I told her how hard it was to dredge up such painful memories of my childhood, and that I had to stop writing. She was very sympathetic and said, "I understand; take your time because what you write can help somebody." Since she knew me well, I believe she knew I would agree.

I said to her, "Yes, and I will get back to it later, but not now. I just can't right now. In addition to the fact that it's really hard, I have another project I'm working on, and when that's done, I'll work on my story."

"No problem. Just take your time, and it will all work out."

Yes, it will. Things have a way of working out at just the right time.

I was done with all the questions. Then I remembered my conversation years earlier with a coworker in Rockville who encouraged me to write my story. I had certainly agreed to do it then, but Dr. Powell's saying "it is time" gave me the *when,* and now the *why* was also crystal clear: *I have a one-of-a-kind story, with messages that can make a difference to people who are receptive. If they are ready to make a change, my story can be a tool to help them,* I confirmed within.

That day in the lab, even though she didn't know the full extent of my story, Dr. Powell gave me an order, and I realized she was right. She knew it and so did I. However, the details were sketchy. Of course, everyone has a story, and while I thought mine was thought provoking, some people would not agree.

At least once or twice every year, she would say to me, "Are you writing?" Most of the time, I would say yes. On other occasions, I told her I had stopped writing again and explained why. She was always supportive but encouraged me to continue.

Finally, she and I actually arranged to meet away from work. We decided to take time to talk about what was unfolding. We met for dinner. *Oh, this is really happening…I don't know how to write a book. I don't know what I'm supposed to write about.*

While I was excited, I was also scared to death. I couldn't procrastinate any longer. The time was now. I took a deep breath, got dressed in my finest outfit, and left the house. I approached the very busy intersection to the east side of the highway and finally spotted the meeting place. There it was to the left. At the green left-turn arrow, I was within minutes of having dinner with Dr. Powell.

Here it is. The time has come to find out exactly what she has been talking about all these years. I'm nervous, but at the same time, I'm very excited.

I parked my car, stepped out, took a deep breath, held my head high, and walked inside.

Instantly I was greeted with smiles and "May I help you?"

"Yes, I'm meeting a friend at seven o'clock." I looked around, but Dr. Powell wasn't there yet.

"Do you want to be seated?"

"No, I'll just wait here. Thank you," I responded with a smile. The piano music was soothing; the dimly lit room and people's laughter were delightful. The tables were draped with crisp white linen coverings, and on them burning candles. The ambience was simply elegant. I was ready to take it all in and enjoy every moment.

Taking it all in is exactly what I did. Instantly one thought came to mind. *These people look like they are rich and famous, and none of them looks like me. But that's OK. I'm here, and I feel good about that. Many years ago, I wouldn't have been able to do this. This never would have happened. Oh, how nice!* I smiled at how human race relationships had changed.

About fifteen minutes later, she walked through the door.

There she is! I thought as I exhaled.

The server greeted us, showed us to our table, gave us the menu, told us about the evening special, took our drink order, and left us to think about what we wanted. We glanced over the menu and started talking.

About ten minutes later, we had not decided what we wanted. We talked a little longer and then decided what we wanted to eat.

Our drinks and our meals were on the table quickly. By this time, I was starving, but more for the conversation than for the food. *What's on her mind that I've been waiting to hear about all these years? What else is there that we'll talk about…?*

She asked me lots of open-ended questions. For example, she said, "Tell me about your children…Tell me about when you got married…" Generally, each answer was followed by another question. We were not in a hurry at all. I really listened to everything she had to say and responded honestly—no holds barred. At times I was quite disturbed, not making eye contact, head down in shame. I struggled to hold back the tears. Nevertheless, I was at peace knowing that the past was indeed behind me, never to be repeated in that same way again.

I began to see her passion about the patients' compliance in seeking the proper health care. We had that in common for sure. Dr. Powell talked about our working together to reach out to the community, bringing awareness to specific issues. That brief part of our conversation was kind of vague. So, I concluded that although she had good ideas about the two of us working together, she would leave it to them to read my story, my book, as she had "read my life." In that way, patients and people everywhere could benefit from examining my issues, stop complaining like victims, take control of their emotional health, and become a victor of their lives.

Basically, we had an awesome time of fellowship together, and she ended our conversation with these words: "You need to write your story because so many people don't make it through these situations like you did. You can help them." The last thing she said to me was, "You are wired differently."

"Yes," I replied immediately, and thought, *Wow! Thank God!* I paused for a few seconds, exhaled again, and said, "Yes, you're right."

On the drive home, I kept thinking about our time together. *She is the messenger; she wants to help people, too, over and beyond her day job as a physician.* I understood that over and beyond her position as a neurologist, she had an agenda to think outside the box. I could see what we had in common. *The idea that she could see something bigger than either of us is absolutely awesome.*

Several years later, another rare moment occurred. Four employees were all working that day. Dr. Powell had been in the physicians' reading room completing her dictation, talking on the phone, and so on. I noticed that one by one all my coworkers had left the lab for various reasons. I was still there, though in another office out of sight from her and other people walking through. I was taking a break and using the time to bring closure to part of my manuscript. I heard her walking toward the room, and then I heard her say, "Anybody here?"

I responded, "Yes, I am," and walked out.

She hugged me and said, "How are you doing?"

"Doing well," I replied. "In fact, I'm finishing the manuscript; that's what I'm doing in there."

"You are!" she said with a bright smile on her face. I could tell she was pleased. She gave me another hug.

We talked about how long I had been working on the book and how awesome it was to be finishing it now. A third time we hugged and continued chatting for a few more minutes.

Was it a coincidence that she and I were alone in the lab just like over ten years ago? I don't think so. It was like bookends in my opinion. Once again, God stepped between us at the right time. The day she was called out as a messenger confirmed for me it was time to write my story, and now we were both getting the message that it was time to finish the story. About a month later, it was done. I thank the Great Physician for using her to reach out to humankind—through me.

My messages for you are threefold:

"Weeping may endure for the night, but joy cometh in the morning" (Psalm 30:5).

"Trust in the Lord with all [your] heart and lead not unto [your] own understanding. In all [your] ways acknowledge him, and he shall direct [your] paths" (Proverbs 3:5–6).

"And we know that all things work together for good to them that love God, to them who are the called according to his purpose" (Romans 8:28).

My question for you again is this: Will
YOU step out and stand under
THE PERFECT COVERING?

The Position

Years have come and years have gone, but now I see it so clearly
The coverings people strive to silence
They plot and they laugh at opportuni-
ties not only to rise above others
But to crush their very souls and to delight in their sorrow.
Why, oh why, I ask. Why? But I know the answer is crystal clear.
It is very clear to me because He reveals everything to me
That is every single thing I *need* to know
And what I *need* to know is who they are and whose they are
The people I come in contact with each day
And I need to recognize who I am in God.
I know who it is that is clothed in truthfulness
And who it is that is clothed in pretense.
Yes, I know some of them
But I also know we are twins in our need for mercy and grace.
We are identical twins indeed with the Coverings
And I know HE wants to remove the covers that divide us.
Open our eyes, oh God, to see you in everyone I pray
Open our minds to understand when we've been deceived
Open our hearts to reject prejudice and tunnel vision
And replace that with a desire to see you, LORD
See you in every man, woman, boy, and girl
You alone are the Covering of all the coverings
Brokenness, deception, and ignorance

Once blinded me to the light of equality
But never again because I am honored
To stand out as a vessel designed by you
And abide in YOU: the Covering of Wisdom, the fountain of life.

Appendix

Through Their Eyes

In the course of my relationships, three beautiful children were born who today are well-grounded adults in their own rights. In their letters, you can get a glimpse into their personal thoughts of me as their mother. In the aftermath of all the trials and tribulations, God clearly had a plan for me and for them. He allowed challenges in our lives; and we thrived.

LETTER FROM MY DAUGHTER—Markela Thatcher

My name is Markela. Most people call me Kitty, the nickname my mother gave me. She came up with that name because she decided my middle name would be Meon. Since it sounded like meow, she thought it was a good idea to call me Kitty. And, of course, she had to choose a nickname because everyone in the family had nicknames. I've always been OK with people calling me Kitty.

Birthday parties—I remember Mama gave me and my brother Frank big birthday parties together because our birthdays are two years and four days apart. We always had lots of fun. We got lots of gifts, and there were a whole lot of people, including parents, at the parties. As with most kids, my birthday parties were a big deal to Mama. Everything was good for me, too, except for one thing—pictures.

I can't tell you why, but I hated getting my picture taken. I always cried when I saw Mama or anybody coming toward me with a camera. To this day, I remember that I was upset, but I honestly don't know why the camera upset me. I just remember that it did, and Mama was always taking my picture. She didn't care that I would cry. She had to have the pictures, and so she tried to comfort me but kept taking my picture anyway.

I'm glad she did because, now as an adult, I have pictures and can look back and remember how things were when I was a little girl. Some things I honestly don't remember, but I have pictures that prove what was happening in my life. I'm really glad about that.

Going to school is the next thing that comes to mind. The first school I attended wasn't close to my house. It was a private school that Mama wanted me to attend because she said I would get a better education there instead of going to the public school, which was just a few blocks away. I was just a little girl, but I remember how different it was from public school. We really learned a lot and had mandatory time to study about the Bible, which was really good for me at such a young age. We wore uniforms, which made it easy to get dressed every day. It was a nice school but, for some reason, Mama sent me to public school the next year. I was OK with that.

The public school was different, but Mama decided it was a good school for me. In fact, I remember that my teacher discovered I had a speech problem that she felt my parents needed to know about, so she sent me home with a note explaining the details of my speech problem.

Mama agreed and, right away, I was attending special speech classes like the teacher recommended. And I continued the classes until I was able to pronounce certain words the right way. I have good memories about elementary school—lots of fun with the kids. Those were the good ol' days for me and for Mama.

Junior high and high school were not the same. I think high school was tough because of the culture shock. We had moved to another city, so now I was attending a predominantly white school for the first time in my life. It was hard to fit in, which made me sad at times. But I tried to make the best of it and got involved in things such as Junior Achievement, which I really enjoyed a lot. I made good grades. In fact, I graduated Junior Achievement with honors.

Later, while I was in high school, things got tough between Mama and me. To be honest, I just didn't like the way she always wanted me to do things her way. After all, I had a mind of my own and was old enough to make my own decisions. Sometimes I just resented her trying to force her opinion on me. That made me mad, and everybody in the family knew it.

I would say to her, "I'm not you; I'm me." And there were times I asked her for things, and she turned me down without even considering what I wanted. She just said no. And during my teenage years, and given the way I was thinking, that wasn't right. Those were the hard years. I definitely wasn't OK with her attitude. I didn't understand why she was acting that way.

Fast-forward to when I became an adult, was married, had children, and continued to disagree with Mama on a lot of stuff, which brought even more discord. That was a really hard time in my life. But I had to trust God because

I couldn't depend on Mama for all my wants and even all my needs. I had decided to do things my way, which was not Mama's way. Yes, those were hard years. At the time, I wasn't mature enough to understand what "tough love" was all about.

Today, one thing that stands out the most to me about my relationship with my mother—the thought that makes me happy—was the time I was in the hospital with a life-threatening illness. Mama was there every day. That meant so much to me. And not only was she there, but she was like my helper (I called her my secretary), explaining to me in layman's terms what the doctors were saying about me and what was happening to my body. She was very honest with me, and at times she and the doctor were making all the decisions. As long as Mama agreed with the doctors, I was comfortable. Mama was there for me when I needed her the most.

Out of everything I can say about my mother, the most important thing is that she taught me not just by words alone but by example to love God. Through the good times and even the bad, she always looked to him to help our family.

As I look back through every stage of my life, my mother consistently tried to be a good role model for me to follow. She has lived out her goal for us kids to know she loves us and to understand how important education is. Yet, at the top of her list was for each of us to have a personal relationship with God. Nothing has been more important to her.

Like Mama, I smile a lot—not because things are always great (I have struggles in my life) but because the joy of the Lord is my strength. That is one of the messages my mother teaches—not just to her children. Her goal, she says, is to reach the world. She has told me that so many times; I can't begin to count the number. There is nothing more important in life to her than to be about

God's business, to bring him glory. And because of that, I am proud to say she's my mother.

I love you, Mama!

Kitty

REFLECTIONS FROM MY SON—Frank Reynolds

My earliest memories of my mother begin when I was between three or four years old. I remember the tremendous amount of love that I had for her. She would always sing to me. I can still hear the words to a song she would sing over and over again, "I love you for sentimental reasons." Those words in my mother's melody are ingrained in my psyche. Likewise, I can also still hear her voice taking on the voices of all the characters in the many stories she used to tell me.

I always wanted to be around my mother when I was a child. I remember going with her when she would get her hair done and falling asleep waiting on her—because it would take hours. I also remember going shopping with her all day long (it seemed) on Saturdays. And if we went to Sears downtown, she would always let me get a hot tamale from the vendor outside the store.

It was also during these early years that my mother would make what I believe to be a pinnacle decision that would lead to many of my successes in life. My feet were developing abnormally, and the doctor recommended that I be fitted for braces. My mother was a single parent with very little income and was being advised by family and friends to just let it be. But that is not the attitude she took. She felt that if there was treatment available that could potentially prevent certain challenges and obstacles in the future, then her son should have it. So, she made that sacrifice. Every morning, I had to put on the device, metal rods from my hips to my feet, attached to my shoes. I remember people looking at me strange, but I didn't care. I thought I was special, because that's what my mother had told me about the braces.

My mother's devotion to my well-being began to manifest in 1979, when my family moved to another city. She took me to register for junior high, and the principal suggested that we meet the football coach. I joined the team the next day and enjoyed a successful season as the team's starting half back. It was my first time in organized sports. That spring, I decided to try out for the track team. I remember having to participate in a trial run so that the coach could determine the students with the fastest times. As I began to run, I could hear the other students comment on my speed. The coach announced the times. I wasn't *one* of the fastest kids. I was *the* fastest kid on the team and would remain that way through my senior year in high school.

I continued my involvement in sports throughout junior and high school and was named the track and field conference and district champ and all-state sprinter three straight years. I was selected to run in the AAU Junior Olympics, and in my senior year, I was the Missouri State champ and qualified for the nationals. This hard work earned me a scholarship to Missouri State University and developed in me a very strong work ethic. My mother's decisions have taught me to always strive for the best, to never give up, and to work hard for what I want.

As a teenager, I was able to talk to my mother about anything. No subject was off limits. If I had girlfriend issues, she would give me the female perspective so that I could better understand how to handle the situation.

To this day, most of my drive and determination comes from the example set by my mother. I watched her take care of her family as a wife and mother, work a full-time job, and go to school. She was always driven to succeed at home and on her job. She taught me to speak well, respect others and, most importantly, to love God. I am the person I am today mainly because of my mother. I am educated because she stressed the importance of a good education. Quitting is never an option for me because I watched my mother work the same job my entire life and advance herself from the very bottom to as far as she can go in her field. I am goal-oriented because I watched her set and attain many personal goals, and she continues to do so. I watched her go back to school and obtain her bachelor's degree and was so inspired that I went back to school and now have a master's degree.

I now have a beautiful family of my own, a lovely wife and two amazing sons. I am guiding them with the values instilled in me from my mother and also with values I obtained on my own, because of her.

I have been told on numerous occasions that I am just like my mother. Typically people mean that I am confident, outgoing, assertive, and driven to succeed…That's my mother.

Letter from my son—Brian Johnson

My name is Brian. I'm the youngest of my mother's children, or, as she would say, the baby. I hated being called that as a kid, but now that I'm in my mid-thirties and know that I'll always be her "baby," I understand.

I've been given an opportunity to say what my mother means to me, and I believe I can do that best by telling a story.

I spent the first four years of my life in one place. But in 1979, my family moved because my father began to pastor a church in another city. He was also the president of a local chapter of the NAACP (National Association for the Advancement of Colored People), so my family was well-known and publicized. I remember watching my older brother and sister go to school every day, and I wanted to go so badly myself, but I was only four years old.

The day finally came in September of 1980, when I got the chance to go to kindergarten. At that time, blacks were a minority where we lived. My school was K–6, and there were maybe ten black students in the entire school. Each grade was made up of two classes with about thirty students in each class, but as a five-year-old, I was just happy to go to school.

I walked in, nervous but excited to meet new people, a little black kid with an Afro, the only one in the class. I was a novelty to my classmates that day. They were curious. Everyone wanted to touch my hair. They wanted to see if they could rub the "dirt" off my skin, and some were amazed to find that it didn't come off. I imagine that for some of those kids, it was the first time they had ever seen a black person in their lives.

It wasn't long before the novelty wore off and I was just another kid, but for a while, they stopped playing with me. I was shy, so it took some time for me to develop friendships. In the interim, I assumed it was because of my color. I went home and told my mom, "I don't want to be brown anymore."

Of course, she asked, "Why?"

I said, "Because people don't like to play with you when you're brown."

My mother decided to take action and did something behind the scenes that I didn't know about until I became an adult. She sent a letter to my teacher explaining what I said and solicited her help.

All of a sudden, Ms. Fisher, my teacher, became more affectionate toward me, always hugging me, making sure I was included in games and asking me how I was. She began to put newspaper clippings on the wall when my dad was in it for his work with the NAACP. She would announce to the students that he was my dad, and I became a semi-celebrity because my dad was in the newspaper. All of these things made me more popular and accepted by the other kids. I didn't know why Ms. Fisher was doing all of those things, but I was glad she did.

My mom is a caring and loving woman. She's always put her kids before herself and would do absolutely anything for us. She's never been one to seek the limelight or be recognized for what she's done.

This is just one example of how great my mom is. I wouldn't be the man I am today if it wasn't for her.

I love you, Mom!

Brian

Every now and then, God sends someone your way and you have no idea why. Sometimes your first impression is that the person has nothing in common with you. Other times you sense that you might become friends because you have academic or spiritual goals in common. You're not quite sure. But you're inquisitive. Eventually the mystery is always uncovered. That is, when it's a divine connection.

Kenny—The Intersection, 1994

At life's crossroads, we find God. This in no way insinuates that *he's* lost but instead reinforces the teaching of the scripture, which reveals that we don't look for him (Romans 3:10–12). We find him there, ready to point us in the lifesaving direction, one that never leaves us as we were before the intersection. The year 1994 was an intersection moment for me.

I was a twenty-two-year-old boy moseying through life with minimal to no purpose. Identity was a word in the dictionary, not something that applied to my life. Without purpose and identity, one is sure to stumble, trip, and fall, and that summed up my existence.

After relocating, I was fortunate to land a job at a hospital as a patient escort. For me, it was simple; I needed money to play. Even though my driver's license had been revoked, I'd met people who could drive, and that was sufficient until that circumstance could be reversed. So, I worked and played.

My job as a patient escort involved transporting patients from their room to various departments for medical testing and procedures. Being an outgoing person, I enjoyed it. It was great exercise and allowed me to interact with many different kinds of people. I also became familiar with various employees as I frequented the same departments. One of those departments was the neurovascular laboratory. While waiting for the lab technologist to finish up charts, I would engage in conversation with the other technologists who weren't seeing patients at that time. The conversations usually centered on sports or my social escapades. They seemed happy to see me each time I came and were constantly curious about any new stories or updates on my social life.

This basically summed up the neurovascular team, with the exception of one. Her name was Rosie, and she was uniquely strange. She was as kind to me and was always adorned with a gracious smile. Initially, I didn't realize it, but she wasn't as interested in my weekends or the girls on my radar. She seemed to take an interest in me apart from those things. On occasion, while waiting for a patient, she would be the only technologist in the laboratory, and so we would visit while she was charting. I couldn't pinpoint what was uniquely strange about her, but by now, I knew that what I normally spoke about with the other technologists didn't fit with Rosie.

One day in the course of a conversation with her, Rosie invited me to her church. I didn't find it out of place, nor did it solve the strange equation about her. I was familiar with church, and I believed in God intellectually—that is, I believed he existed. Beyond that, I had no interest, nor did I have answers. At the time, I was actually attending a church regularly. But what raced through my mind when Rosie invited me was the imagery of a nice young lady awaiting me at this church. Rosie was nice, and I was sure her church had nice young ladies as well, and so why not? On a warm, bright, and sunny Kansas Sunday, clothed in a gray three-piece polyester suit with maroon shoes, I descended upon the parking lot of the church.

Rosie greeted me and escorted me into the building where, within seconds, I was spellbound. There were people everywhere, and there were all kinds of them! There were black ones, white ones; some were in shorts, and some were in jeans. The energy and the joy that filled the room were refreshing and confusing at the same time because I had never experienced that. I never knew that blacks and whites went to church together, and if I knew anything about sin, not wearing a suit to church had to be in the top ten.

As I entered the auditorium, which felt more like a small arena to me, I was captivated by the various flags that represented countries all over the world. *What is this place and what kind of church am I in?* I thought to myself. I remember the pastor's scripture text was 1 Peter 5:10, and he was explaining how we struggle in life, but God uses those struggles for our growth. What I found most interesting was that I seemed to grasp what he was saying and was very interested. Looking around the 1,200-seat auditorium, I noticed people were writing things on notepads during the sermon. Leaning over to Rosie, I whispered, "What are people writing down?" She explained that they were taking notes from the sermon. I thought that was interesting.

After the service, I was introduced to Rosie's husband, David. He greeted me in the church lobby, and we quickly became acquainted. He asked if I liked sports, and I explained that I did. He then inquired if I would be interested in playing on his softball team for the summer, and I was excited to do that. As I left that day, there were two things I found to be immaterial. The first was girls. I did not walk away preoccupied with vain thoughts about a woman. The second thing I found immaterial was the gray three-piece suit with maroon shoes that I had put so much thought into. What I had experienced on that bright, warm, and sunny day shook me like nothing before.

In a follow-up discussion with Rosie, she encouraged me and invited me to attend a Monday night Bible study at the church. She was also careful to inform me that it was a very relaxed environment and that people wore shorts and "stuff like that." In other words, no need for the suit, young man. The Bible study was as amazing as the service I'd attended a week before. About five hundred people were there. I thought it was interesting that five hundred people were interested in the Bible on a Monday night in the summer.

The format was somewhat interactive. People in the audience would raise their hand to be acknowledged by the pastor, and once they were, they would ask a question. From there, the pastor would provide an answer from the Bible.

I was taken aback greatly by the scope of the scripture. I had no idea that the Bible had that much to say about everyday life. To be honest, as a child, I used to observe my grandmother reading the Bible in her rocking chair, and so I thought the scriptures were for the elderly or the clergy. As the Bible study came to a close, the pastor instructed everyone to enter into an atmosphere of prayer. Bowing my head and closing my eyes, I listened to his words. At one point, he asked this question: "If you died tonight, do you know for sure that you would spend eternity with Jesus Christ in heaven?" I wrestled inside myself. I began taking inventory of all the good I'd done while comparing it to the bad things I'd done. This was a big struggle because I knew that I'd done some good, but I also knew enough about God to know that he knows everything, and that presented a big problem for me in giving a definitive yes to the question.

The pastor then followed his first question with, "If you're not sure, raise your hand, and I'll pray for you." I slowly lifted my hand toward heaven and listened as he prayed for me and others. I felt somewhat relieved and hoped that his prayer would somehow satisfy the big guy upstairs, but the pastor wasn't done. He then said, "If you raised your hand and would like to know how you can leave tonight knowing that you're saved and that you'll spend eternity with Jesus in heaven, just stand up, and I'll have someone come and take you away privately and show you how you can know for sure that you're saved."

All bets were off now. There was no way I was going to stand up in the midst of five hundred people and be taken away by a stranger. I didn't budge.

Rosie and her husband, David, walked with me to my car as we stood in the parking lot. They wanted to know what I thought. I shared that I was blown away by how well the pastor knew the Bible and how relevant the Bible was to everyday life. I then confessed that I really didn't understand what it meant to be saved. I explained to them that in my mind, I wasn't perfect, but I was a pretty good guy.

After hearing that, David asked, "Would you like to know for sure?"

And I replied, "Tonight?"

And with a nod from David, I was following him to his home.

As I sat at their kitchen table, David began to explain to me the death, burial, and resurrection of Jesus Christ. I was somewhat familiar with it, but when he was done, I told him that I'd heard that before but was still unclear on how to be saved. David said to me, "I know you know it in your head, but have you accepted it in your heart?"

Looking at him strangely, I had no idea what he was referring to and admitted that I didn't understand. He then explained to me that what Jesus did on the cross was both universal and personal. It was specifically for my sins, and because of that, a personal response was required on my behalf.

Sitting at David's kitchen table, I cried out to Jesus Christ for forgiveness of sin and personally received him as my only Savior and King. That was the greatest night of my life. As I drove home, I felt a peace and joy unlike ever before. I knew that something incredible had happened to me. Little did I know that it was only the beginning.

That glorious night was June 6, 1994. From there, David began meeting with me weekly for discipleship. I was for the most part biblically illiterate. But David was faithful and patient. For the next year, we met weekly to study the Bible, and he taught me how to practically live out the teachings of scripture. He became a big brother, best friend, mentor, and father. This was big because I had lost my father at a very young age and never experienced a father–son relationship, and I desperately needed it. There was nothing that was off limits with David. Our relationship was open and safe, and it helped me walk away from the vices and habits that owned me as an unsaved man.

As I was getting ready for church fifteen years later on Sunday, May 10, 2009, I sat on my couch and studied my beautiful wife of six and a half years as she prepared herself for church. I also looked over and watched my five-year-old son and my three-year-old daughter sitting at the table eating their Cheerios and loving life. May 10, 2009, was Mother's Day, and that's a special day. It's special for my wife, but it's also special because since June of 1994, I think of Rosie.

Rosie is who she was in the neurovascular lab at the hospital, but to me in 2009, she's Mom. I have not called her Rosie in years. I call her Mom, and David is Pops. As I thought further that morning about God's goodness to me over the years, I marveled not only at how he'd led me to himself, but also at how he led me to the privileged calling of full-time ministry as an ordained pastor of the Lord Jesus Christ. But it's impossible to reflect on all of that without going back to the intersection at the neurovascular lab.

I called Mom on the morning of Sunday, May 10, 2009, and essentially said these words: "Thank you for allowing God to use you in my life fifteen years ago. That was literally a life-or-death season in my life. I know that you love me, but you loved me fifteen years ago when I was much harder to love. I am forever grateful and indebted to you. I love you, and Happy Mother's Day."

As I began to grow in my relationship with Jesus Christ, I realized what it was about Rosie that was uniquely strange. She was God's child and his ambassador. She saw a young man who was lost and perishing. In faith, she obeyed her Lord and was led by him to the intersection where he knew I would be. That intersection saved my soul and changed my life!

Thanks, Mom. I love you!

Kenny

About the Author

Rosie M. Hill has authored three books: *Neurotheology Reveals the Covert Bondage of Unforgiveness*, the workbook *Forgiveness versus the Covert Bondage of Unforgiveness*, and *Forgiving Them*. She is a graduate of the Shepherd School of Ministry, a four-year Bible institute where she received the Christian Leadership Award. Rosie and her husband, David, live in Kansas City, Missouri, and are the cofounders of the Fruit of Forgiveness Ministry Inc. www.fruitof-forgiveness.org

Through tenacity, I know that what happened to me was not accidental—was not coincidental, but providential. I was born to tell the story.

From left: my little sister Rita, Mama Doe, and me at age fifteen

Taking my baby Brian home from the hospital

This is my beautiful mother, Mama Doe